A类/G类通用

雅思语法

主　编：何国武

副主编：叶　彤

编　委：张芳芳　刘晓君　谭凯茵

　　　　杨宇畅　李琦琪

 中国出版集团有限公司　　 世界图书出版公司
广州·上海·西安·北京

懂方法 更有效
www.huayan-edu.com

前言 *PREFACE*

您在备考雅思时是否会遇到这些问题？

- 雅思成绩 5 分以下，做真题错误太多，没提升
- 记了半年词汇，阅读文章还是看不懂
- 背了各种作文模板，写作分数还是在 5 分徘徊
- 多次参加考试反复刷分，却无法提分

如果您遇到以上问题，说明您的语法基础不扎实！为此，本书对症下药，专门讲解雅思阅读和写作中需要掌握的基础语法知识，并辅以针对性练习，考什么学什么，考什么练什么。解决语法根源问题，才能有效提分。

一 阅读篇：零基础看懂英文句子

➡ 14 节句法讲解 + 双语例句 + 单句拆分训练

本书摒弃传统语法书烦琐的语法体系，避开晦涩难懂的语法术语，针对性地解决看得懂单词，看不懂句子的问题。设置【真题句解读·实战演练】版块，指导考生利用简化、拆分等手段划分句子意群，提取出句子的关键信息，从而达到解题的终极目标！

每个句法点均配套对应的例句，在语境中学语法，便于理解和运用所学语法知识。且所有例句均选自雅思真题或与真题同等难度的句子，只学考试要用到的语法点，省时省力！

每个句法点后均有针对性的习题，以便即时检测学习成果，从简单句到复杂的长句，循序渐进，逐步达到看懂长难句的目的。

➡ 200 道真题句训练 + 图解难句 + 词汇注释

阅读篇第 3 章设有 200 道雅思单句训练，分为基础训练和提高训练，一页一练，并附有【词汇注释】，考生可免查词典，同步积累词汇。答案部分以图解方式分析句子成分，清晰易懂（如下图）。

5 The Massachusetts Institute of Technology	investigated	automated mobility	in Singapore.
主语	谓语	宾语	后置定语

【参考译文】麻省理工学院研究了新加坡的自动化出行情况。

【理解要点】本句的主语是 The Massachusetts Institute of Technology，谓语是 investigate 的过去式，后接宾语 automated mobility in Singapore，其中 in Singapore 是 automated mobility 的后置定语，说明是哪里的自动化出行情况。

写作篇：零基础写对英文句子

➡ 7大常见错误

写作篇第1章总结了写作中常见的7大基础性错误，包括拼写、标点以及用词错误，帮助考生减少不必要的丢分。每一节后均附有改错、填空等针对性练习，提高考生对写作易错点的敏感度。

➡ 6类组句方式

攻克基础性错误后，考生需要掌握组句方式，才能写出正确的句子。写作篇第2章讲解了6类在雅思写作中常用的基本句式，包括简单句、并列句、被动句、定语从句、名词性从句和状语从句，通过具体实例分析和相应的练习，帮助考生一步步写出语法正确的句子。

➡ 12大写作技巧

根据语法多样性的评分标准，考生写出的句子仅仅做到没有语法错误是不够的，在此基础上，句子还要出彩，才能拿到高分。写作篇第3章分别从句式变换、同义改写和论证句型的使用三个方面讲解写作技巧，帮助考生从"写对句子"进阶到"写好句子"。

➡ 句子写作训练

写作篇第4章精选150个句子和10篇雅思例文，从基础到提高，训练考生综合运用写作语法点的能力。

视频精讲，解读真题句和写作语法点

阅读篇的【真题句解读·实战演练】和写作篇的第2、3章均附有配套视频，由一线雅思老师讲解，扫描内文和封底二维码即可获取，方便考生随时随地学习。

▶ 真题句解读·实战演练

在做雅思阅读时，实际上同学们并不需要将每个句子成分都分析透彻，**关键是要找准句子的谓语动词**。找到谓语动词，再根据谓语动词判断前后的成分，理解句子的基本结构即可。

例1 Composer David Cope invented a program called Experiments in Musical Intelligence, or EMI. 真

译1 作曲家大卫·柯普发明了一个名为"音乐智能实验"的程序，也称EMI。

编　者

CONTENTS 目录

第 1 章　英语语法基本概念

语法从根本上说是语言组织的规律，而英语语法可分为四个主要层次：

单词（word）　　　　**短语（phrase）**　　　　**分句（clause）**　　　　**句子（sentence）**

句子是最高的语法层次，由一个或一个以上的分句构成；分句由一个或一个以上的短语构成；短语由一个或一个以上的单词构成。

第 1 节　单词、短语、分句与句子

1. 单词（word）

从语法角度来说，掌握单词的词性非常重要。如果我们在记单词时只记住其拼写和读音，不记住词性，就无法知道如何使用它们。因此，记单词的同时，要注意记住其词性。英语中主要的词性如下表所示：

词性		缩写	示例
名词	noun	*n.*	people, man, woman, child
动词	verb	*v.*	do, play, hit, bite
形容词	adjective	*adj.*	happy, excited, annoying
副词	adverb	*adv.*	sadly, greatly, generally
介词	preposition	*prep.*	in, on, of, with
代词	pronoun	*pron.*	he, them, mine, this
连词	conjunction	*conj.*	and, but, because, that
冠词	article	*art.*	a, an, the
感叹词	interjection	*int.*	oh, hey
数词	numeral	*num.*	one, two, first, third

2. 短语（phrase）

短语(又称"词组")是大于"单词"的一个语法单位。

常用短语分类	示例
名词短语	three close friends 三个要好的朋友 some red roses 一些红玫瑰 the bird in the tree 树上的小鸟 the development of China 中国的发展 the way to the hotel 去酒店的路 the life in the future 未来的生活 the cute boy wearing blue jeans 穿蓝色牛仔裤的可爱男孩
介词短语（介词＋宾语）	according to the law 根据法律　　　in spite of the rain 尽管下雨 of great importance ……是很重要的

形容词短语	more and more careful 越来越小心	strong enough 足够强壮
副词短语	as carefully as possible 尽可能小心	again and again 再三地，反复地
动词短语（包含分词短语、不定式短语）	tried desperately 不顾一切	having been waiting 已经在等了

3. 分句（clause）

从结构形式上看，分句包括一个或一个以上的短语，是若干单词在一定语境中构成主谓关系的组合。分句至少含有一个主语（subject）和一个谓语动词（verb）。

分句常见的分类有以下两种：独立分句(independent clause)和从属分句(dependent clause)；主句(main clause)和从句(subordinate clause)。在复合句中，其中一个信息比另一个或其他信息更重要，较重要的信息为独立分句(即常说的"主句")，较不重要的信息属于从属分句(即常说的"从句")。

（1）独立分句

独立分句包含主语和谓语动词，且表达完整的语义。独立分句相当于一个句子（sentence）。独立分句除主语和谓语动词外，常还带有其他补充成分。

例1 The scientists　were combining　methodologies.
主语　　　　　谓语　　　　　补充成分（宾语）

译1 科学家们正在结合各种方法。

例2 They　finally　emerged　from the den with their cubs.
主语　补充成分（状语）　谓语　补充成分（状语）

译2 它们最终带着幼崽从洞穴中出来。

析 这两句都包含主谓结构并具有完整语义，为独立分句。

（2）从属分句

从属分句的开头是从属连词（subordinator），比如 when、while、if、that 和 who 等。从属分句不是完整的句子，不能独立成句。如果不是依附于独立分句，而是单独出现的话，从属分句就是一种语法错误。从属分句由从属连词、主语、谓语和其他补充成分构成。

例1 Because　the scientists　were combining　methodologies
从属连词　　主语　　　　谓语　　　　　补充成分（宾语）

译1 因为科学家们正在结合各种方法

改1 Because the scientists were combining methodologies,　they were able to obtain an
从属分句　　　　　　　　　　　　　　　主句（独立分句）

portrait of music in the brain. 真

改译1 因为科学家们正在结合各种方法，所以他们能够获得音乐在大脑中的详细信息。

例2 When　they　finally　emerged　from the den with their cubs
从属连词　主语　补充成分（状语）　谓语　补充成分（状语）

译2 当它们最终带着幼崽从洞穴中出来时

改2 When they finally emerged from the den with their cubs,　there was no evidence of
从属分句　　　　　　　　　　　　　　　主句（独立分句）

significant loss of bone density. 真

改译2 当它们最终带着幼崽从洞穴中出来时，没有证据表明它们的骨密度有明显下降。

析 例句1和2均由从属连词开头，都不是完整的句子，不具有完整的句义，为从属分句。虽然它们包含主谓结构，但需要和独立分句（即主句）结合，才具有完整语义（如修改后的句子所示）。另外，直接删除从属连词，如分别删除这两个例句中的 Because 和 When，也可改正这类句子错误。

<table>
<tr><td>Tips</td><td>短语（phrase）</td><td>vs</td><td>分句（clause）</td></tr>
<tr><td></td><td>①若干单词的组合；
②不含主谓结构；
③语义不完整</td><td>特点</td><td>①若干短语的组合；
②包含主谓结构；
③语义有可能完整，也有可能不完整</td></tr>
<tr><td></td><td>名词短语、动词短语、介词短语等</td><td>分类</td><td>从属分句、独立分句；从句、主句</td></tr>
<tr><td></td><td>a good girl 一个好女孩
a friend of mine 我的一个朋友
is dancing 在跳舞
being injured 受伤了
in the classroom 在教室里</td><td>例子</td><td>从属分句：
when I went home 在我回家的时候
who is standing next to you 站在你旁边的人
独立分句：
Everyone was eating. 每个人都在吃。
The sun rises. 太阳升起。
People enjoyed the dinner. 人们很喜欢这顿晚餐。</td></tr>
</table>

4. 句子（sentence）

按照使用目的和交际功能，句子可划分为陈述句、疑问句、祈使句和感叹句。

● **陈述句——用来描述一件事情或表明说话人的看法、态度等**

例1 From our earliest origins, man has been making use of glass. 真

译1 从我们最早的起源开始，人类就一直在使用玻璃。

例2 What's more, your efforts to improve the situation can end up making you feel worse. 真

译2 更重要的是，你改善现状的努力最终会让你感觉更糟。

● **疑问句——用来提出问题**

例1 But what was it? 真

译1 但那是什么呢？

例2 Does that mean that we should actively cause pain? 真

译2 这是否意味着我们应该主动让自己感受痛苦？

● **祈使句——表示请求、命令、建议、劝告等**

例1 Don't go on to the north gate. 真

译1 不要去北门。

例2 Just look at the ways in which everything under the sun has been marketed. 真

译2 看看天底下所有东西的营销方式。

- **感叹句——表示喜、怒、哀、乐等情感**

  例1 How little we know about music! 真

  译1 我们对音乐知之甚少!

  例2 What a fresh interpretation! 真

  译2 多么让人耳目一新的诠释!

  按照结构形式,句子可以划分为简单句、并列句和复合句。

- **简单句**

  只有一个主谓结构而且各个成分均由短语构成的句子叫简单句。在简单句中,主语和谓语可以分别由一个单词或短语充当,也可以分别由两个或两个以上的单词或短语充当,组成并列的主语或并列的谓语。除了主语和谓语外,简单句中还可以有宾语、定语、状语、补语等。

  例1 **Language co-activation** *occurs*. 真

  译1 语言协同激活发生。

  析1 此句只包含一个主语和一个谓语。

  例2 **The ancient Greeks and Romans** *used* <u>cork</u> for anything from beehives to sandals. 真

  译2 古希腊人和古罗马人将软木用于从蜂房到凉鞋的任何东西。

  析2 本句的主语由 The ancient Greeks 和 (The ancient) Romans 组合而成,为并列主语。除了主语、谓语和宾语外,本句还包含状语 for anything from beehives to sandals,其中 from beehives to sandals 为 anything 的后置定语。

  例3 **Bilingual experience** *may keep* <u>the cognitive mechanisms</u> sharp. 真

  译3 双语经验可以使人的认知机制保持敏锐。

  析3 本句中的 sharp 为宾语 the cognitive mechanisms 的补语,即宾语补语。

- **并列句**

  两个或两个以上的简单句由并列连词或其他并列手段连接起来,便构成并列句。其基本结构为:简单句 + 并列连词 + 简单句。

  在并列句中,除了使用并列连词 and、but、so、or 外,还可使用并列连词短语 either... or、not only... but also 连接分句,有时甚至只用分号、冒号等。

  例1 There is at least one dog collar museum in existence, **and** it grew out of a personal collection. 真

  译1 现存至少一个狗项圈博物馆,它是从个人收藏发展而来的。

  例2 This ant might be unique, **or** it might represent a broader pattern among other social bugs. 真

  译2 这只蚂蚁也许是独一无二的,或者它也许代表存在于其他社会性昆虫中的更广泛的生存模式。

  例3 Archaeologists have even found evidence of man-made glass which dates back to 4000 BC; this took the form of glazes used for coating stone beads. 真

  译3 考古学家甚至发现了可以追溯到公元前4000年的人造玻璃的证据;这是一种用于涂抹石珠的釉料。

- **复合句**

    由一个主句和一个或一个以上从句构成的句子是复合句，所以复合句又称为"主从复合句"。

    例1 Financially I didn't really benefit from it, I never filed for a patent. ×

    Financially I didn't really benefit from it **because** I never filed for a patent. √ 真

    译1 在经济上，我并没有真正从中受益，因为我从未申请过专利。

    析1 第一个句子中，两个分句不能用逗号连接。依据句意，可以把第二个分句变成由 because 引导的原因状语从句，从而与第一个分句一起构成复合句。

    在复合句中，主句是全句的主体，从句充当某种句子成分(核心成分或修饰成分皆可)。一般说来，从句在复合句中充当什么成分就称为什么从句。比如，从句在复合句中用作主语，就叫主语从句；在复合句中用作宾语，就叫宾语从句；在复合句中用作状语，就叫状语从句，以此类推。

    例2 **What Beethoven does instead** is suggest variations of the pattern. 真 （主语从句）

    译2 相反，贝多芬所做的是暗示模式的变化。

    例3 Schimmelpennink cannot see **that this changes Amsterdam's need for a bike-sharing scheme**. 真 （宾语从句）

    译3 Schimmelpennink 认为这并不能改变阿姆斯特丹对自行车共享计划的需求。

    例4 The other attitude is **that the purpose of marketing is irrelevant**. 真（表语从句）

    译4 另一种态度是，市场营销的目的无关紧要。

语法点精练·小试牛刀

Exercise 1 请写出画线单词的词性及其中文意思。

1. The spice then travelled from that great trading city to markets all around Europe. 真

2. Before Europeans arrived on the island, the state had organised the cultivation of cinnamon. 真

3. The original idea for an urban bike-sharing scheme dates back to a summer's day in Amsterdam in 1965. 真

4. However, Tehrani found no significant difference in the rate of evolution of incidents compared with that of characters. 真

5. One way to answer the question is to look at the music and not the neurons（神经元）. 真

Exercise 2 判断画线部分属于短语还是分句。

1. You will not have the same health concerns as someone who lives in a different geographical region. 真

2. Bilingual people often excel at tasks such as this, which tap into the ability to ignore competing perceptual information. 真

3. When people experience art, they wonder what the artist might have been thinking. 真

4. One of the findings is that ecosystems without large predators behave in completely different ways. 真

5. The prominent historian would say exploration was a thing of the past. 真

（答案见 p. 156）

第 2 节 英文句子的基本成分

组成句子的各部分叫作句子的成分。按功能划分，句子的成分包括主语、谓语、表语、宾语、定语、状语、补语、同位语、独立成分等，其中主语和谓语是最重要的句子成分。

1. 主语

主语是一个句子叙述的主体对象，一般位于句首。名词、代词、数词、名词化的形容词、不定式、动名词、从句均可用作主语。

主语的类别	例句
名词	例 **Their journey** ended when they reached Alexandria. 真 译 当他们到达亚历山大时，他们的旅程就结束了。
代词	例 **They** hunted the tortoises and destroyed their habitat to clear land for agriculture. 真 译 他们猎杀象龟并破坏它们的栖息地，以便为农耕清理土地。
不定式	例 **To get medical attention** is very difficult in the area. 真 译 在该地区，获得医疗救治是非常困难的。
动名词	例 **Protecting large areas of the sea** would result in some losses to the fishing industry. 真 译 保护大片海域将给渔业带来一些损失。
从句	例 But **what they often lack** is the evidence to base policies on. 真 译 但他们通常缺乏支撑政策的证据。

2. 谓语

谓语表述主语的动作或状态，一般位于主语之后，由动词或动词短语充当，有人称、数和时态的变化。

例1 The sounds **arrive** in sequential order. 真
译1 声音按顺序到达。

例2 Many forms of collecting **have been dignified** with a technical name. 真
译2 很多种类的收集都有一个专业名称使之变得更高级。

3. 表语

表语说明主语的身份、特征和状态，位于系动词后。表语一般由名词、代词、形容词、数词、分词、不定式、动名词、介词短语、从句等充当，某些副词也可作表语。

表语的类别	例句	
名词	例 It's **a process of cultural resuscitation**. 真	译 这是一个文化复苏的过程。
形容词	例 They are **ignorant** about the ideas. 真	译 他们对这些想法一无所知。
现在分词	例 The conclusion is **empowering**. 真	译 这个结论赋予人们权力。
介词短语	例 Those objects are **of interest to archaeologists**. 真	译 考古学家对那些物品感兴趣。
从句	例 An idea is **that Machu Picchu was a country estate built by an Inca emperor**. 真 译 有一种观点认为马丘比丘是由一位印加皇帝建造的乡村庄园。	

4. 宾语

宾语表示动作的承受者，一般位于及物动词或介词之后。名词、代词、数词、不定式、动名词、从句等均可用作宾语。

宾语的类别	例句	
名词	例 They lacked **a control group**. 真	译 他们缺少一个对照组。
代词	例 We believe **you**. 真	译 我们相信你。
动名词	例 This might involve **trying to see every locomotive of a particular type**. 真 译 这可能涉及争取看到每一种特定类型的机车。	
从句	例 I predict **that changes in public attitudes will be essential for changes in businesses' environmental practices**. 真 译 我预计，公众态度的改变对企业环保实践的改变至关重要。	

5. 定语

定语修饰名词或代词，用来说明人或事物的品质或特征。形容词、名词、代词、数词、副词、介词短语、分词、不定式、动名词、从句等均可用作定语。单个单词作定语通常放在被修饰词的前面；短语或从句作定语则放在被修饰词的后面。

定语的类别	例句
形容词	例 The Dutch treated the **native** inhabitants harshly. 真 译 荷兰人粗暴对待当地的原住民。
名词	例 The **trade** route allowed for only small quantities of the spice to reach Europe. 真 译 这条贸易路线只允许少量香料运送到欧洲。
介词短语	例 The key **to understanding what the hormone does** lies in pinpointing its core function. 真 译 了解激素作用的关键在于明确其核心功能。
过去分词	例 The ME2 counteracted some of the widely **perceived** negative impacts of digital gaming devices. 真 译 ME2 电子游戏消除了人们普遍认为的数字游戏设备的一些负面影响。
从句	例 Oxytocin could also make things worse for people **who are overly sensitive or prone to interpreting social cues**. 真 译 对于过于敏感或爱解读社交信号的人来说，催产素也可能使事情变得更糟。

6. 状语

状语用来修饰动词、形容词、副词以及整个句子。形容词、副词、介词短语、分词、不定式、从句等均可用作状语。状语的位置很灵活，可置于句首、句中或句末。按其用途，状语可表示时间、地点、原因、结果、目的、条件、让步、方式、伴随情况等。

状语的类别	例句
副词	例 Zoos are now **increasingly** sophisticated in their communication and outreach work. 真（程度状语） 译 现在动物园在沟通和推广工作方面越来越成熟。
形容词	例 **Exhausted**, the trading economy broke down. 真（原因状语） 译 筋疲力尽的贸易经济崩溃了。
介词短语	例 **After a few years**, contrasting findings began to emerge. 真（时间状语） 译 几年后，开始出现截然不同的发现。
从句	例 She can't say for sure **because her study wasn't designed to follow an ant's final moments**. 真（原因状语） 译 她不能肯定，因为她的研究并不是为了追踪蚂蚁的最后时刻而设计的。

7. 补语

英语中有些及物动词接宾语后，意义仍不完整，还需要其他的句子成分来补充说明宾语的意义、状态等，这就是宾语补语。宾语和宾语补语构成复合宾语，它们在逻辑上有主谓关系。含有宾语补语的句子变为被动句时，宾语补语便成了主语补语。名词、形容词、介词短语、分词、不定式及少数副词皆可作补语。

补语的类别		例句
宾语补语	形容词	例 Visitors to New Zealand find activities **special**. 真 译 新西兰的游客觉得活动很特别。
	副词	例 They lever it **away**. 真 译 他们用杠杆把它撬开。
	省略 **to** 的不定式	例 We must adopt policies that let peasants **diversify the plant**. 真 译 我们必须采取让农民种植多样化作物的政策。
	现在分词	例 You may notice customers **replacing this product with another**. 真 译 你可能会注意到客户用另一种产品替换了这个产品。
主语补语	形容词	例 In 83 percent of cases, the perceived dangers of ocean trash were proven **true**. 真 译 在83%的案例中，已知的海洋垃圾危害被证明是真实存在的。

8. 同位语

同位语用来说明或解释同一事物，通常放在其所说明的名词或代词之后。名词、代词、数词、动名词、从句等均可用作同位语。

同位语的类别	例句
名词	例 This pronouncement by Richard Layard, **an economist and advocate of 'positive psychology'**, summarises the beliefs of many people today. 真 译 经济学家及"积极心理学"倡导者理查德·莱亚德的这一声明概括了当今许多人的信仰。
代词	例 They **each** set their own particular criteria. 真 译 他们各自设定了自己的特定标准。
数词	例 You **two** are much older. 真 译 你们两个年纪大多了。
从句	例 The idea **that governments should be responsible for promoting happiness** is always a threat to human freedom. 真 译 一直以来，促进幸福感是政府的责任这个想法是对人类自由的一种威胁。

✏️ 语法点精练·小试牛刀

判断以下句子是简单句、并列句还是复合句，并标出句中的主语和谓语。

1. Happiness is the ultimate goal. 真

2. If we didn't have physical pain, bad things would happen to us. 真

3. We can predict some of the notes, but we can't predict them all. 真

4. The ship's next captain was an excellent navigator, who got the best out of both his ship and his crew. 真

5. Music triggers the production of dopamine. 真

（答案见 p. 157）

第2章 基础句法精讲精练 240 句

第1节 简单句及五种基本句型

一 简单句的核心

简单句是英文中最基础的句子类型，一个简单句陈述一个事实，其结构的核心是主语和谓语。其中，主语表明陈述的对象，一般由名词（短语）或代词充当；谓语表明主语的动作，由动词（短语）充当。一个简单句有且只有一个主谓结构。英语中，根据谓语动词的种类及其后所跟的成分，划分出了五种基本句型，如下图所示：

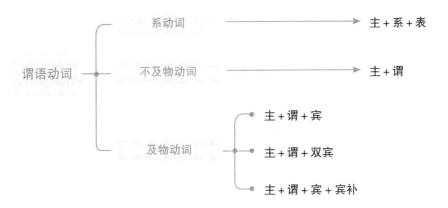

Tips

1. 系动词

系动词也称"连系动词"，其后接表语。雅思阅读真题中常见的系动词，包括以下几类：

• **be 动词**（意为"是"）

例词：am、is、are

例 Most cork forests **are** family-owned. 真

译 绝大多数的软木橡树林是家庭所有的。

• **感官动词**

例词：look "看"、sound "听"、taste "尝"、feel "感觉"、smell "闻"

例 1 The future is **looking** good.

译 1 未来看起来一片光明。

例 2 The problems **sound** dramatic. 真

译 2 这些问题听起来很有戏剧性。

• **变化系动词**（意为"变得，成为"）

例词：become、turn、get、grow、go

例 1 The tortoises eventually **become** too large to transport. 真

译 1 这些象龟最终会变得过于巨大而难以运输。

例2 The climate **turned** cold. 真

译2 气候变冷了。

- **终止系动词**

例词：prove "证明"、turn out "结果是"

例 It **proved** invaluable to the optical industry. 真

译 事实证明，它对光学业非常有价值。

- **持续系动词**（意为"保持，处于"）

例词：keep、remain、stay、stand

例 The information provided **remained** accurate. 真

译 所提供的信息仍然准确。

- **表象系动词**（意为"似乎"）

例词：seem、appear

例 At times, he **seemed** to abandon the human figure altogether in his work. 真

译 有时，他的作品似乎完全舍弃了人体特征。

2. 及物动词（vt.）与非及物动词（vi.）

这两类都属于实义动词，即"有实在动作含义的动词"，其区别在于动词后是否可以直接加宾语。从本质上说，这代表这个动作是否可以由主语独立完成。不及物动词就是指该动作可以由主语独立完成，不需要涉及其他事物，如 arrive、happen、fly；而及物动词就是主语不能独立完成的动作，后面需要加上动作涉及的事物（即宾语），如 put、send、say。

二 简单句的五种基本句型

1. 主语 + 系动词 + 表语

例 Cork **is** a remarkable material. 真

译 软木橡树是一种重要的资源。

析 系动词作谓语时后面必须有形容词或名词等词语作表语，与其构成系表结构。表语实质上是对主语状况的说明，因此表语属于主语补语（简称"主补"）的一种。本句中，is 是系动词，后接表语 a remarkable material 是对主语 Cork 的说明。

2. 主语 + 谓语（不及物动词）

例 The soil **will disappear** completely. 真

译 土壤将会完全消失。

析 本句的谓语动词是 will disappear（disappear 的一般将来时），意为"将会消失"，动作由主语 The soil 单独完成，不涉及别的事物，即 disappear 为不及物动词（后不可直接加宾语），故本句"主 + 谓"的结构已经完整。

3. 主语 + 谓语 + 宾语

例　The bark of the cork oak **has** a particular cellular structure. 真

译　软木橡树的树皮有一种特殊的细胞结构。

析　本句谓语动词是 has, 意为"有", 为及物动词, 其后需接"有"的内容, 即宾语 a particular cellular structure, "主 + 谓 + 宾"结构才完整。

4. 主语 + 谓语 + 间接宾语 + 直接宾语

例　The British **would give** them the island. 真

译　英国人会把这个岛给他们。

析　本句谓语动词是 would give (give 的过去将来时), 意为"给", 该动作涉及两个对象: 一是给"谁", 在例句中是 them, 此为间接宾语; 二是给"什么东西", 在例句中为 the island "岛屿", 此为直接宾语。此句为"主 + 谓 + 双宾"结构。

5. 主语 + 谓语 + 宾语 + 宾语补语

例　These two unique aspects **make** food production vulnerable and different from any other business. 真

译　这两点特征使得粮食生产业高度脆弱, 有别于其他行业。

析　有时句子有"主 + 谓 + 宾"结构, 但句意还是残缺的。例如, 本句如果只有 These two unique aspects make food production "这两点特征使得粮食生产业", 很明显, 句意不完整, 没有提到粮食生产业到底怎么了。因此, 还需加上补充说明宾语"粮食生产业"的内容, 即宾语补语 (简称"宾补")。例句中 vulnerable 和 different from... 就是宾补。这就构成了"主 + 谓 + 宾 + 宾补"结构。

> **Tips**
>
> 宾补是对宾语的补充说明, 实际上它与宾语有逻辑上的主谓关系。简单来说, 我们在理解时, 可以在宾语和宾补之间加上"是"。如上面的例子, 传达的意思是 food production is vulnerable and different from any other business "粮食生产业是脆弱的, 且是有别于其他行业的"。同学们在理解句意时, 只需知道该部分补充说明宾语即可, 不用深究"宾语补语"的具体定义。

▶ 真题句解读·实战演练

在做雅思阅读时, 实际上同学们并不需要将每个句子成分都分析透彻, **关键是要找准句子的谓语动词**。找到谓语动词, 再根据谓语动词判断前后的成分, 理解句子的基本结构即可。

例1　Composer David Cope invented a program called Experiments in Musical Intelligence, or EMI. 真

译1　作曲家大卫·柯普发明了一个名为"音乐智能实验"的程序, 也称 EMI。

步骤一: 确定真正的谓语动词

按正常语序读句子, 发现本句有 2 个动词, 分别是 invented 和 called, 但一个简单句不能同时有几个非并列的谓语动词, 那么谓语动词究竟是哪一个呢?

假设 called 是谓语，那么 invented 只能是过去分词作后置定语，表示"被发明的"，修饰 Composer David Cope，而这明显逻辑不通，也不能连上后面的 a program，因此假设不成立，invented 是谓语动词。由此可以判断 called 才是过去分词作定语，意为"被称作……"，修饰 a program，句子意思也说得通了。

Composer David Cope **invented** a program *called* Experiments in Musical Intelligence, or EMI.
           谓语

步骤二：确定句子主干，理解基本结构

确定谓语动词是 invented 后，则可确定本句的主干是 Composer David Cope invented a program。Composer David Cope 是句子的主语，a program 是宾语，called Experiments in Musical Intelligence, or EMI 则是非谓语动词作后置定语，修饰宾语 a program。

Composer David Cope **invented** a program *called* Experiments in Musical Intelligence, or EMI.
    主语   谓语   宾语   宾语的定语

- -

例2 Some of the most compelling evidence, called 'language co-activation', comes from studying eye movements. 真

译2 一些最有力的证据，被称为"语言协同激活"，来自对眼球运动的研究。

步骤一：确定真正的谓语动词

谓语动词究竟是 called 还是 comes 呢？此处可从语法结构和语义上判断。从语法结构上看，called 除了可以是过去式，还可能是过去分词作后置定语，called 'language co-activation' 意为"被称为'语言协同激活'的……"；而 comes 是一个第三人称单数形式的动词，没有别的可能，只能作谓语动词。从语义上看，若 called 为谓语，则 evidence 应为主语，宾语为 language co-activation，句意则为"该证据称语言协同激活为……"，后面应接宾补，说明把这个 language co-activation 称为什么，而不应该是动词形式的 comes from。从这点也可判断 called 不是谓语。

Some of the most compelling evidence, called 'language co-activation', **comes from**
                                                  谓语

studying eye movements.

步骤二：确定句子主干，理解基本结构

确定谓语为 comes from 后，则可确定主语中心词应为 evidence，修饰成分 Some of the most compelling 和过去分词短语 called 'language co-activation' 都是 evidence 的定语。而 comes from 后的宾语为动名词短语 studying eye movements。实际上，在理解句意时，同学们可以将 comes from doing sth."来自做某事"这部分看作整体，不用细分究竟这个 doing sth. 是作什么成分。

Some of the most compelling   evidence,   called 'language co-activation',
        主语的定语   主语   主语的定语

comes from studying eye movements.
     谓语部分

Exercise 1 画出以下句子的核心成分（主语、谓语、宾语、表语、宾语补语）。

1. Several disasters have happened. 真

2. The cleanup devices closer to shore would more effectively reduce pollution over the long term. 真

3. Buying cheap and selling dear can give the collector a sense of triumph. 真

4. Those designs appear counter-intuitive. 真

5. Being bored makes us more creative. 真

Exercise 2 划分以下句子的句子成分，找出谓语动词。

1. New Zealand is a small country of four million inhabitants. 真

2. Over two millennia ago, the Greek philosopher Plato extolled its virtues as a means of developing skills for adult life. 真

3. Rochman and her colleagues examined more than a hundred papers on the impacts of marine debris（废弃物）. 真

4. Our blaming of businesses also ignores the ultimate responsibility of the public for creating the conditions. 真

5. They later passed on their knowledge of the qanat method（暗渠法）to the Romans.

Exercise 3 划分以下句子的句子成分，判断句子属于哪种基本句型。

1. In 1999, Tourism New Zealand launched a campaign. 真

2. Nutmeg（肉豆蔻）was a highly prized and costly ingredient in European cuisine. 真

3. Providing support to employees gives them the confidence to perform their jobs better. 真

4. Ideas about play-based learning have been developing since the 19th century. 真

5. He considers the perceived dangers of ocean trash as a potential alarm.

（答案见 pp. 157~159）

第2节 简单句基本成分的变化

英语的基本句型虽然只有五种，但在此基础上句子可以千变万化，使简单句变得"不简单"。本节主要讲解简单句中各个成分的变化，帮助同学们打好理解长难句的基础。

一 谓语动词的变化

谓语动词是简单句的核心，而谓语动词有四种变化，分别为时态、情态、语态和否定形式，即"**三态一否**"。同时由于这些变化，谓语动词在长难句中不一定是一个单词，有可能是由几个单词组成一个整体，同学们需要将这个整体看作谓语动词。下面将从这四个方面讲解具体的变化形式。

1. 谓语动词的时态

英语中的时态应从两个维度去理解，分别是动作发生的"**时间**"和"**状态**"。

"**时间**"分为四种：**过去、现在、将来、过去将来**。

"**状态**"也分为四种：**一般、进行、完成、完成进行**。

将这两个维度两两组合，就构成了英语的 16 种时态，如下表所示。但雅思常考的只有 8 种时态（表格中有底色的部分），同学们需熟知这 8 种时态的构成形式和用法。

时间＼状态	一般	进行	完成	完成进行
过去	一般过去时 was/were; did	过去进行时 was/were doing	过去完成时 had done	过去完成进行时 had been doing
现在	一般现在时 is/am/are; do/does	现在进行时 is/am/are doing	现在完成时 have/has done	现在完成进行时 have/has been doing
将来	一般将来时 is/am/are going to do; will do	将来进行时 will be doing	将来完成时 will have done	将来完成进行时 will have been doing
过去将来	一般过去将来时 was/were going to do; would do	过去将来进行时 would be doing	过去将来完成时 would have done	过去将来完成进行时 would have been doing

2. 谓语动词的情态

谓语动词的情态就是"**情态动词+动词原形**"的形式。在句子中，"情态动词+动词原形"应视作一个整体，充当一个谓语动词。常见的情态动词有 must"必须"、can/could"能够，可以"、will/would"愿意"、may/might"可能；可以"、should"应该"。关于情态动词，注意以下几点即可：

① 情态动词一般只有现在时和过去时两种时态，个别情态动词如 must 和 need，没有过去时。

② 情态动词没有人称的变化，任何人称都用情态动词的同一形式。

③ 变否定句和疑问句时，情态动词的变化与助动词一样：变否定句时，情态动词后加 not 即可；变一般疑问句，则将情态动词提前至句首。

④ 情态动词也可以表示推测，推测的可能性由大到小排列为：must > should > can > may > might。

3. 谓语动词的语态

谓语动词的语态分为"**主动语态**"和"**被动语态**"两种。主语是谓语动词动作的发出者，即为主动语态。主语为谓语动词动作的承受者，则为被动语态。被动语态的基本构成是"be+done"。其中，be随着时态和主语人称的单复数而变化。同学们需要熟知各种时态下的被动语态形式，把"be+done"这个被动形式当作整体来看，视作一个谓语动词。

常用时态的被动形式如下：

时态	被动形式	时态	被动形式
一般过去时	was/were done	过去进行时	was/were being done
一般现在时	is/am/are done	现在进行时	is/am/are being done
一般将来时	will be done	过去完成时	had been done
一般过去将来时	would be done	现在完成时	have/has been done

上一节我们学习了简单句的五种基本句型，除了"主+系+表"和"主+谓"结构不能转化为被动形式，其他句型的被动形式如下：

● **主语+谓语+宾语**

例 | A witch called Nannie chases Tam, a farmer. （主动语态） ➡ Tam, a farmer, is chased by a witch called Nannie. （被动语态）真

译 农民谭被一个叫南妮的女巫追赶。

析 "主+谓+宾"结构转化为被动形式时，主动语态中的宾语（此处为Tam）转化成被动语态中的主语。

● **主语+谓语+间接宾语+直接宾语**

例 | Researchers gave all participants a frustrating task. （主动语态） ➡ All participants were given a frustrating task by researchers. （被动语态）真

译 研究人员给了所有参与者一个令人沮丧的任务。

析 "主+谓+双宾"结构转化为被动形式时，间接宾语（此处为all participants）转化成被动语态中的主语。

● **主语+谓语+宾语+宾语补语**

例 | The appearance of the first of standing figures in bronze proved critics wrong. （主动语态） ➡ Critics were proven wrong by the appearance of the first of standing figures in bronze. （被动语态） 真

译 第一批站立铜像的出现证明了批评家是错误的。

析 主动形式转换成被动形式后，原来的宾语（此处为critics）变成主语，宾语补语（此处为wrong）也相应变成主语补语。

4. 谓语动词的否定形式

肯定句变否定句，只需要把谓语动词变成否定形式。具体分为两种情况：

① 谓语动词只有实义动词：动词前加助动词的否定式"do/does/did+not"，实义动词变原形；

② 谓语动词为系动词或包含助动词、情态动词：只需要在相应的系动词、助动词或情态动词后加not即可。

（注：若谓语动词同时包含系动词、助动词和情态动词，只需在首词后加一个not即可。）

真题句解读·实战演练 1

熟知谓语动词的四种变化，有助于同学们快速、准确地找出句子的谓语动词，而确定谓语动词是解读长难句的关键。

例 The public must accept the necessity for higher prices for products to cover the added costs. 真

译 公众必须接受产品价格务必会提高以弥补额外成本的事实。

步骤一：找出句子的谓语动词

句中有两个动词，分别是must accept和cover。如果熟知谓语的四种变化，就会发现must accept是一个"情态动词＋动词原形"的结构，也就能判断其为本句真正的谓语动词。

The public **must accept** the necessity for higher prices for products to cover the added costs.
     谓语

步骤二：观察分析谓语动词前的内容

通过观察，可判断 must accept 前面的名词 The public 就是主语。

The public   **must accept**   the necessity for higher prices for products to cover the added costs.
主语   谓语

步骤三：观察分析谓语动词后的内容

谓语动词 must accept 后是宾语 the necessity for higher prices for products，而 to cover the added costs 则是后置定语，对 higher prices 进行补充说明。

The public   **must accept**   the necessity for higher prices for products   to cover the added costs.
主语   谓语   宾语   后置定语

二 主语、宾语、补语的变化

简单句中，除了重点掌握谓语动词的变化外，同学们还需注意主语、宾语、补语（表语实质上也属于补语的一种）的变化。这三种成分常由名词（短语）和代词充当，或由从句充当（这部分详见第6、7节名词性从句），也可以由非谓语动词 doing 和 to do 短语充当。本节主要讲述 doing 和 to 短语作主语、宾语和补语。

非谓语动词，顾名思义，即为"不可作谓语的动词"。非谓语动词可以充当多种成分，如主语、宾语、补语、定语、状语等。**非谓语动词分三类：doing**（动名词和现在分词）、**to do**（不定式）**和 done**（过去分词）。其中 doing 和 to do 都可以当作名词来用，故可以充当主语、宾语和补语。

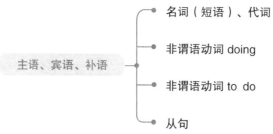

1. doing 充当句子的主语、宾语和补语

例1 Finally, **understanding implicit theories of intelligence** can help elucidate developmental and cross-cultural differences. 真

译1 最后，理解内隐智力理论有助于阐明发展差异和跨文化差异。

析1 本句中的主语由 doing 短语 understanding implicit theories of intelligence 充当，指"理解内隐智力理论"这件事。

例2 He himself started **carving a variety of subjects in stone**, including depictions of reclining women, mother-and-child groups, and masks. 真

译2 他自己开始在石头上雕刻各种主题，包括斜倚的妇女、"母与子"以及面具。

析2 及物动词 started 后面要接宾语，宾语则由 doing 短语 carving a variety of subjects in stone 充当。

例3 I see governments **seizing** the opportunity. 真

译3 我看到政府抓住了机会。

析3 本句的谓语动词是 see，后接宾语 governments，而 doing 短语 seizing the opportunity 则为宾语补语，对宾语做补充说明。

2. to do 充当句子的主语、宾语和补语

例1 **To continue the project** is not easy. 真

译1 要继续这个项目并不容易。

析1 此处 to do 短语 To continue the project 作主语，谓语动词用单数形式。

例2 Health geographers can attempt **to identify the reasons** behind an increase or decrease in illnesses. 真

译2 健康地理学家可以试图找出疾病增加或减少背后的原因。

析2 与 doing 不同，to do 作宾语，只能位于及物动词之后，不能位于介词之后（介词之后要用 doing）。此处 attempt 的宾语由 to identify the reasons 充当。

例3 A fast-food company encouraged the government **to introduce legislation**. 真

译3 一家快餐公司鼓励政府立法。

析3 句中出现 encourage sb. to do sth. 结构，to introduce legislation 在句中充当宾语 the government 的补语。

Tips

1. 非谓语动词 doing 和 to do 作主语时，谓语动词均用单数形式。若出现两个或以上的 doing 和 to do 的非谓语动词并列作主语，谓语动词则用复数形式。

2. doing 和 to do 作句子成分时，要注意其完整性。如果使用的是及物动词，后面要接宾语，这时的 doing sth. 或 to do sth. 应被看作一个整体。

3. to do 作某些动词的宾补时，会省略 to。这些动词主要是感官动词和某些使役动词，比如 see sb. do sth.、let sb. do sth. 等用法。

例1 Consumers are tending to purchase access to a range of vehicles through a mobility provider. 真

译1 消费者倾向于在一个汽车供应商处购买多种车辆的使用权。

步骤一：判断谓语动词

这个句子有两个动词，分别是 are tending 和 purchase。注意，purchase 前有 to，说明这是 to do 结构，是非谓语动词，故句子真正的谓语动词是 are tending，此为 tend 的现在进行时态。

Consumers **are tending** to purchase access to a range of vehicles through a mobility provider.
　　　　　谓语

步骤二：分析句子其他成分

同学们只要意识到 to do 结构可以作主语、宾语或补语，那么这个句子就很好理解了。句子的宾语由 to do 短语充当，即 to purchase access to a range of vehicles，意指"购买多种车辆的使用权"。当然，也可以利用 tend to do sth. "倾向于做某事"结构将谓语动词和 to do 合起来理解。需要注意 access 可作动词或名词，在本句中，其位于及物动词 purchase 后面，因此可判断其为名词。

Consumers	**are tending**	to purchase access to a range of vehicles	through a mobility provider.
主语	谓语	宾语	状语

例2 Refusing to accept the advantages of AI could place a large group of people at a serious disadvantage. 真

译2 拒绝接受人工智能的好处可能会使一大群人处于严重的劣势。

步骤一：判断谓语动词

速读句子，可发现句中有三个动词，即 Refusing、to accept、could place。其中，Refusing 是 doing 结构，而 to accept 则是 to do 结构，两个都是非谓语动词，故判断句子真正的谓语动词是 could place。

Refusing to accept the advantages of AI **could place** a large group of people at a serious disadvantage.
　　　　　　　　　　　　　　　　　谓语

步骤二：分析句子其他成分

谓语动词的前面是 Refusing to accept the advantages of AI，是 doing 短语作主语，而谓语动词后的宾语 a large group of people 则为宾语，介词短语 at a serious disadvantage 为宾语补语，补充说明宾语被置于何种处境。

Refusing to accept the advantages of AI	**could place**	a large group of people
主语	谓语	宾语

at a serious disadvantage.
宾语补语

语法点精练·小试牛刀

Exercise 1 画出以下句子的谓语动词。

1. Children must enjoy the activity. 真

2. More papers on the subject have been published since 2013. 真

3. In an oral context, a story won't survive because of one great teller. 真

4. Knowing more than one language can cause speakers to name pictures more slowly. 真

5. He asked both expert musicians and non-experts to assess six compositions. 真

Exercise 2 用所给动词的正确形式填空。

1. Many insect species _____ (encounter) infrequently by human. 真

2. From the tiny proportion of insects that have been investigated, several promising compounds _____ (identify). 真

3. The meaning and value of happiness _____ (explore) for many years. 真

4. But _____ (blame) alone is unlikely to produce change. 真

5. When the experiments were repeated, activation _____ (observe) in all areas of the brain. 真

（答案见 pp. 159~160）

第 3 节 简单句的扩展（一）

除核心成分外，简单句还能添加很多起修饰作用的非核心成分，而这些扩展的部分常常是理解难句的障碍。接下来两节将分别从"词性"和"句子成分"两个角度讲解简单句的扩展。

本节是从词性角度来看简单句的扩展。

一 名词的限定词和修饰语

主语、宾语、表语、补语都可由名词充当，而名词的前后通常会有限定词和修饰语。限定词包括冠词、数词、代词、名词所有格等。修饰语通常为形容词、名词（名词也可修饰名词）和介词短语。一个名词可以同时带有多个限定词和修饰语。

例1 **The crop varieties** should be more resilient to **new climate trends** and **extreme weather patterns**. 真

译1 作物品种应更能适应新的气候趋势和极端天气模式。

析1 主语 The crop varieties 的中心词是名词 varieties，前有名词 crop 修饰构成名词短语，冠词 The 为限定词；new climate trends 的中心词是名词 trends，名词 climate 为其修饰语，共同构成名词短语"气候趋势"，形容词 new 是整个短语的修饰语；同样地，extreme weather patterns 也是"形容词修饰语 + 名词修饰语 + 中心词"结构的名词短语。

例2 According to the latest figures, **a majority of the world's population** is now bilingual or multilingual. 真

译2 根据最新数据，现在世界上大多数人都掌握两种或多种语言。

析2 本句的主语是 a majority of the world's population，中心词是 population，名词所有格 the world's 和量词短语 a majority of 为其限定词。

二 介词短语

所谓的介词短语，就是"介词 + 名词/代词/doing"，介词后的成分是介词的宾语，因此介词短语也被称为"介宾短语"。介词短语是一种很常见的修饰语（作状语或定语），这时它并非句子的主要成分，分析句子时可先不看。雅思阅读中常见的介词及用法如下。

1. 表示时间的介词

at/on/in 在	例 **In 1796**, the English arrived on Ceylon, thereby displacing the Dutch from their control of the cinnamon monopoly. 真 译 在 1796 年，英国人抵达锡兰，从而取代了荷兰人控制肉桂的垄断。
from 从……之后 since 自从 after 之后	例 **After every weekend** there would always be a couple of bikes missing. 真 译 每个周末过后，总会有几辆单车不见了。
from... to... 从……到…… during 在……期间	例 **During a period of three days**, a group of volunteers from the breeding centre worked around the clock to prepare the young tortoises for transport. 真 译 在三天时间里，育种中心的一群志愿者夜以继日地工作，为运输幼龟做好准备。

by 直到 until/till 直到	例 **Until the late 18th century**, it only grew in one place in the world: a small group of islands in the Banda Sea. 真 译 18 世纪末之前，它只在世界上一个地方生长：班达海的一小群岛屿上。
for ……以来	例 **For years**, repatriation efforts were carried out in small numbers. 真 译 多年来，野外放归工作都是小规模进行的。

2. 表示地点和方位的介词

at/in 在	例 The bikes were then left unlocked **at various locations** around the city, to be used by anyone in need of transport. 真 译 之后，这些没有上锁的单车就放置在城市各处，以供任何有需要的人代步。
on/above/over 在……上面 under/below 在……下面	例 Well **above the treeline in Norway's highest mountains**, ancient fields of ice are shrinking as Earth's climate warms. 真 译 在挪威最高山脉的林木线之上，古老冰原的面积正随着全球气候变暖而缩减。
near 在……附近 by/beside 在……旁边	例 In 1944, Harlow, a town **near London**, offered Moore a commission for a sculpture depicting a family. 真 译 1944 年，伦敦附近的一个小镇哈洛委托摩尔做一个家庭雕像。
across 跨过 through/past 穿过	例 The secret of glass making was taken **across Europe** by the Romans during this century. 真 译 玻璃制造的秘密在该世纪被罗马人带到了整个欧洲。
to/towards 去，朝	例 This fantasy is helping her take her first steps **towards her capacity for creativity**. 真 译 这种幻想正在帮助她向创造力迈出第一步。
in front of 在……前面 behind 在……背后 around 在……周围	例 Many of their houses were built **around a courtyard** and were constructed of stone. 译 他们的许多房子分布在庭院四周，是用石头建造的。

3. 其他介词

of ……的…… （表从属关系）	例 Many collectors collect to develop their social life, attending meetings **of a group of collectors** and exchanging information on items. 真 译 很多收藏者通过收藏开展社交，他们参加收藏者群体的会议，交流藏品信息。
about 关于	例 The answer to my question **about marketing principles** was obvious: *no*. 真 译 对于我提出的关于市场营销道德准则的问题，答案很明显是否定的。
with 有 without 没有	例 He made the ascent **without having the least expectation**. 真 译 他在登顶时并未抱有一丝期望。
for 为了；因为；对于	例 By custom, Pachacuti's descendants built other similar estates **for their own use**. 真 译 按照惯例，帕查库蒂的后代建造了其他类似的庄园供自己使用。

by 通过	例 His recently published research answers the question **by looking at the causes of unemployment**. 真 译 他最近发表的研究通过研究失业的原因，回答了这一问题。
despite 尽管	例 **Despite this recognition of the importance of employee development**, the hospitality industry has historically been dominated by underdeveloped HR practices. 真 译 尽管酒店业认识到员工发展的重要性，但长期以来不完善的人力资源管理做法在该行业一直占主导地位。

真题句解读·实战演练

虽然简单句的句子结构较为单一，但由于可以加入限定词以及形容词、介词短语等修饰语，简单句也可以很长，有时句子很难一眼看懂。无论如何，解剖长难句的关键始终是找出句子的核心部分，即主谓部分，然后再去剖析修饰成分。

例 The implementation of robotic car manufacture from the 1970s onwards led to significant cost savings and improvements in the reliability and flexibility of vehicle mass production. 真

译 自动机械从 20 世纪 70 年代开始用于制造汽车，这大大节省了成本，并极大提高了汽车大规模生产的稳定性和灵活性。

步骤一：找谓语

这句虽长，但只有一个动词 led to，实际上是个简单句。

The implementation of robotic car manufacture from the 1970s onwards **led to** significant cost

　　　　　　　　　　　　　　　　　　　　　　　　　　　　　　　　　　谓语

savings and improvements in the reliability and flexibility of vehicle mass production.

步骤二：找主语

找到谓语后，找主语。led to 前的名词短语 The implementation 即主语。主语后的两个介词短语 of robotic car manufacture 和 from the 1970s onwards 是主语的修饰语，可先略去不看。

The implementation ~~of robotic car manufacture from the 1970s onwards~~ **led to** significant cost

　　主语　　　　　　　　　　　　　　　　　　　　　　　　　　　　　　谓语

savings and improvements in the reliability and flexibility of vehicle mass production.

步骤三：找宾语

led to 的 to 为介词，后面需接宾语。led to 之后的部分中，significant 为形容词，修饰后面的 cost savings and improvements，而 cost 为名词，修饰名词 savings，因此此句的宾语为 savings and improvements。improvements 后面的介词短语是 improvements 的修饰语。至此，句子的主干很明显是 "The implementation led to savings and improvements."。

The implementation	of robotic car manufacture from the 1970s onwards	**led to**
主语	后置定语	谓语
significant cost	**savings and improvements**	in the reliability and flexibility of vehicle mass
修饰语	宾语	后置定语
production		

语法点精练·小试牛刀

Exercise 1　用所给单词的正确形式填空。

1. At the same time, _____ (culture) values are highly entrenched (根深蒂固的) in food and agricultural systems worldwide. 真

2. When futures markets become excessively financialised, they can contribute to short-term price volatility, which increases _____ (farmer) food insecurity. 真

3. EMI created replicas (仿制品) which still rely completely on the original artist's _____ (create) impulses. 真

4. If the designers had had the tools to think with _____ (they) bodies, there might have been a better solution. 真

5. Fun may have a _____ (benefit) effect, but the framing of that fun must be carefully aligned with both organizational goals and employee characteristics. 真

Exercise 2　为以下句子选择恰当的介词。

1. _____ (In/By) the Middle Ages, Europeans used the spice to flavour food, particularly meat. 真

2. Arab traders and European sailors are likely to have moved coconuts _____ (between/from) South and Southeast Asia to Africa. 真

3. _____ (Through/Without) these efforts there would be fewer species alive today. 真

4. Governments can significantly reduce risks for farmers _____ (by/to) providing basic services like roads to get produce more efficiently to markets. 真

5. In fact, studies show that sixty percent _____ (about/of) beneficiaries of subsidies are not poor, but rich landowners and non-farmer traders. 真

Exercise 3　画出以下句子中名词的修饰成分 (限定词、形容词或介词短语等)，并判断其修饰对象。

1. It might represent a broader pattern among other social bugs. 真

2. Animals in good zoos get a varied and high-quality diet with all the supplements required. 真

3. Mobility will change in such potentially significant ways and in association with so many other technological developments, such as telepresence and virtual reality. 真

4. In many large cities, the wind is not strong enough to clear the air of the massive amounts of smog. 真

5. A hybridised band-tailed pigeon (斑尾鸽), with the added nesting habits of a passenger pigeon (旅鸽), could, in theory, re-establish that forest disturbance. 真

Exercise 4　画出以下句子中的介词短语，并判断其充当的成分。

1. By understanding why and how we get sick, we can change the way we treat disease. 真

2. In Britain, the modern glass industry only really started to develop after the repeal of the Excise Act in 1845. 真

3. Modern glass plants are capable of making millions of glass containers a day in many different colours. 真

4. Scientists collected thousands of 30-second conversations between parents and their babies. 真

5. Given the current concerns about environmental issues, the future of this ancient material once again looks promising. 真

(答案见 pp. 160~162)

简单句的核心成分有五种：**主语、谓语、宾语、表语和补语**。其中只有主语和谓语是**必备成分**，而宾语、表语和补语则视乎谓语的类型和句意来决定是否需要。

除此之外，英文句子的基本成分还包括"定语""状语""同位语"等，这一节将从这几个成分的角度讲解简单句的扩展。

一　定语和状语

定语和状语是同学们容易混淆的成分。简单来说，定语就是修饰说明名词（或代词）的品质与特征的成分，可以是单个单词，也可以是短语或从句。而这个修饰成分，可放在被修饰词的前面（即前置定语）或被修饰词的后面（即后置定语）。例如，在短语 a useful book 中，形容词 useful 就是定语，修饰名词 book；在短语 a man of a good temper 中，介词短语 of a good temper 就是定语，且这个定语是后置的，修饰名词 man，整个名词短语的意思是"一个好脾气的人"。

对于定语，关键是确定被修饰词。

状语则是用来修饰动词、形容词、副词以及全句的句子成分，同样可以是单个单词、短语或从句。状语可出现在句首、句中或句末。例如，在句子 "It rained heavily." 中，副词 heavily 修饰的是动词 rained，作状语；在句子 "Unfortunately, the message never arrived." 中，副词 Unfortunately 则是修饰整个句子，也是作状语。

至于我们常见到的诸如"伴随状语""方式状语"和"让步状语"等术语，只是根据状语所起的作用而定的名字，本质上还是要从状语本身表达的意思来判断。**同学们在看句子时不必纠结于某部分是"伴随状语"还是"结果状语"等问题，只需明白其意思即可。**

一般来说，除了相应的从句外，定语常由形容词和介词短语充当，状语由副词和介词短语充当。此处介绍定语和状语的特殊形式，即由非谓语动词 doing、to do 和 done 充当定语和状语。

1. 非谓语动词充当定语

非谓语动词作定语，用来修饰名词。其中，doing 和 done 既可置于名词前，也可置于名词后；不定式 to do 则常置于名词后。这些定语在翻译时，常放到名词前，即译成"……（定语）的……（名词）"。

例1　The **growing** unpredictability of weather patterns increases farmers' difficulty in managing weather-related risks. 真

译1　天气模式变得越来越难以预测，使农民更难应对与天气有关的风险。

例2　The Travel Planner offered **suggested** routes and public transport options between the **chosen** locations. 真

译2　旅程安排表为选定的地点提供了往来的建议路线和可选择的公共交通。

析　以上两个例子中，现在分词 growing "越来越多的"、过去分词 suggested "建议的" 和 chosen "选中的" 都是前置的定语，用法与形容词类似。

例3　In ancient Rome, mourners **attending funerals** burnt cinnamon to create a pleasant scent. 真

译3　在古罗马，参加葬礼的送葬者会燃烧肉桂来制造令人愉悦的香气。

例4　People belonging to the ethnic group **called the Salagama** would peel the bark off young shoots of the cinnamon plant in the rainy season. 真

译4　萨罗人会在雨季从肉桂植株的嫩芽上剥下树皮。

例5　Oxytocin makes us more likely to look others in the eye and improves our ability **to identify emotions**. 真

译5　催产素使我们更有可能直视他人的眼睛并提高我们识别情绪的能力。

以上三例中，三个非谓语动词均位于所修饰的名词后面，作后置定语。doing 和 done 短语的逻辑主语就是它修饰的名词，注意区分两者在语态上的区别，doing 表主动，done 表被动。例如，mourners attending funerals，参加葬礼的是送葬者，mourners 与 attend 是主动关系；而 the ethnic group called the Salagama 实际上是 the ethnic group is called the Salagama，"该种族被称为萨罗"，为被动语态。不定式 to do 与被修饰语之间既可以是主谓关系，也可以是动宾关系，或是对名词的解释，根据具体句意理解即可。例5中，ability to identify emotions 意思是"识别情绪的能力"。

Tips

非谓语动词作定语时，不一定只有 doing、done 或 to do 单独一两个单词，如果是及物动词，还可能带上宾语及其他修饰成分，构成一个较复杂的非谓语动词短语，同学们在分析句子时，**一定要找到完整的非谓语动词短语**，才能理清句意。

2. 非谓语动词充当状语

非谓语动词作状语，修饰句子的谓语，补充说明时间、目的、原因、结果、条件等。该部分的逻辑主语就是句子的主语。

例1 Activities are the key driver of visitor satisfaction, **contributing 74% to visitor satisfaction**. 真

译1 活动是影响游客满意度的关键因素，占比为74%。

析1 本句已有完整的"主＋系＋表"结构，另一个动作 contribute 就要变成非谓语动词，且 contribute 与主句的主语 Activities 是主动的关系，意思是"活动贡献了……"，故此处用了表主动的 doing 形式。contributing 后接上宾语和其他修饰成分，就构成了整个非谓语动词短语 contributing 74% to visitor satisfaction，补充说明"活动是关键因素"的原因。

例2 From Britain, visits to New Zealand grew at an average annual rate of 13% between 2002 and 2006, **compared to a rate of 4% overall for British visits abroad**. 真

译2 2002 年至 2006 年间，英国到新西兰的访问人次年均增长率为13%，而英国人出国次数的总体增长率为 4%。

析2 本句的主谓结构是 visits... grew...，故另一个动词 compare 就要变成非谓语动词形式。而句子主语 visits 与 compare 是被动关系（访问量被比较），故 compare 用了 done 形式表被动。

例3 Eventually, the Dutch began cultivating their own cinnamon trees **to supplement the diminishing number of wild trees available for use**. 真

译3 可供使用的野生肉桂树不断减少，为了补上这一缺口，最终，荷兰人开始自己种植肉桂树。

析3 本句的主、谓、宾已完整，在已有谓语 began 的情况下，另一个动词 supplement 要改成非谓语动词形式。supplement 与句子主语 the Dutch 是主动关系，且表示目的(荷兰人种植肉桂树是为了……)，故用了不定式 to do 结构。同学们注意，不定式结构作状语时多数表示目的。

二 同位语和插入语

同位语，用来解释名词，一般紧跟在其所说明的名词之后，可以是一个单词、一个短语甚至是一个从句（即同位语从句）。而插入语则是插入到句子中间，一些表明态度、看法等解释性的词语。与同位语相似，插入语可以是一个单词、短语甚至是一个从句。

同位语和插入语都是句子的非核心成分，它们会使句子出现分隔结构（见本章第 13 节），增加句子理解的难度。

例1 On one occasion, in 1872, the ship and a rival clipper, *Thermopylae*, left port in China on the same day. 真

译1 有一次，在1872年，这艘船和与之匹敌的一艘快船塞姆皮雷号在同一天离开了中国的港口。

析1 *Thermopylae* 是对主语之一 a rival clipper 的补充，作其同位语，说明船的具体名字。

例2 In order to protect their hold on the market, the Dutch, **like the Portuguese before them**, treated the native inhabitants harshly. 真

译2 为了保持自己对市场的控制，荷兰人和在他们之前的葡萄牙人一样，粗暴对待当地的原住民。

析2 句中的 like the Portuguese before them 是插入语，补充说明荷兰人如何对待原住民。

Tips
　　同位语和插入语的作用均为补充说明，常伴有一些标志性的标点符号，如逗号、括号、破折号或冒号。这些标点符号都可以帮助同学们进行判断，从而快速划分出句子主干。

真题句解读·实战演练

　　解读长难句的关键并不在于对从句的理解，而在于**对简单句基本结构的掌握**。所有句子都是在基本句型的基础上进行变化，只要掌握好简单句的构成，再复杂的句子我们也能化繁为简，手到擒来。

　　化繁为简时重要的一步是去掉句子的修饰成分，找出句子的主干。

例 In November 2010, the environmentalist and Galapagos National Park liaison officer Godfrey Merlin, a visiting private motor yacht captain and a helicopter pilot gathered around a table in a small cafe in Puerto Ayora on the island of Sant Cruz to work out more ambitious reintroduction. 真

译 2010 年 11 月，加拉帕戈斯国家公园联络官、环保主义者戈弗雷·梅林、一位外地来访的私人摩托艇船长和一名直升机飞行员坐在圣克鲁斯岛阿约拉港一家小咖啡馆的桌子旁，制定目标更远大的放生计划。

步骤一：找核心成分

　　先去掉修饰成分，只留下核心成分，句子就可以简化成 Godfrey Merlin, a captain and a pilot gathered，整个句子的大意就一目了然，即"戈弗雷·梅林、一位船长和一名飞行员三人聚在一起"。

~~In November 2010, the environmentalist and Galapagos National Park liaison officer~~ *Godfrey Merlin,* ~~a~~ *visiting private motor yacht* captain ~~and a~~ helicopter *pilot* gathered ~~around a table in a small cafe in Puerto Ayora on the island of Sant Cruz to work out more ambitious reintroduction.~~

步骤二：分析主语的修饰成分

　　对修饰成分逐个进行观察：除了句首的 In November 2010，人名 Godfrey Merlin 前面的一长串单词都是这个主语的同位语，用于表明其身份；captain 前面的 a visiting private motor yacht 是它的修饰语；同样 pilot 前面的名词 helicopter 也是修饰语，都用于补充说明具体身份。

In November 2010, <u>the environmentalist and Galapagos National Park liaison officer</u> **Godfrey Merlin**, <u>a visiting private motor yacht</u> **captain** and <u>a helicopter</u> **pilot** gathered around a table in a small cafe in Puerto Ayora on the island of Sant Cruz to work out more ambitious reintroduction.

步骤三：分析其他成分

　　句首的 In November 2010 为时间状语。谓语动词 gathered 后面还有很长一部分，around a table、in a small café、in Puerto Ayora、on the island of Sant Cruz 这几个都是表示地点的介词短语，由小到大进行排列。最后 to work out... 是非谓语动词短语，放在句子结尾作目的状语。

In November 2010, the environmentalist and Galapagos National Park liaison officer *Godfrey Merlin,* *a* visiting private motor yacht *captain and a* helicopter *pilot* **gathered** <u>around a table</u> <u>in a small café</u> <u>in Puerto Ayora</u> <u>on the island of Sant Cruz</u> *to work out more ambitious reintroduction.*

Exercise 1 画出以下句子的主干。

1. In the past—and nowadays, too, though to a lesser extent—a popular form of collecting, particularly among boys and men, was trainspotting. 真

2. Vehicles with limited self-driving capabilities have been around for more than 50 years, resulting in significant contributions towards driver assistance systems. 真

3. A team made up of more than 30 psychological scientists, anthropologists, and biologists then played these recordings to listeners from 24 diverse societies, from indigenous tribes in New Guinea to city-dwellers in India and Europe. 真

4. At first glance, spending resources to incorporate elements of a seemingly irrelevant trend into one's core offerings sounds like hardly worthwhile. 真

5. A major milestone in the history of glass occurred with the invention of lead crystal glass by the English glass manufacturer George Ravenscroft. 真

Exercise 2 用所给动词的正确形式填空。

1. _____ (travel) around Thailand in the 1990s, William Janssen was impressed with the basic rooftop solar heating systems on many homes. 真

2. _____ (make) it easier to plan motoring holidays, the site catalogued the most popular driving routes in the country, _____ (highlight) different routes according to the season and indicating distances and times. 真

3. The Massachusetts Institute of Technology investigated automated mobility in Singapore, _____ (find) that fewer than 30 percent of the vehicles currently used would be required in case of fully automated car sharing. 真

4. Relatively immobile and capable of surviving for months without food or water, the tortoises were taken on board these ships _____ (act) as food supplies during long ocean passages. 真

5. Rewilding means the mass restoration of _____ (damage) ecosystems. 真

Exercise 3 找出以下句子中的同位语及非谓语动词充当的状语或定语，并画出句子的主干。

1. Dr David Beresford-Jones, archaeobotanist（考古植物学家）at Cambridge University, has been studying the role of the huarango tree in landscape change. 真

2. In 1866, he gave up his business to open a photographic studio, advertising himself as a portrait and landscape photographer. 真

3. Supported by a rope and harness（安全带）, you can stand on branches no bigger than your wrist. 真

4. The BLFC arranged games between teams representing the north and the south of England. 真

5. Our biggest challenge is to address the underlying causes of the agricultural system's inability to ensure sufficient food for all. 真

（答案见 pp. 162~164）

第5节 / 并列句

在雅思阅读中，并列句出现的频率非常高。而要理解阅读篇章的各种并列句，我们需熟悉表示不同逻辑关系的并列连词。

一 并列句的基本概念

两个或两个以上的简单句用并列连词连在一起构成的句子，叫作并列句。其基本结构是"**简单句 + 并列连词 + 简单句**"（有时也可不用并列连词，而是用分号、冒号等把分句隔开）。并列句中各个分句的关系是平行的，没有从属关系。但各个分句之间却可以有不同的逻辑关系，分句之间的逻辑关系要靠并列连词来体现。

二 常见的并列连词

1. 表示顺承的并列连词

表示顺承的并列连词包括 and、both... and、not only... but (also) 和 neither... nor 等。其中 neither... nor 含有否定意味，表示"既不……，也不……"，其他连词则表示"……和……"以及"不但……，而且……"。

例1 From the planting of a cork sapling to the first harvest takes 25 years, **and** a gap of approximately a decade must separate harvests from an individual tree. 真

译1 从种植软木橡树苗到第一次收成需要25年的时间，而且每棵树必须间隔大约10年才能再次有收成。

析1 此句由简单句 From... to... takes 25 years 和 a gap... must separate harvests... 构成，并由表示顺承的并列连词 and 连接在一起。

例2 **Not only** would extinction of polar bears mean the loss of potential breakthroughs in human medicine, **but** more importantly, it would mean the disappearance of an intelligent, majestic animal. 真

译2 北极熊的灭绝不仅意味着人类医学失去潜在的突破，更重要的是，它意味着一种聪明、威严的动物消失。

析2 本句为 not only... but (also) 连接的并列句，其中第一个分句用了部分倒装结构（由于 Not only 置于句首），其正常语序为 extinction of polar bears would not only mean the loss of...。

2. 表示转折的并列连词

表示转折的并列连词包括 but、yet、while 和 whereas 等，意为"但是，然而"。

例1 There are endless ways I could have approached this assignment, **but** I took my cue from the title of the course. 真

译1 我有很多方法可以完成这个任务，但我选择按照课程的标题来。

析1 此句由前后两个分句 There are endless ways... 和 I took my cue from... course 构成，并由表示转折的并列连词 but 连接在一起。

例2 The ancient Egyptians sealed their sarcophagi (stone coffins) with cork, **while** the ancient Greeks and Romans used it for anything from beehives to sandals. 真

译2 古埃及人用软木来密封石棺，而古希腊人和古罗马人将软木用于从蜂房到凉鞋的任何东西。

析2 while 连接两个简单句，分别描述软木对古埃及人以及古希腊人和古罗马人有着不同的用途。同学们要注意，while 和 whereas 引导并列句时，强调前后两个分句的对比。

3. 表示选择的并列连词

表示选择的并列连词包括 or 和 either... or 等,表示"或者",两者选其一。

例 The cities could not cope with an increasing population, so they exhausted their resource base **or** they succumbed to invasion and conflict. 真

译 这些城市无法应对不断增长的人口,所以它们耗尽了资源基础,或者屈服于入侵和冲突。

析 表示选择的并列连词 or 将简单句 they exhausted their resource base 和 they succumbed to invasion and conflict 连接在一起。

4. 表示原因或结果的并列连词

表示原因或结果的并列连词包括:for"因为",表原因;so"所以",表结果。

例 No mechanical means of stripping cork bark has been invented, **so** the job is done by teams of highly skilled workers. 真

译 剥离软木树皮的机械方法还未发明出来,所以这项工作是由熟手工人群体完成的。

析 逗号前后两个简单句由并列连词 so 连接在一起,表明前后具有因果关系。

真题句解读·实战演练

例 Not only was a monopoly of cinnamon becoming impossible, but the spice trade overall was diminishing in economic potential, and was eventually superseded by the rise of trade in coffee, tea, chocolate, and sugar. 真

译 不仅肉桂的垄断变得不可能,而且香料贸易整体的经济潜力也在下降,最终在咖啡、茶、巧克力和糖贸易的崛起中被取代。

步骤一:速读句子,找出并列连词

速读句子,马上可发现句中有并列连词 Not only... but,同时后面还有一个 and。往下读找出句中的谓语动词,可发现句子中有三个谓语动词,即 was becoming、was diminishing 和 was superseded,可据此将句子分为三部分。

第一部分:**Not only** <u>was</u> a monopoly of cinnamon becoming impossible,

第二部分:**but** the spice trade overall <u>was diminishing</u> in economic potential,

第三部分:**and** <u>was</u> eventually <u>superseded</u> by the rise of trade in coffee, tea, chocolate, and sugar.

步骤二:分析并列句

并列连词 Not only... but 将 a monopoly of cinnamon was becoming impossible 和 the spice trade overall was diminishing in economic potential 这两个分句连接在一起;

分析第三部分时,可以发现这部分缺少主语。根据上下文我们可知,是香料贸易最终被其他物品的贸易取代,所以第三部分和第二部分共用一个主语 the spice trade,这两个部分合起来是一个含有并列谓语的简单句——并列连词 and 将 was diminishing 和 was superseded 这两个谓语连接起来。

分句1:**Not only**　　　<u>was</u>　　　a monopoly of cinnamon　　　becoming　　　impossible,
　　　　　　　　　　　助动词　　　　　　主语　　　　　　　系动词　　　表语

分句2(第二部分+第三部分):**but**　　　the spice trade overall　　　was diminishing　　　in
　　　　　　　　　　　　　　　　　　　主语　　　　　　　　　谓语1

economic potential,　　**and**　　was eventually superseded　　by the rise of trade in coffee, tea,
　　　　　　　　　　　　　　　　　　谓语2

chocolate, and sugar.

Exercise 1 画出句子中的并列连词及其连接的分句。

1. By the early 20th century, this region had become the world's largest producer of cork, and today it accounts for roughly half of all cork production around the world. 真

2. He can get you treated by himself, or he'll send you off somewhere else if necessary. 真

3. From the 17th century, pirates took a few tortoises on board for food, but the arrival of whaling ships in the 1790s saw this exploitation grow exponentially. 真

4. Corkboard and cork tiles are ideal for thermal and acoustic insulation, while granules of cork are used in the manufacture of concrete. 真

5. Her work tracked the ants from the time the pupae（蛹）became adults, so she knew their exact ages. 真

Exercise 2 选择合适的并列连词填空。

1. Collecting must be one of the most varied forms of human activities, _____ (and/but) it's one that many of us psychologists find fascinating. 真

2. Each person comes to the program and course with his or her own plans, _____ (and/so) these need not even concern the acquisition of marketing expertise as such. 真

3. The field of health geography is often overlooked, _____ (and/but) it constitutes a huge area of need in the fields of geography and healthcare. 真

4. Research shows that activities are the key driver of visitor satisfaction, contributing 74% to visitor satisfaction, _____ (so/while) transport and accommodation account for the remaining 26%. 真

5. Imagining is helping her take her first steps towards her capacity for creativity, _____ (so/while) it will have important repercussions（持续影响）in her adult life. 真

Exercise 3 根据句子逻辑，使用恰当的并列连词合并句子。

1. In the 19th century, many collectors amassed（积聚）fossils, animals and plants from around the globe.
   Their collections provided a vast amount of information about the natural world.

2. Oxytocin（催产素）probably does some very basic things.
   These basic processes could manifest in different ways depending on individual differences and context.

3. Intrinsically（发自内心地）motivated free play provides the child with true autonomy.
   Guided play can help parents and educators provide more targeted learning experiences.

4. In some versions of *Little Red Riding Hood*, the wolf swallows up the grandmother.
   In others it locks her in a cupboard.

5. They don't have the money to buy the diesel（柴油）to run the desalination plants（海水淡化厂）.
   It is a really bad situation.

（答案见 pp. 164~165）

第6节 复合句——名词性从句（一）

　　由于复合句可以带有多个从句，而且往往主句和从句的分隔并不明显，于是很多复合句变成了长难句。因此，掌握各类从句的性质是解读这类长难句的突破口。从句尽管形式多变，但根据其作用，可以分为三大类：名词性从句、定语从句和状语从句。本节先讲解名词性从句和其中的宾语从句。

一　名词性从句的基本概念与分类

　　名词性从句就是指把从句看作一个名词，放在主句中可充当主语、宾语、表语和同位语等，因此名词性从句可以分为**主语从句、宾语从句、表语从句和同位语从句**等。

　　四种名词性从句的结构基本相同，只是出现的位置和充当的成分不同，重点学会其中一种从句的构成，其他三种自然就会了。

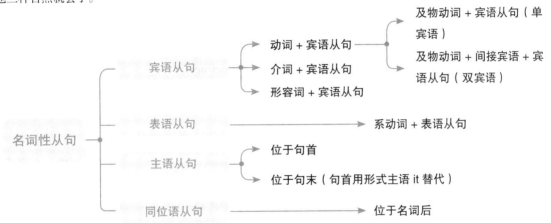

引导名词性从句的连接词可分为 3 类：

① 从属连词（不充当句子成分）：that、whether、if、as if/though。that 用来引导陈述句，本身没有意义，在宾语从句中一般可以省略；但在引导其他名词性从句时，that 不能省略。whether 和 if 引导一般疑问句（从句中的一般疑问句要用陈述语序）。as if/though 引导表语从句。

② 连接代词：who、whom、whose、what、which、whatever、whichever、whoever 等，由于它们在从句中充当相应的句子成分，因此一般不能省略。

③ 连接副词：when、why、how、where 等，在从句中充当状语。

二　宾语从句

　　所谓宾语从句，就是在主句中充当宾语的从句。

例 Their documentation states **that** other methods should be considered. 真

译 他们的文档资料声明其他方式也应该被考虑。

析 Their documentation　　states　　**that** other methods should be considered.

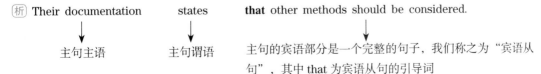

　　　主句主语　　　　主句谓语　　　主句的宾语部分是一个完整的句子，我们称之为"宾语从句"，其中 that 为宾语从句的引导词

1. 宾语从句的转换

（1）主句 +that+ 宾语从句（陈述句）

例 句A：Many of the students immediately assumed+ 宾语

句B：The answer to my question about marketing principles was obvious: no.

= Many of the students immediately assumed **(that)** the answer to my question about marketing principles was obvious: no. 真

译 许多学生立刻认为，对于我提出的关于市场营销道德准则的问题，答案很明显是否定的。

析 宾语从句前的that作引导词，没有实际意义，不充当从句成分，只起到连接主句和从句的作用，可以省略。

> **Tips**
>
> 若一个句子中有多个宾语从句，只有第一个宾语从句前的that可省略，第二个及之后的宾语从句不能省略 that。

（2）主句 +whether/if+ 宾语从句（改为陈述语序的一般疑问句）

例 句A：The farmer should think about+ 宾语

句B：Can the job be performed on a workbench?

= The farmer should think about **whether/if** the job can be performed on a workbench. 真

译 农民应该考虑是否可以在工作台上完成这项工作。

析 当要放入的句子是一般疑问句时，要将一般疑问句调整成陈述语序，同时加上表示"是否"的引导词 whether 或者 if。

（3）主句 + 连接代词 / 连接副词（即原句的疑问词）+ 宾语从句（改为陈述语序的特殊疑问句）

例 句A：The person lifting needs to be able to see+ 宾语

句B：Where are their feet going?

= The person lifting needs to be able to see **where** their feet are going. 真

译 举重物的人需要能够看到他们的脚步要往哪走。

析 与一般疑问句相似，如果要把特殊疑问句放入主句当中，那么就要把句子变为陈述语序，而原句子的特殊疑问词保持不变，作从句的引导词。

> **Tips**
>
> 综合上述三个例子可知，无论充当宾语从句的句子原来是陈述句、一般疑问句还是特殊疑问句，最终的句式都是"引导词 + 陈述句"，至于引导词用什么，则取决于陈述句所缺的成分。缺"谁"，则用 who；缺"地点"，则用 where；缺"时间"，则用 when；缺"是否"，则用 whether 或 if；什么都不缺，则用 that 或省略引导词。

2. 宾语从句的分类

宾语从句根据其所处的位置，可以分为以下几类：

（1）及物动词 + 宾语从句 // 及物动词 + 间接宾语（人）+ 宾语从句（作直接宾语）

例1 That **means** it can be attached to almost anything. 真

译1 这意味着它几乎可以附着在任何东西上。

析1 及物动词 means 后为宾语从句，从句意思完整，故可省略引导词 that。

例2 The app **tells** people where they can fill their bottles with water for free. 真

译2 该应用程序告诉人们在哪里可以免费给瓶子装水。

析2 例句中所涉及的搭配为 tell sb. sth.，句中的 people 是及物动词 tells 的间接宾语，而 where 引导的宾语从句则为 tells 的直接宾语。

及物动词除了在作为谓语动词时后可接宾语从句外，用作非谓语动词 doing 和 to do 时也可以。

例 This starts with **assessing** <u>how qualified each builder is</u>. 真

译 这从评估每个建造者的资质开始。

析 由 "how+ 形容词" 引导的从句作非谓语动词 assessing 的宾语。

（2）介词 + 宾语从句

例 We want people to clip their bottles **onto** <u>what they are wearing</u>, to show that they are recycling— and to look cool. 真

译 我们希望人们把瓶子扣在他们所穿戴的衣物配饰上，展示自己在循环利用，同时看起来很酷。

析 由 what 所引导的宾语从句跟在介词 onto 后，构成介宾结构。

（3）形容词 + 宾语从句

例 We **are aware** <u>that the product is mainly finding application in the developing world and humanitarian sector</u>. 真

译 我们意识到，这个产品主要在发展中国家和慈善领域中寻求应用。

析 表示情感等心理状态的形容词（如 ashamed、anxious、aware、convinced、disappointed 等）作表语时，后可接介词短语补充情感涉及的对象，如 be aware of sth.。当介词后面的宾语是从句时，介词往往省略，这就构成了"系动词 + 形容词 + 宾语从句"的结构。

3. 形式宾语 it 与宾语从句

在"动词 + 宾语 + 宾语补语"结构中，当宾语为从句，且较长时，往往用 it 作形式宾语，占据宾语的位置，同时将宾语从句置于宾语补语之后，构成了"动词 +it+ 宾语补语 + 宾语从句"的结构。注意，这种情况下宾语从句的引导词 that 不可省略。

例 I find **it** strange <u>that she doesn't want to go</u>.

译 她居然不想去，我觉得很奇怪。

析 这句话中，that 引导的从句 that she doesn't want to go 才是动词 find 的真正宾语，由于这个宾语从句比宾语补语长很多，故用 it 作形式宾语，放在动词 find 的后面，而宾语从句则放在了宾语补语 strange 的后面。本句的结构原本应是 I find that... strange "我发现某事很奇怪"。

真题句解读·实战演练

例 It's fascinating to see how what we learn about the past is relevant to what's going on in the world now. 真

译 看看我们对过去的了解如何与现在世界上所发生的事情产生关联是很让人入迷的事情。

步骤一：判断宾语从句的存在

动宾结构或介宾结构有助于我们快速判断宾语从句的存在。在例句中，主句中的 see 为及物动词，后需接宾语。通过动宾结构，可知 how 引导的从句正是非谓语动词 to see 的宾语，因此 how 引导的从句为宾语从句。

It's fascinating to *see* **how** what we learn about the past is relevant to what's going on in the world now.

how 引导的宾语从句

步骤二：分析宾语从句

我们知道，在没有并列关系的情况下，一个简单句只能有一个谓语动词，但在例句中，由 how 引导的宾语从句里一共有三个谓语动词——learn about、is 和 -'s going on，因此可判断此宾语从句中还含有两个从句。由关键短语 be relevant to 可知，how 所引导的宾语从句整体的结构为 how A is relevant to B，再结合两个引导词 what，我们马上得知，另外两个从句分别在短语前后。

how **what** we *learn about* the past *is relevant to* **what**'s *going on* in the world now.

　　　　从句 2　　　　　　　　　　　　　　　　　　从句 3

　　　　　　　　　　　　从句 1（宾语从句）

步骤三：分析从句中的从句

根据短语 A is relevant to B，前后两个在 A 和 B 位置上的由 what 所引导的从句，分别作 how 引导的宾语从句中的主语和宾语，因此它们分别为主语从句和宾语从句。

how **what** we learn about the past is relevant to **what**'s going on in the world now

　　　　　　　　A　　　　　　　　　　　　　　　　　B

　　　　（主语从句）　　　　　　　　　　　　（宾语从句）

语法点精练·小试牛刀

Exercise 1　为以下句子选择恰当的引导词。

1. He stated _____ (who/that) the company would produce bottles in grey and white. 真

2. Oxytocin's effects vary depending on _____ (who/that) we are interacting with. 真

3. Wiggins condemned him for his deliberately vague explanation of _____ (what/how) the software worked. 真

4. Students need to study both how to achieve a thing, and also _____ (what/that) the thing is. 真

5. For instance, depending on _____ (what/where) you live, you will not have the same health concerns as someone who lives in a different geographical region. 真

Exercise 2　划分以下句子的句子成分，找出其中的宾语从句。

1. We know how the land surface of our planet lies. 真

2. This emerging technology could be used to fully understand why various species went extinct. 真

3. In the developing world, the price will depend on what deal aid organisations can negotiate. 真

4. Prices will vary according to where the device is bought. 真

5. The UK's Transport Research Laboratory has demonstrated that more than 90% of road collisions involve human error as a contributory factor. 真

6. He wondered whether it could have been the birthplace of the very first Inca, Manco the Great. 真

7. Indeed, environmentalists estimate that by 2050 there will be more plastic in our oceans than fish. 真

8. They wonder what the artist is trying to tell them. 真

9. They carried out a survey of how the larger area was settled in relation to sources of water. 真

10. Prospective arson investigators can learn all the tricks of the trade for detecting whether a fire was deliberately set. 真

（答案见 pp. 165~167）

第7节 复合句——名词性从句（二）

在上一节中，我们已经学习了宾语从句的用法，本节将继续聚焦于名词性从句的另外几种从句，包括**主语从句、表语从句以及同位语从句**。

一 主语从句

所谓主语从句，就是在主句中充当主语成分的从句。主语从句分两类：一类位于句首，在谓语动词之前；一类位于句末，句首则用形式主语 it 来代替，这样做是为了平衡句子结构，避免句子头重脚轻。雅思阅读中常考的是第二类。

例1 **How you treat your customers** has a direct impact on your profit margins. 真

译1 你对待客户的方式直接影响你的利润率。

析1 本句的谓语动词是 has，在谓语动词之前，是由 How 引导的从句，位于句首，作整个主句的主语部分，由此判断 How you treat your customers 为主语从句，意思是"你对待客户的方式"。

例2 *It* is uncertain **whether** Closca will succeed in its goal. 真

译2 目前还不确定 Closca 公司能否成功实现目标。

析2 句首的 It 为形式主语，真正的主语是 whether 引导的从句部分，意为"Closca 公司能否成功实现目标"。该句也可写成 **Whether** Closca will succeed in its goal is uncertain，只是这样会显得句子头重脚轻，于是我们常采用 it 作形式主语，把真正的主语后置。

> Tips
>
> **1. 常见的 it 作为形式主语的结构有：**
>
> | it 作为形式主语的结构 | 例词 |
> | --- | --- |
> | It+be+ 形容词 +that 从句 | necessary, important, obvious, likely, essential |
> | It+be+ 过去分词 +that 从句 | believed, known to all, estimated, decided |
> | It+be+ 名词 +that 从句 | no wonder, a pity, luck, common knowledge |
> | It+ 动词 +that 从句 | matter, surprise sb., occur to sb. |
>
> **2. 单独一个从句作主语时，谓语动词使用第三人称单数形式。**

二 表语从句

所谓表语从句，就是在主句中充当表语成分的从句，构成"主语 + 系动词 + 表语"的结构。表语从句除了可用其他名词性从句通用的引导词外，还可以用 because、as if、as though 来引导。

例1 But the truth was **that** nobody had yet tested those perceived threats. 真

译1 但事实是，还没有人验证过那些已被察觉到的威胁。

析1 由 that 引导的从句位于系动词 was 之后，作整个主句的表语，因此为表语从句，意指"还没有人验证过那些已被察觉到的威胁"。

例2 So it looks **as if** the problem might have another explanation. 真

译2 所以这个问题看似还有另一种解释。

析2 从句由 as if 引导，位于系动词 looks 之后，是主句的表语，因此为表语从句，意思是"这个问题似乎还有另一种解释"。

三 同位语从句

所谓同位语从句，就是在主句中充当同位语成分的从句，解释说明抽象名词。

that是同位语从句最常见的引导词，不能省略。同位语从句还可以用whether、how、when、where、why等连接。

例1 The fact **that** geoglyphs can disappear easily, along with their associated rituals and meaning, indicates that they were never intended to be anything more than temporary gestures. 真

译1 地质印痕和与其相关的仪式、意义一起很快消失，这个事实表明它们从来都只是一种暂时性的表达方式。

析1 画线部分的从句由that引导，解释说明抽象名词fact的具体内容，意为"地质印痕和与其相关的仪式、意义一起很快消失的事实"，因此画线部分在主句中充当同位语，为同位语从句。而主句的结构则为"主语The fact+ 同位语从句that...+ 谓语indicates+ 宾语从句that..."。

例2 What do you think about the idea **that** our dreams may predict the future? 真

译2 你认为我们的梦或许可以预测未来这个想法怎么样？

析2 主句为特殊疑问句"What do you think about the idea?"，that引导的从句that our dreams may predict the future表意和语法结构完整，解释说明了前面的抽象名词idea的具体内容，意为"我们的梦或许可以预测未来的这个想法"，故该从句为同位语从句。

> **Tips**
>
> 在雅思阅读中，同位语从句常修饰的抽象名词包括：
>
> | | | | |
> |---|---|---|---|
> | hope（希望） | fact（事实） | news（消息） | problem（问题） |
> | conclusion（结论） | agreement（意见一致） | belief（信仰） | concept（观念，概念） |
> | idea（想法） | question（问题） | suggestion（提议） | thought（想法） |
> | doubt（怀疑） | assumption（假定，设想） | evidence（迹象，证据） | |

▶ 真题句解读·实战演练

当句子出现较多从句时，找到从句的始末能帮助我们快速分解长难句。从句的开始是引导词，一般结束于标点符号、下一个引导词或第二个谓语动词。

例 What is amazing is that the number of human cells in the average person is about 30 trillion. 真

译 令人惊讶的是，人类平均拥有大约30万亿个细胞。

步骤一：判断从句的存在

这句话出现两个引导词，分别为What和that。另外，句子里有三个谓语动词（都是is），因此可推断此句含有两个从句。

第一个从句，始于引导词What，从What后开始数，第一个is是从句内的谓语动词，What从句到第二个is前结束。

第二个从句，始于引导词that，一直到句号结束。

综上可知，第二个谓语动词is是主句的谓语，主句的主语即What引导的从句，主句的表语则是that引导的从句。

What *is* amazing *is* **that** the number of human cells in the average person *is* about 30 trillion.

主谓结构   系表结构

步骤二：分析从句

由步骤一已知该句子（句1）中含有两个从句。由 What 引导的位于句首的从句（句2），是主句的主语，故为主语从句；由 that 引导的从句（句3）位于系动词 is 后，作主句的表语，故为表语从句。两个从句本身皆为"主 + 系 + 表"结构。

What *is* amazing *is* **that** the number of human cells in the average person *is* about 30 trillion.
句2（主语从句）   句3（表语从句）

句1（主句）

语法点精练·小试牛刀

Exercise 1　为以下句子选择恰当的引导词。

1. The fact _____ (what/that) any ancient hill figures survive at all in England today is testament to the strength and continuity of local customs and beliefs 真

2. _____ (What/How) I'm interested in is what idea this bird refers to. 真

3. _____ (What/That) was surprising, according to Barrett, was the timing of these periods. 真

4. _____ (What/It) is remarkable how much people can vary in their wisdom from one situation to the next. 真

5. This is _____ (how/that) plants compete to escape each other's shade. 真

Exercise 2　划分以下句子的句子成分，找出其中的名词性从句。

1. The additional information may be what they did.

2. It's unlikely that they'll come back. 真

3. This is why the tree is so suited to life there. 真

4. It is clear whether a dominant laugh is produced by a high- or low-status person. 真

5. There is little doubt that birth order has less influence on academic achievement than socio-economic status. 真

6. How successful they were is a matter of opinion. 真

7. What many millennials prefer to post on social media are 'real' (refillable) bottles or even the once widespread Thermos bottles. 真

8. They never mind the fact that these stainless-steel vacuum-insulated water bottles feel oddly out-of-date to anyone over the age of 40 or that teenagers in the 1970s would have avoided ever being seen with one. 真

9. What seems entirely predictable and controllable on screen has unexpected results when translated into reality. 真

10. It also seems that the neurological roots（神经根）of the bilingual advantage extend to brain areas associated with sensory processing（知觉处理）. 真

（答案见 pp. 167~168）

第 8 节　复合句——定语从句

在雅思阅读中，定语从句是一大重点，也是一大难点。熟练掌握定语从句，对理解阅读篇章的长难句有重要的帮助。

一　定语从句的基本概念

定语从句在句中充当定语，本质上相当于一个形容词，用以修饰名词或代词，故又称为"形容词性从句"。被定语从句修饰的词称为"先行词"，引导定语从句的连接词叫"关系词"。

关系词有两个作用：一是"引导"，作为定语从句的引导词，连接主句与从句；二是"替代"，关系词在从句中充当成分，替代的是先行词，简单来说就是"关系词 = 先行词"。

例 This book presents the details	This book presents **the details**.
主句	译 这本书给出了细节。(怎样的细节？)
that illustrate the mathematical style of thinking. 真	**The details** illustrate the mathematical style of thinking.
that 引导的定语从句，修饰先行词 the details	译 这些细节展示了思维的数学特点。

析 这句话中，关系词 that 后的从句是"谓语 + 宾语"的结构，缺乏主语。在语法上，把 that 前的名词 the details 代入从句中，它充当的正是从句中的主语，从句复原后为 the details illustrate the mathematical style of thinking；在语义上，把 the details 放在从句中，表示"这些细节展示了思维的数学特点"，意思成立。由此可知，that 引导的是一个修饰 the details 的定语从句。

Tips
　　定语从句的特征：在语法上，先行词（由关系词替代）在从句中充当成分；在语义上，把先行词代入从句后，从句的意思成立。

二　定语从句的构成

由上面的例子可知，定语从句的构成就是"关系词 + 陈述句"，而关系词的选择需要看先行词的内容和关系词在从句中充当什么成分，具体见下表：

（注：以下表格只适用于限制性定语从句，非限制性定语从句有细微区别，详见本节第三点。）

先行词的内容	关系词充当的成分	选用的关系词	关系词可否省略
事 // 物	主语、宾语	which // that	作宾语时可省
人	主语、宾语	who // that // whom（作宾语时）	作宾语时可省
物 // 人	定语(表示所属关系)	whose // of which（指物）// of whom（指人）	否
时间	状语	when // 介词 +which	可
地点	状语	where // 介词 +which	可
原因	状语	why（先行词只能是 reason）	可
方式	状语	that // in which （先行词为 the way）	可

例1 Archaeologists have even found evidence of <u>man-made glass</u> **which** dates back to 4,000 BC. 真

译1 考古学家甚至发现了人造玻璃的证据，这玻璃的年代可以追溯到公元前 4,000 年。

析1 先行词是 man-made glass（物），代入从句中充当主语，故关系词用 which。

例2 Participants **who** watched the humorous video spent significantly more time working on this tedious task. 真

译2 观看搞笑视频的受试者明显坚持了更长的时间来完成这项烦琐的任务。

析2 先行词是 Participants（人），代入从句中充当主语，故关系词用 who。

例3 What was more, the old ants didn't experience any drop in the levels of either serotonin or dopamine—<u>brain chemicals</u> **whose** decline often coincides with aging. 真

译3 更重要的是，老年蚂蚁的血清素和多巴胺水平都没有下降，要知道，这两种大脑化学物质往往随着年龄增加而下降。

析3 先行词是 brain chemicals（物），代入从句中充当定语，表示所属关系，意为"大脑化学物质的下降"，故关系词用 whose。

例4 The Arab-Venetian dominance of the trade finally ended in <u>1512</u>, **when** the Portuguese reached the Banda Islands and began exploiting its precious resources. 真

译4 阿拉伯人与威尼斯人的贸易主导地位于 1512 年迎来了终结，那一年葡萄牙人抵达了班达群岛，并开始开采当地的宝贵资源。

析4 先行词是表示年份的 1512（时间），代入从句中作时间状语，关系词用 when，也可用 in which 代替。定语从句还原后相当于 the Portuguese reached the Banda Islands and began exploiting its precious resources in 1512。

例5 Being able to undertake research on animals in <u>zoos</u> **where** there is less risk and fewer variables means real changes can be effected on wild populations. 真

译5 动物园里的风险更小，变量更少，能够在动物园里对动物进行研究意味着真正的变化也可以发生在野生种群中。

析5 先行词是 zoos（地点），代入从句中作地点状语，关系词用 where。定语从句还原后相当于 there is less risk and fewer variables in zoos。

例6 There are many <u>reasons</u> **why** technology is advancing so fast. 真

译6 技术发展如此之快有很多原因。

析6 先行词是 reasons（原因），代入从句中作原因状语，关系词用 why，也可用 for which 代替。定语从句还原后相当于 technology is advancing so fast for many reasons。

例7 We have studied only 5% of the <u>species</u> we know. 真

译7 我们仅研究了 5% 的已知物种。

析7 读到 species 时会发现，species 后的 we know 是另一个句子结构（主语＋谓语），缺失了宾语，由此判断这是一个省略了关系词的定语从句。实际上，这句话的先行词是 species，代入从句中作 know 的宾语，故可省略关系词 that。如果不省略关系词，句子可写作 "We have studied only 5% of the species that we know."。

三　定语从句的分类

　　定语从句可分为限制性定语从句(或称"限定性定语从句")和非限制性定语从句(或称"非限定性定语从句"),两者最明显的区别是定语从句前是否有逗号,但两者最本质的区别是先行词的范围是否明确,是否需要修饰限定。

例1　*People* **who** travel on the underground don't carry their bikes around. 真

译1　坐地铁的人不会随身携带自行车。

例2　*Theo Molennaar*, **who** was a system designer for the project, worked alongside Schimmelpennink. 真

译2　Theo Molennaar 是这个项目的系统设计师,他和 Schimmelpennink 一起工作。

析　例1是限制性定语从句,先行词 People 语义范围不明确("人们"是泛指),故需要定语进行限定,说明是哪些人,这个定语从句不能省略,否则句子语义不完整。

　　例2是非限制性定语从句,先行词 Theo Molennaar 语义明确(指名为 Theo Molennaar 的这个人),即使没有定语进行限定,也能让人知道说的是谁,非限制性定语从句起补充说明的作用。句子省略从句后,语义还是完整的。

Tips

在做雅思阅读时,同学们只需读懂句意,所以两者在语义上的区别同学们大概了解即可。

而在使用上则需注意以下两点:

1. 非限制性定语从句的关系词不可省略,且不能用 that;

2. 非限制性定语从句的先行词既可是关系词前的某个名词(短语),又可以是整个分句。

四　一些特殊的定语从句

1. which/as 引导的非限制性定语从句,修饰分句

　　一般来说,定语从句用以修饰名词或代词,但有一种特殊情况是非限制性定语从句修饰整个分句,此时关系词只能用 which 或 as,两者在用法上没有区别,区别主要是在位置上:which 引导的非限制性定语从句只能位于被修饰的分句后;而 as 引导的从句位置灵活,在句前、句中、句末都可以。

例1　Many insect species are infrequently encountered and very difficult to rear in captivity, **which**, again, can leave us with insufficient material to work with. 真

译1　许多昆虫种类很少偶遇到,且在圈养状态下很难养育,这又会使我们缺乏足够的研究材料。

析1　定语从句修饰的并非主句的主语 insect species,而是前面整句话,即 Many insect species are infrequently encountered and very difficult to rear in captivity。

例2　**As we have seen**, someone could use the very same knowledge of means to achieve a much less noble end. 真

译2　正如我们所见,有人会用同样的关于"手段"的知识来达到一个不那么高尚的目的。

析2　As 引导的定语从句中,have seen 后缺少宾语,关系词 As 正好充当这个成分,而 As 指代的内容是后面整一句话,即 someone could use the very same knowledge of means to achieve a much less noble end 这件事。此时 As 引导的从句位于句首,关系词不能用 Which 代替。

Tips

as 引导非限制性定语从句时,as 只能指代分句。as 引导的非限制性定语从句多为固定搭配,如:as was discussed before、as is pointed out、as is well-known、as is often the case、as was expected、as is shown in the figure 等。

2. "介词 + 关系词" 引导的定语从句

在定语从句中，当关系词作介词后的宾语时，为了引导定语从句，关系词会被提前，而与之搭配的介词也可随关系词提前，也可不提前。如果介词提前，那么就构成了"介词 + 关系词"引导定语从句。

例1

The classic cork stopper's traditional image is more in keeping with that of the type of *high quality goods* **which** it has long been associated **with**. (介词在后)	The classic cork stopper's traditional image is more in keeping with that of the type of *high quality goods* **with which** it has long been associated. 真（介词在前）

译1 鉴于传统的软木塞长久以来都与高质量产品联系在一起，它的传统形象与该类产品更相称。

析1 介词 with 与形容词 associated 构成 be associated with sth. 结构，关系词 which 提前了，就造成了介宾结构 with sth. 的分隔。此时也可以把介词 with 一同提前，将介宾短语放一起。

例2 First, the students performed *a tedious task* **in which** they had to cross out every instance of the letter 'e' over two pages of text. 真

译2 首先，学生们要完成一项烦琐的任务，在这个任务中，他们必须圈出两页文本中的每一个 e 字母。

例3 Guided play is *an avenue* **through which** parents and educators can provide more targeted learning experiences. 真

译3 通过引导式游戏这一途径，父母和教育工作者可以提供更有针对性的学习体验。

▶ 真题句解读·实战演练

例 Building designs are now conceived and stored in media technologies that detach the designer from the physical and social realities they are creating. 真

译 如今，建筑设计是在媒体技术中构思和储存的，这些技术将设计师与他们所创造的实体和社会现实相分离。

步骤一：断句，分开主句与从句

句中出现明显的从句引导词 that，故句子可在此先断句。that 前面是主句，主语是 Building designs，谓语是 are conceived and stored，被动语态，表示"被构思和储存"，in media technologies 为状语。主句部分意思完整。that 后的部分有谓语动词 detach 和 are creating，可知存在从句。

Building designs are now conceived and stored in media technologies // **that** *detach* the designer

　　　　　　　　　　主句

from the physical and social realities they *are creating*.

步骤二：分析从句结构

鉴于 that 之后出现了两个谓语动词，所以应该有两个从句。

第一个从句从引导词 that 开始，难点在于这个从句到哪里结束。读句子至 social realities 时，发现其后的 they are creating 是另一个主谓结构，因此可以先在此将两个从句分开。

第一个从句为"引导词 + 谓语 + 宾语"结构，缺少主语。第二个从句为"主语 + 谓语（及物动词）"结构，缺少宾语。

第一个从句：**that**　　detach　　the designer　　from the physical and social realities

　　　　　　　　　　　谓语　　　宾语

第二个从句：they　　　　are creating

　　　　　　　主语　　谓语（及物动词）

步骤三：判断从句类型

第一个从句前是名词 media technologies。在语法上，将其代入 detach the designer from the physical and social realities 中，media technologies 充当主语；再从语义判断，media technologies 放在从句中，表示"媒体技术将设计师与实体和社会现实相分离"，意思成立。由此可见，that 引导的是定语从句，media technologies 为先行词，that 是关系词。

而第二个从句缺少宾语，前面是名词 the physical and social realities，熟悉定语从句的同学们应该马上能想到，这是一个省略了关系词的定语从句。由于先行词在从句 they are creating 中充当宾语，关系词 that 可省略，句子还原后为 they are creating the physical and social realities，意为"他们在创造实体和社会现实"。

... <u>media technologies</u> // **that** detach the designer from <u>the physical and social realities</u> // (**that**)

they are creating

语法点精练·小试牛刀

Exercise 1 为以下句子选择恰当的关系词。

1. Cork is a sustainable product _____ (who/that) can be recycled without difficulty. 真

2. More evidence that boredom has detrimental（有害的）effects comes from studies of people _____ (which/who) are more or less prone to boredom. 真

3. The opportunities for free play, _____ (which/that) I experienced almost every day of my childhood, are becoming increasingly scarce. 真

4. In this book about the exploration of the earth's surface, I have confined myself to those _____ (who/whose) travels were real and _____ (who/whom) also aimed at more than personal discovery. 真

5. _____ (As/Which) work in neurosciences（神经科学）indicates, the acquisition of literacy necessitated（需要）a new circuit in our species' brain more than 6,000 years ago. 真

Exercise 2 划分以下句子的句子成分，找出其中的定语从句。

1. Psychologically, this can give a purpose to a life that otherwise feels aimless. 真

2. Collecting gives a feeling that other hobbies are unlikely to inspire. 真

3. In the Middle Ages, Europeans who could afford the spice used it to flavour food. 真

4. People who collect dolls may develop an interest in the way that dolls are made, or the materials that are used. 真

5. This allowed them to determine the genes that have allowed polar bears to survive in one of the toughest environments on Earth. 真

6. Mangen's group asked subjects questions about a short story whose plot had universal student appeal. 真

7. There are still areas around the world where certain health issues are more prevalent. 真

8. Another solution may be to reveal more about the algorithms which AI uses and the purposes they serve. 真

9. A third approach, known as 'counteract and reaffirm', involves developing products or services that stress the values traditionally associated with the category. 真

10. A radical solution, which may work for some very large companies whose businesses are extensive and complex, is the professional board supported by their own dedicated staff and advisers. 真

（答案见 pp. 168~170）

第9节 复合句——状语从句

状语从句也是一类非常常见的从句，且种类多样。若要更好地理解雅思阅读的长难句，对状语从句的学习是必不可少的。

一 状语从句的基本概念

所谓状语从句，就是用一个从句作状语，修饰句子或句子中的成分。状语从句的位置灵活，可在主句前面、后面或插入到主句中间。状语从句的构成是"从属连词＋完整的陈述句"，可以表示时间、地点、原因、条件等。

例 **If the bark is stripped on a cold or damp day, the tree will be damaged.** 真

译 如果在天气很冷或很潮湿的日子剥树皮，树木就会受到破坏。

析 本句中 the tree will be damaged 是主句，逗号前的部分为条件状语从句。If 是从属连词，意为"如果"，后面引导一个完整的陈述句 the bark is stripped on a cold or damp day。

> **Tips**
>
> 状语从句一共分成 9 大类，状语从句的种类是由从属连词的含义决定的，从属连词表达什么含义（逻辑关系），就引导什么从句。
>
> 雅思阅读常考的状语从句包括：时间状语从句、原因状语从句、条件状语从句、让步状语从句、结果状语从句。此外，状语从句还包括地点状语从句、目的状语从句、方式状语从句和比较状语从句。

二 状语从句的分类

1. 时间状语从句

用表示时间的连词连接一个从句作状语，这样的从句就是时间状语从句。时间状语从句常用的从属连词有以下几类：

（1）when、while、as（当……的时候）

例 You can squash the cork and watch it spring back to its original size and shape **when you release the pressure.** 真

译 你可以挤压软木，然后在你松开后，看着它恢复到原来的大小和形状。

析 本句的主句是 You can squash... and watch... shape，从句为 when you release the pressure，修饰第二个谓语动词 watch，说明这个动作发生的时间。

（2）before（在……之前）、after（在……之后）

例 Glass making developed from traditional mouth-blowing to a semi-automatic process, **after factory-owner HM Ashley introduced a machine capable of producing 200 bottles per hour.** 真

译 在工厂主 HM 阿什利引进了一台每小时能生产 200 个瓶子的机器后，玻璃制造从传统的口吹工艺发展成了半自动加工。

（3）once（一旦）

例 **Once the microorganisms that give soil its special properties have been lost**, it may take the soil thousands of years to recover. 真

译 一旦失去赋予土壤特性的微生物，土壤可能需要数千年才能恢复。

（4）since（自从）

例 **Since** Google announced in 2010 that it had been trialling self-driving cars on the streets of California, progress in this field has quickly gathered pace. 真

译 自 2010 年谷歌宣布已经在加州街道上测试自动驾驶汽车以来，该领域开始加速发展。

（5）until、till、not until（直到）

例 Captive-bred tortoises can't be reintroduced into the wild **until** they're at least five years old and weigh at least 4.5 kilograms. 真

译 人工繁殖的象龟，至少要到 5 岁且体重不低于 4.5 公斤，才能重新放归野外。

（6）as soon as、no sooner... than、hardly... when（一……就……）

例 **As soon as** the white bikes were distributed around the city, the police removed them. 真

译 这些白色自行车一放置在城市各处，警察就把它们搬走了。

Tips
时间状语从句除了可以用以上的从属连词来引导外，还可以用**名词短语**（如 the moment、every time、the next time）、**副词**（如 immediately、directly）和**介词短语**（如 by the time）。这些词的作用相当于从属连词，后面接完整的陈述句。

例 I want to see him **the moment** he arrives.

译 我希望他一到我就能见到他。

析 主句是 I want to see him，从句为 the moment he arrives，说明 see 这个动作发生的时间。从句引导词为名词短语 the moment，意为"一……就……"，引导时间状语从句。

2. 原因状语从句

原因状语从句指在句中用来说明主句原因的从句。引导原因状语从句的常见连词包括 because、since、as、for、now that、in that 等，均表"因为"的意思。这些词所表示的因果关联程度有细微差别，但不会影响句意理解，同学们不必深究。

例1 There are the people who collect **because** they want to make money. 真

译1 有些人收藏物品是因为他们想赚钱。

析1 主句是 There are the people，之后是定语从句 who collect... make money，修饰先行词 people。定语从句中包含一个原因状语从句 because they want to make money，说明这类人收藏物品的原因。

例2 One polar bear called Agee has formed a close relationship with her owner Mark Dumas. This is even more astonishing **since** polar bears are known to actively hunt humans in the wild. 真

译2 一只名叫艾吉的北极熊和她的主人马克·仲马建立起了亲密的关系。这更令人吃惊，因为众所周知，北极熊在野外会主动捕猎人类。

析2 第二句的主句是 This is even more astonishing，从句为 since polar bears are known to actively hunt humans in the wild，说明为何北极熊与主人建立亲密关系让人吃惊。从句的连词为 since，根据上下文可判断其意为"因为"，引导原因状语从句。

3. 条件状语从句

条件状语从句是由连词 if 以及 unless 等引导的状语从句。在英文中，"条件"是指某一件事情实现之后（状语从句中的动作），其他事情（主句中的动作）才能发生，通常译作"假如""如果"。引导条件状语从句的连词有以下几类：

（1）if、provided、providing that、supposing that、on condition that（如果，倘若）

例 **If** we don't slow the decline of soil, all farmable soil could be gone in 60 years. 真

译 如果我们不减缓土壤退化的速度，所有可耕种的土壤将在 60 年内消失。

（2）as long as、so long as（只要）

例 **So long as** there is a demand for these drugs, the financial incentive for drug dealers will be there.

译 只要这些毒品还有需求，毒贩的经济动机就不会消失。

（3）unless（除非）

例 The grass would soon grow over the geoglyph again **unless** it was regularly cleaned or scoured by a fairly large team of people. 真

译 除非有相当庞大的一队人马定期清理或冲刷，否则地质印痕上很快就会重新长草。

析 unless 相当于 if not，所以此例句中的条件状语从句又可写为 if it was not regularly cleaned...。

4. 让步状语从句

在句子中作让步状语的从句被称为"让步状语从句"，一般翻译为"尽管……"或"即使……"等，与主句之间存在转折的逻辑关系。常见的引导让步状语从句的连词有表示"虽然"的 although、though，表示"即使"的 even if、even though，表示"然而"的 while 等。

例1 **Although** there are plenty of promising chemical compounds in nature, finding them is far from easy. 真

译1 尽管自然界中有许多有价值的化合物，但找到它们远非易事。

例2 **Even though** music says little, it still manages to touch us deeply. 真

译2 尽管音乐说得很少，但它仍然能深深地打动我们。

Tips

"疑问词 +ever"构成的复合词亦可引导让步状语从句，含义是"不管……""无论……"，与"no matter+ 疑问词"可以互换使用，即 whatever=no matter what、whoever=no matter who、wherever=no matter where、whenever=no matter when、however=no matter how。

例1 **Whatever** its intellectual pedigree, the idea that governments should be responsible for promoting happiness is always a threat to human freedom. 真

译1 无论其思想渊源是什么，一直以来，促进幸福感是政府的责任这个想法是对人类自由的一种威胁。

析1 主句主干是 the idea is always a threat to human freedom。Whatever its intellectual pedigree 是省略了系动词 is 的让步状语从句，从句引导词为 Whatever，意为"无论什么"。

例2 Maybe being swallowed whole by a wolf, then cut out of its stomach alive is so gripping that it helps the story remain popular, **no matter how** badly it's told. 真

译2 也许被狼整个吞下，然后从它肚子里被救出来，（这个情节）太扣人心弦，以至于这个故事一直广受欢迎，无论讲述的方式有多糟糕。

析2 主句主干是 being swallowed..., then cut out of its stomach alive is gripping（so... that it helps the story remain popular 为结果状语从句）。no matter how 引导让步状语从句，意为"不管多么……"。

5. 结果状语从句

结果状语从句说明主句所描述的事情产生的结果，可由 so/such... that "如此……以至于……"或 so that "结果，所以"引导。需要注意的是，so... that 与 such... that 意思相同，区别只在于 so 后接形容词或副词，such 后接名词。

例1 Indeed, play is **such** an instrumental component to healthy child development **that** the United Nations High Commission on Human Rights recognized play as a fundamental right of every child. 真

译1 实际上，玩游戏对儿童的健康发展而言是一个重要的要素以至于联合国人权高级委员会认为玩游戏是每一位儿童的基本权利。

析1 so/such... that 引导的结果状语从句中，that 之后的从句往往用来强调 so/such 之后的内容。

例2 Process may take the place of discussion and be at the expense of real collaboration, **so that** boxes are ticked rather than issues tackled. 真

译2 流程取代了讨论，从而失去了真正的通力合作，所以一切只是例行公事而没有真正解决问题。

6. 其他状语从句

（1）地点状语从句

连词：where（在某个地方）；anywhere、wherever（在任何地方）；everywhere（所有地方）

例 **Where** there is a will, there is a way.

译 有志者，事竟成。

析 Where there is a will 是 Where 引导的地点状语从句，直译为"有意志力的地方"。

（2）目的状语从句

连词：so that、in order that（为了）；lest、in case（以防）；for fear that（唯恐）

例 But defining boredom **so that** it can be studied in the lab has proved difficult. 真

译 但经证实，给无聊这种情绪下定义，以便我们可以在实验室里研究它，是很困难的一件事。

析 连词 so that "为了，以便"引导目的状语从句 so that it can be studied in the lab，该从句放在动名词形式的主语 defining boredom 后，说明给"无聊"下定义的目的。

（3）方式状语从句

连词：as（按照……的方式）、as if（似乎，好像）

例 They write **as if** nothing of any importance had been thought on happiness. 真

译 他们的文章似乎表明人们从未认真思考过幸福这个话题。

析 主句是 They write，连词 as if "似乎，好像" 引导方式状语从句 as if nothing of any importance had been thought on happiness。从句中所表达的"人们从未认真思考过幸福这个话题"的含义与过往的事实不符，因此要用虚拟语气，即 had done。

（4）比较状语从句

连词：than（比）、as（和……一样）

例 Bilingual adults acquire a third language better **than** monolingual adults master a second language. 真

译 双语者对第三语言的掌握要比单语者对第二语言的掌握要好。

真题句解读·实战演练

例 If we can understand how geography affects our health no matter where in the world we are located, we can better treat disease, prevent illness, and keep people safe and well. 真

译 如果我们不论身处何方，都能够了解地理环境如何影响我们的健康，我们就可以更好地治疗疾病、预防疾病，并保证人们的安全和健康。

步骤一：判断从句的存在，并简化句子

这句话出现三个引导词，分别为 If、how 和 no matter where，因此此句含有三个从句。

第一个从句：If we can understand how geography affects our health no matter where in the world we are located,

第二个从句：how geography affects our health

第三个从句：no matter where in the world we are located

步骤二：分析主从句

由步骤一可知，该句有三个从句。从句子划分可以看出，第二、三个从句（句2、3）包含在第一个从句（句1）中。

句1为 If "如果" 引导的条件状语从句，说明主句所述情况成立的条件；

句2的引导词为 how "如何，怎样"，该从句跟在句1的谓语动词 understand 后面，作其宾语，因此为宾语从句；

句3为 no matter where "无论哪里" 引导的让步状语从句，修饰 we can understand…；

主句为逗号后的部分，含有三个并列谓语动词 can treat、prevent 和 keep。

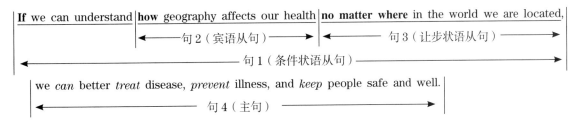

Exercise 1 为以下句子选择恰当的引导词。

1. I realized this problem anew _____ (when/if) I was invited to speak before a class in marketing. 真

2. A Russian-English bilingual asked to 'pick up a marker' from a set of objects would look more at a stamp than someone who doesn't know Russian, _____ (as if/because) the Russian word for 'stamp', sounds like the English word, 'marker'. 真

3. The fastest commercial sailing vessels of all time were clippers, built to transport goods around the world, _____ (for/although) some also took passengers. 真

4. _____ (If/Although) we know what's going to happen next, then we don't get excited. 真

5. Their objective is to make AI technologies more trustworthy and transparent, _____ (as if/so that) organisations and individuals understand how AI decisions are made. 真

Exercise 2 划分以下句子的句子成分，找出其中的状语从句，并判断其类型。

1. If we are asked why happiness matters, we can give no further external reason. 真

2. The Dutch took over the cinnamon trade from the Portuguese as soon as they arrived in Ceylon. 真

3. They may feel empty, now that the goal that drove them on has gone. 真

4. This chapter addresses how people conceptualize (使概念化) intelligence, whatever it may actually be. 真

5. If the customer's credit card is declined at the till (收银机), keep your voice down and enquire about an alternative payment method quietly so that the customer doesn't feel humiliated (丢人的). 真

6. If we want our soils to survive, we need to take action now. 真

7. Although the study involves plenty of fancy technology, the experiment itself was rather straightforward (简单的). 真

8. Since most of the seats in most cars are unoccupied, this may boost production of a smaller, more efficient range of vehicles for individual use. 真

9. When futures (期货) markets become excessively financialised, they can contribute to short-term price volatility. 真

10. When I ask the students to articulate (阐明) the purpose of their field, they eventually generalize to something like, 'The safety and welfare of society'. 真

（答案见 pp. 170~172）

在雅思阅读中，除了前面讲解的基本句型和从句之外，我们还会经常遇到一些特殊句式，增加我们理解长难句的难度，其中一种就是倒装结构。在本节，我们将学习如何还原倒装结构的真面目，从而正确理解阅读篇章的长难句。

一 倒装的基本概念

英语陈述句的正常语序是主语在前，谓语在后。但有时为了强调和突出部分内容，会颠倒原有语序，构成倒装结构。倒装结构一般有两种：**完全倒装**和**部分倒装**。

二 完全倒装

将整个谓语放在主语前面，这种结构称为"完全倒装"。完全倒装句通常将形容词、介词、副词短语置于句首。

例 <u>Among the less appealing case studies</u> **is** one about a fungus that is wiping out entire populations of frogs. 真

译 其中一个不那么吸引人的案例研究是围绕一种正在消灭整个青蛙种群的真菌展开的。

析 本句为"介词短语 +be+ 主语"的倒装结构，其正常语序为"One (study) about a fungus that is wiping out entire populations of frogs is among the less appealing case studies."。

> **Tips**
>
> 我们常见的 There be 句型，实际上就是一种完全倒装句。例如，句子"There is a boy.",原意为"那有一个男孩"，正常语序是"A boy is there."。There be 句型后来引申为表示客观存在的"有"，意为"(某地方)有……"。There be 句型是雅思阅读真题中常出现的句型，其中 be 还可以有不同的时态和情态。
>
> 例 **There seem to be** two main attitudes toward that question. 真
>
> 译 对于这个问题似乎主要有两种态度。
>
> 析 本句的句型为 There seem to be…，源于 There be 句型，而 There be 句型是一种倒装形式，原来的句型应该为 sth. be there,因此该句的正常语序为"Two main attitudes toward that question seem to be there."。

三 部分倒装

部分倒装就是把谓语动词的一部分置于主语之前。简单来说，就是把陈述句的语序变成一般疑问句的语序，即将助动词 do/does/did、am/is/are/was/were、have/has/had、情态动词 will/can 等置于主语前。

在雅思阅读中，使用部分倒装结构的句子多为下列几种情况。

1. 句首为否定词或含否定意义的短语

含有否定意义的副词或连词（短语）置于句首时，句子要部分倒装。常见的这类副词或连词（短语）有：never、no、neither、hardly、scarcely、little、seldom、nowhere、on no account、by no means、in no way、not only、not until 等。

例 **Not only** _was_ a monopoly of cinnamon _becoming_ impossible, but the spice trade overall was diminishing in economic potential. 真

译 不仅肉桂的垄断变得不可能，而且香料贸易整体的经济潜力也在下降。

析 本句是由 not only... but 连接两个并列分句构成。前一个分句中，含有否定意义的 Not only 置于句首，故该分句使用了部分倒装，正常语序是 Not only a monopoly of cinnamon was becoming impossible。

2. 句首为 "only+ 状语"

only 出现在句首修饰介词短语、副词、状语从句时（包括 only if 引导状语从句的情况），主句部分要使用部分倒装结构。

例 **Only if** these conditions are fulfilled *can* the application *proceed* to the next stage.

译 只有这些条件都满足，申请才能进入下一程序。

析 本句句首是 Only if 引导的条件状语从句，所以主句部分用了部分倒装结构，句子的正常语序是 "The application can proceed to the next stage only if these conditions are fulfilled."。

Tips
> 只有当置于句首的 only 是修饰状语时，句子才需要倒装。当 only 属于主语的一部分时（如 only 修饰名词），句子不用倒装结构。
>
> 例 Only a few people understood what he said.
>
> 译 只有很少人懂得他在说什么。
>
> 析 在这个句子中，句首的 Only 修饰主语 a few people，所以句子不用倒装。

3. 省略 if 的条件句

非真实条件句可以省略连词 if，把从句中的助动词（主要包括有 were、should/could/might、had）移至主语前，形成部分倒装。

例 *Had* I *known*, I would have come home sooner.

译 我要是知道的话，就早一点回家了。

析 本句使用了虚拟语气，是对过去情况的假设。句中 Had I known 是倒装句，还原后为 If I had known。

▶ 真题句解读·实战演练

例 Government regulation has arisen precisely because it was found that not only did moral principles need to be made explicit, they also needed to be enforced. 真

译 政府监管之所以出现，正是因为人们发现，道德准则不仅要清楚确立，而且还需要强制执行。

步骤一：寻找引导词，判断从句的存在

这句话出现两个引导词，分别为 because 和 that，因此此句含有两个从句。

主句：Government regulation has arisen precisely

从句1：**because** it was found that not only did moral principles need to be made explicit, they also needed to be enforced

从句2：**that** not only did moral principles need to be made explicit, they also needed to be enforced

步骤二：分析从句

由步骤一可知，该句包含两个从句。

从句1中，because 引导原因状语从句，说明 Government regulation has arisen 的原因。而该从句中又含有一个 that 引导的从句。

从句2是 that 引导的主语从句，it was found 中的 it 是形式主语，真正的主语是 that 后的从句。该从句是由 not only... also 连接两个并列分句构成，前一个分句中，含有否定意义的 not only 置于从句句首，所以该分句使用了部分倒装，正常语序是 moral principles not only needed to be made explicit。

- 50 -

because it was found | that not only *did* moral principles *need* to be... needed to be enforced.

not only 位于分句句首，该分句使用部分倒装

←————————— 从句 2（主语从句）—————————→

←————————————— 从句 1（原因状语从句）—————————————→

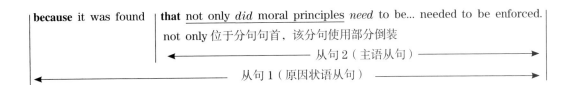
语法点精练·小试牛刀

Exercise 1 选择正确语序的短语，补全句子。

1. Hardly _____ (had we sat/had sat we) down at the table, when the phone rang.

2. Here _____ (are some recent studies/some recent studies are) that explore the science behind baby talk. 真

3. There _____ (are obvious risks/obvious risks are) to this practice and it would be important to establish clear guidelines. 真

4. Never _____ (has the technology succeeded/has succeeded the technology) in replicating that structure. 真

5. Only when we have shed our magnificent light on this world, _____ (will we experience/will experience we) real purpose, real fulfilment, and real joy.

Exercise 2 将以下倒装句还原为正常语序。

1. Not only did EMI create compositions in Cope's style, but also that of the most revered classical composers, including Bach, Chopin and Mozart. 真

2. And yet there are millions of collectors around the world. 真

3. Bingham didn't realise the extent or the importance of the site, nor did he realise what use he could make of the discovery. 真

4. Only in bilingual situations were the babies able to successfully learn the new rule. 真

5. Among the many cited reasons are low compensation, inadequate benefits, poor working conditions and compromised employee morale and attitudes. 真

Exercise 3 根据提示，把以下句子改为倒装句。

1. None of the donors has a stake in his idea, and he has no debt either. （nor）

2. *Cutty Sark* never lived up to the high expectations of her owner. （never）

3. It only grew in one place in the world: a small group of islands in the Banda Sea. （only）

4. Direct food distribution systems not only encourage small-scale agriculture, but also give consumers more control over the food they consume. （not only... but also）

5. All people are equal as human beings, and one person would serve as well as another in almost any position of responsibility in terms of their competencies. （not only... but also）

（答案见 pp. 172~173）

第11节　特殊句式——强调句型

强调句型也是雅思阅读中常见的一类特殊句式，熟练掌握强调句型有助于我们简化长难句。

一　强调句型的基本构成

在英语书面语中，如果想要强调一个句子中的某些信息点，可以采用强调句型。强调句型的基本构成是"it is+ 强调内容 +that..."（其中的 it 无实义），具体写法就是把一个正常的陈述句分成两部分，把要强调的部分放到 it is 和 that 中间，其他部分则放到 that 后面。

例　**It is** at this point **that** 'Arson for Profit' becomes supremely relevant. 真

译　正是从这一点看，谋利型纵火罪变得极其切题。

析　本句 It is 和 that 中间的部分为所强调的内容，即强调 at this point "从这一点"。此句的正常语序为 "'Arson for Profit' becomes supremely relevant at this point."。

二　强调句型的变化

1. 时态变化

在强调句型中，强调现在的事物用 is，强调过去的事物则用 was。换句话说，如果原来的陈述句用的是与过去有关的时态（如一般过去时，过去完成时等），则用 "it was+ 强调内容 +that..."，否则用 "it is+ 强调内容 +that..."。

例　**It was** not until 1500 BC **that** the first hollow glass container was made by covering a sand core with a layer of molten glass. 真

译　直到公元前 1500 年，人们才通过将一层熔融玻璃覆盖在砂芯上制造出第一个中空玻璃容器。

析　本句强调的是 not until 1500 BC，其为过去的时间点，应用与过去有关的时态，故该句使用 "it was+ 强调内容 +that..." 结构。

2. 引导词的变化

如果强调的成分是"人"，that 可以换成 who，即用 "it is/was+ 强调内容（人）+who..." 结构。但不论强调的是什么成分，都可以用 that。

例　**It was** the philosopher Jeremy Bentham (1748—1832) **who** was more than anyone else responsible for the development of this way of thinking. 真

译　要对这种思维方式的发展负上最大责任的人是哲学家杰里米·边沁（1748—1832）。

析　本句所强调的内容为 the philosopher Jeremy Bentham，指人，因此引导词可以用 who。

三　强调句型的辨别

雅思阅读中常会出现 it is... that... 的结构，但不一定都是强调句型，有可能是主语从句的后置形式。可通过以下两种方法，进行快速判断。

1. 看强调部分的词性

强调句型不能强调形容词和动词，所以如果 it is 和 that 之间的部分是形容词或动词的话，那这一定不是强调句型。

例1 It is therefore **assumed** that the end is good in an ethical sense. 真

译1 因此，人们预设这个目的从伦理层面看是好的。

析1 本句中 It is 和 that 中间是 assumed（assume 的过去分词形式），由于强调句型不能强调动词，因此可判断该句不是强调句，而是类似 it is said that... "据说……"的结构。It 是形式主语，实际指代后面的 that 从句，因此 that 引导的是主语从句。

例2 It is **clear** that the role of a board director today is not an easy one. 真

译2 很明显，今天董事会成员这个角色并不轻松。

析2 本句中 It is 和 that 中间是形容词 clear "明显的"，故本句不可能是强调句，而是主语从句后置，还原后即为"that 从句 + is clear"，表示"某事是显而易见的"。

2. 看去掉强调结构的句子是否完整

根据强调句型的构成原理，如果去掉了 it is... that... 结构之后，**余下部分仍能构成一个完整的句子**，则句子为强调句，反之则不是。

例 **It is** therefore essential for hotel management to develop HRM practices **that** enable them to inspire and retain competent employees. 真

译 因此，酒店管理层有必要制定人力资源管理措施，使他们能够激励并留住有能力的员工。

析 这个句子去掉 It is 和 that 后，therefore essential for hotel management to develop HRM practices 并不能与后面的从句 enable them to inspire and retain competent employees 结合形成完整的句子，故可判断原句子不是强调句。根据句子逻辑，使酒店能够激励和留住员工的是上文所提到的 HRM practices "人力资源管理措施"，所以 that 引导的是定语从句，其修饰的先行词为 HRM practices，句子还原后应为 HRM practices enable them to inspire and retain competent employees。而句子开头的 It is 实则是"it is+形容词+for sb. to do sth."句型的一部分。

真题句解读·实战演练

与倒装结构类似，对于强调句型的解读，同学们只需要将其还原成正常语序即可。

例 It was not until their empire collapsed in 476 AD that glass-making knowledge became widespread throughout Europe and the Middle East. 真

译 直到他们的帝国在公元 476 年覆亡，玻璃制造的知识才在欧洲和中东地区广泛传播。

步骤一：判断句子是否是强调句

该句中，有 It was... that... 结构，将其去掉后，剩下的部分可以组成一个完整的"主+系+表"结构的句子："Glass-making knowledge didn't become widespread throughout Europe and the Middle East until their empire collapsed in 476 AD."，因此该句是强调句。

步骤二：分析 It was... that... 结构所强调的内容

It was 和 that 中间的部分是 not until their empire collapsed in 476 AD，是由 not until 引导的时间状语从句，因此这句话强调的是玻璃制造知识在欧洲和中东地区广泛传播的时间节点。It was not until... that... 翻译为"直到……才……"。

It was not until their empire collapsed in 476 AD that glass-making knowledge became widespread
　　　　　　时间状语从句

throughout Europe and the Middle East.

Exercise 1 为以下句子选择恰当的引导词。

1. It is thanks to Ravenscroft's invention _____ (that/which) optical lenses, astronomical telescopes, microscopes and the like became possible. 真

2. It was Franklin _____ (who/whom) discovered that storms generally travel from west to east. 真

3. It is those objects _____ (that/when) are of interest to archaeologists. 真

4. It is now known _____ (that/what) the building process went through many different stages. 真

5. It is possible _____ (that/who) the carving represents a goddess in native mythology. 真

Exercise 2 找出以下句子中强调的部分，并将句子还原为正常语序。

1. It is cutting down native woodland that leads to soil erosion (水土流失). 真

2. It is in situations like these that the field of health geography comes into its own. 真

3. It is this uncertainty that triggers the surge of dopamine (多巴胺) in the brain. 真

4. It is this research that shows we should continually question whether or not our existing assumptions work. 真

5. It is over the past 50 years that the number of business schools and graduates has massively increased. 真

6. It is this simple and ancient molecule (分子) that has been used for many different functions. 真

7. It was through various studies focusing on animals that scientists first became aware of the influence of oxytocin (催产素). 真

8. It is this easily understood target that can help shape expectations and encourage action. 真

9. It was not until the early 20th century that mathematics and physics became part of meteorology (气象学). 真

10. It is the suspenseful (充满悬念的) tension of music, arising out of our unfulfilled expectations that is the source of the music's feeling. 真

(答案见 pp. 173~174)

第 12 节　特殊句式——虚拟语气

由于使用虚拟语气的句子所述内容是非真实的，因此学会判断虚拟语气十分重要，这决定了我们能否准确理解句意。虚拟语气的判断依据主要是谓语动词形式，本节将详细讲解不同句型使用虚拟语气时所使用的动词形式。

一　虚拟语气的基本概念

虚拟语气，顾名思义，就是指描述的是"非真实的情况"，表示说话者一种主观的意愿、假设或建议等。使用虚拟语气的句子所描述的内容一般与真实情况相反，或假设的情况不太可能成真（即成真的可能性很小）。例如，当一个女孩说"我是一个男的"时，其所述与事实不符，在英语中需用虚拟语气 I were a boy 来表述。

在雅思阅读中，虚拟语气主要出现在两种情况中：**一是 if 引导的非真实条件句；二是名词性从句**。

二　if 非真实条件句中的虚拟语气

if 引导的条件状语从句可分为"真实条件句"和"非真实条件句"。如果假设的情况是真的，或者可能成真，就是真实条件句。反之，如果假设的情况不是真的，或者不可能成真的，那就是非真实条件句，也称为"虚拟条件句"，要用虚拟语气。

if 引导的非真实条件句，对不同的情况进行假设，主句和从句的谓语需要用不同的形式，如下表：

假设的类型	if 从句谓语形式	主句谓语形式
与过去的情况相反	had done	would/could/might/should+have done
与现在的情况相反	did/were	would/could/might/should+do
与将来的情况相反	did/were were to do should do	would/could/might/should+do

上表看似复杂，实际上只要记住几个要点，就可以轻易记住并理解虚拟语气的用法。

①**从句时态往前推**：对现在情况的虚拟，从句用过去时；对过去情况的虚拟，从句用过去完成时。

②**主句共用四个情态动词**：观察上表可发现，无论哪种情况，主句的谓语都带有 would、could、might、should 这四个情态动词中的一个，之后再加上动词原形或 have done。

③**将来与现在一致**：对将来情况的虚拟实际上与对现在情况的虚拟所用谓语形式相同（只是对将来情况的虚拟中，从句谓语多了 were to do 和 should do 两种形式）。

例1　If you **employed** the 'principles of marketing' in an unprincipled way, you **would not be** doing marketing. 真

译1　如果你无原则地使用"营销原则"，你就不是在做营销。

析1　本句是对现在或将来情况的虚拟假设，实际上说话的对象 you 并没有在无原则使用"营销原则"，或说话者主观认为 you 在未来也不会这样做。

例2　If they **hadn't interviewed** participants face-to-face, they **could have used** a much bigger sample size. 真

译2　如果他们当时不是面对面地采访受试者，他们可以使用更大的样本量。

析2　本句是对过去情况的虚拟假设，根据句意得知实际上他们面对面地采访了受试者。

例③ If the soil **lost** its ability to perform its functions, the human race **could be** in big trouble soon. 真

译③ 如果土壤无法发挥其作用，人类很快就会陷入大麻烦。

析③ 本句是对将来情况的虚拟假设，实际上土地还没有失去发挥其作用的能力。

例④ **Were you introduced** to someone called Charlie, you **might make** the connection with your uncle. 真

译④ 如果有人介绍你认识一个叫查理的人，你可能会联想到你叔叔（和他同名）。

析④ Were you introduced to someone called Charlie 是倒装句，还原后为 If you were introduced to someone called Charlie。在英语中，if 引导的非真实条件句，可以把 if 省略，句子使用部分倒装结构，把助动词或 be 动词放到主语前面去。本句是对现在或将来情况的虚拟假设。

三　名词性从句中的虚拟语气

　　虚拟语气也可用在名词性从句（包括宾语从句、表语从句、主语从句和同位语从句）中，但用法与 if 的非真实条件句完全不一样。如果主句中有表示"建议""命令""要求"之类意思的词（无论词性是什么），其对应的名词性从句都需要使用虚拟语气。名词性从句的虚拟结构是把谓语动词变成"should+ 动词原形"，其中 should 可以省略，这种虚拟语气亦称为"should 型虚拟"。

<table>
<tr><td colspan="3" align="center">宾语从句中的虚拟</td></tr>
<tr><td rowspan="3">动词</td><td>advise　建议
suggest　建议
recommend　推荐
propose　提议</td><td>例 I **suggest** we <u>meet</u> there for coffee at 10. 真
译 我建议我们 10 点在那里见面喝咖啡。</td></tr>
<tr><td>ask　要求
request　请求
demand　要求
require　要求</td><td>例 This situation **required** that he <u>be</u> present.
译 这种情形需要他在场。</td></tr>
<tr><td>insist　坚决要求
intend　打算
order　命令</td><td>例 He **insists** that she <u>should come</u>.
译 他执意要她来。</td></tr>
<tr><td colspan="3" align="center">主语从句中的虚拟</td></tr>
<tr><td rowspan="2">形容词</td><td>desirable　想要的
essential　必需的
imperative　命令的
important　重要的
necessary　必要的
urgent　紧急的</td><td>例 It is **essential** that we <u>obtain</u> more climate data from areas close to the two great cities at Mohenjodaro and Harappa and also from the Indian Punjab. 真
译 我们必须从摩亨佐达罗和哈拉帕这两个大城市附近的地区以及印度旁遮普地区获得更多的气候数据。</td></tr>
<tr><td>过去分词</td><td>desired　渴望
requested　请求
suggested　建议
recommended　推荐
required　必需
demanded　要求</td><td>例 It's **recommended** that we <u>use</u> melted snow for washing to conserve supplies. 真
译 有人建议我们用融雪水洗刷以节约物资。</td></tr>
</table>

		表语从句和同位语从句中的虚拟
名词	**suggestion** 建议 **proposal** 提议，建议 **advice** 建议 **recommendation** 推荐 **demand** 要求 **requirement** 要求 **request** 要求	例1 Some scientists' **suggestion** is that we <u>should think of</u> each species and its microbes as a single unit, dubbed a 'holobiont'. （表语从句） 真 译1 一些科学家的建议是，我们应该把每个物种及与其共生的微生物视为一个整体，称为"全生物"。 例2 In fact, she offers us her **suggestion** that we <u>should seek out</u> more boredom in our lives. （同位语从句） 真 译2 事实上，她给我们的建议是，我们应该多寻找生活中的无趣之处。
	order 命令 **desire** 愿望，要求	例 Our **desire** is that we <u>discover</u> and then <u>share</u> new-found knowledge. （表语从句） 真 译 我们的愿望是发现并分享新发现的知识。

四 其他句型中的虚拟语气

1. wish/would rather 后的宾语从句

wish 之后的宾语从句，表示一种没有实现或根本不可能实现的愿望，常用虚拟语气。

would rather、had rather、would sooner 等之后的宾语从句常表示与客观事实不相符的一种愿望，也使用虚拟语气。

这两种句型对应的虚拟语气谓语形式如下：

从句假设的类型	wish 句型	would rather 句型
与过去的情况相反	had done 或 would/could/might/should+have done	had done
与现在的情况相反	did/were	did/were
与未来的情况相反	would/could/might/should+do	

例1 **Wish** I <u>had</u> that amount of time to spend! 真

译1 真希望我有那么多时间！

析1 本句是对现在情况的虚拟假设，言下之意是目前不可能有这么多时间。

例2 I **wish** I <u>hadn't eaten</u> so much.

译2 我倒希望我没有吃那么多。

析2 本句是对过去情况的虚拟假设，根据句意得知实际上"我"吃了很多。

例3 I **would rather** you <u>came</u> with us next week.

译3 我倒愿意你下周和我们一块儿去。

析3 本句是对未来情况的虚拟假设，根据句意得知实际上"你"不会和"我们"一起去。

2. It is (high/about) time that 句型

It is (high/about) time that 中的从句要用虚拟语气,谓语动词通常用过去式,有时也用"should+动词原形"(should不可省略),意为"该是干……的时候了"。

例 It's **about time** you <u>cleaned</u> your room!

译 你该打扫自己的房间了!

析 本句为It is (high/about) time that 句型,that 从句用虚拟语气,即谓语动词用一般过去式或"should+动词原形",句中you cleaned your room 也可写为you should clean your room。

真题句解读·实战演练

例 On the other hand, if Watson generated a recommendation that contradicted the experts' opinion, doctors would conclude that Watson wasn't competent. 真

译 另一方面,如果沃森提出了一个与专家意见相矛盾的建议,医生就会得出沃森不称职的结论。

步骤一:判断虚拟语气

这句话包含一个主句和一个if引导的从句,主句的谓语动词形式为would do,if从句的谓语动词形式为did,由此同学们可以联想到此处是if引导的非真实条件句中的虚拟语气。

On the other hand, **if** Watson *generated* a recommendation that contradicted the experts' opinion, doctors *would conclude* that Watson wasn't competent.

步骤二:分析虚拟语气

if引导的非真实条件句中,谓语动词形式为did,而主句谓语动词形式为would do,由此判断,这是对现在或将来情况的假设,也就是说,实际上沃森并没有提出相矛盾的建议,也没有人认为它不称职。

步骤三:分析其他成分

在if引导的非真实条件句中,含有一个that引导的定语从句,修饰先行词recommendation;而在主句中,则含有一个that引导的宾语从句,作conclude的宾语。

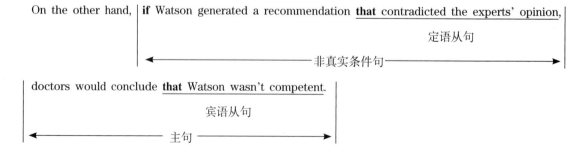

语法点精练·小试牛刀

Exercise 1　根据句意，选择恰当的动词形式填空。

1. It would be better if it _____ (followed/had followed) a chronological pattern. 真

2. The Industrial Revolution couldn't _____ (take place/have taken place) at all without these new sources of power.

3. If their designers _____ (had had/had) the tools to think with their bodies, there might have been a better solution. 真

4. He wrote to the Home Office suggesting that the departments of government _____ (are linked/be linked) together through a set of 'conversation tubes'. 真

5. It is high time you _____ (made/had made) the preparation for the speech. 真

Exercise 2　判断以下句子中虚拟语气的假设类型，并划分句子成分。

1. If I were you, I'd start looking for another job.

2. What would life be like if people didn't have to work? 真

3. I wish I'd taken a diploma in business skills instead of on IT. 真

4. I wish you wouldn't leave your clothes all over the floor.

5. You would know what was going on, if you had listened.

6. His proposal that the system should be changed was rejected.

7. If everyone accessed books from their own computers at home, libraries would be obsolete (淘汰的). 真

8. What would life have been like if the Industrial Revolution hadn't taken place? 真

9. The US government's Food and Drug Administration introduced rules demanding that the meat industry abandon practices associated with the risk of the disease spreading. 真

10. It is suggested that fathers use less familial (家庭特有的) language to provide their children with a bridge to the kind of speech they'll hear in public. 真

（答案见 pp.174~176）

第13节 / 特殊句式——分隔结构

分隔结构是特殊句式的一种，在雅思阅读中频繁出现，而且往往伴随着长句，使句法结构错综复杂，给理解文意带来一定的困难。因此，理解分隔结构对扫除阅读障碍有很大的帮助。

英语分隔结构并非杂乱无章，是有一定的规律的。掌握这些规律，就能更好地拆解长难句。

一 分隔结构的基本概念

分隔结构 (split structure) 是指依照正常的语序和句法结构，关系密切、本应紧连在一起的两个句子成分被另一些句子成分所隔开，或者是词语的习惯搭配关系被拆开，从而使这两部分产生分隔的现象。

分隔结构的出现往往是为了保持句子结构平衡，将复杂的成分、语义重点移至句末；又或者是某些成分带有补充信息，只能插入到句子当中。在阅读时，同学们需要把原来属于一个整体的各部分找出来，才能从结构和语义上弄清楚句子的意思，避免理解上的错误。

例 My proposal, **which I believe would also be Kane's**, is that neither of these attitudes captures the significance of the end to the means for marketing. 真

译 我的提议是，这两种态度都没有抓住目的对于营销手段的意义。我相信我的提议也会是凯恩的意见。

析 此句中，修饰My proposal的定语从句which I believe would also be Kane's将主句分成了两部分，造成了主谓结构的分隔(主语是My proposal，谓语是系动词is)。这句话可以分开两句理解："My proposal is that neither of these attitudes... for marketing. I believe my proposal would also be Kane's."。

二 插入式分隔结构

最常见的分隔结构是将同位语、插入语、从句等成分插入句子中间，这种插入式的分隔结构，通常会在插入成分的前后两端加上标点进行分隔，如成对的逗号或破折号。

1. 同位语和插入语造成的分隔结构

例1 In his essay, Kanayo F. Nwanze, **President of the International Fund for Agricultural Development**, argued that governments can significantly reduce risks for farmers by providing basic services. 真

译1 国际农业发展基金会主席卡纳约·F. 恩万泽在他的文章中指出，通过提供基础服务，政府能大大降低农民面临的风险。

析1 本句出现的成对的逗号，提示句中含有分隔结构，President of the International Fund for Agricultural Development 为插入成分，把主句的主语 Kanayo F. Nwanze 和谓语 argued 分隔开。这个插入成分是主语 Kanayo F. Nwanze 的同位语，补充说明该人物的身份。

例2 The typical way of talking to a baby—**high-pitched, exaggerated and repetitious**—is a source of fascination for linguists who hope to understand how 'baby talk' impacts on learning. 真

译2 对希望了解"模仿儿语"如何影响学习的语言学家来说，与婴儿交谈的典型方式——高音调、夸张和重复——让他们着迷不已。

析2 可轻易判断本句破折号中间的 high-pitched, exaggerated and repetitious 为插入成分，是对主语 The typical way of talking to a baby 的补充说明，插入成分将句子的主语和系动词 is 分隔开来。

尽管分隔结构的典型标志是逗号和破折号，但不是所有插入成分都会有标点符号分隔。在有些句式中，插入语的前后两端或其中一端没有标点符号作为分隔符号，比如以 such as、like 引导的用来举例的插入语。

[例] Procedures **such as capturing and moving at-risk or dangerous individuals** are bolstered by knowledge gained in zoos about doses for anaesthetics. 真

[译] 在动物园获得的关于麻醉剂量的知识，能优化诸如捕获和转移个别需要特别保护的动物或危险动物等程序。

[析] 本句并没有出现典型的分隔标点符号，但 Procedures 后出现 such as 短语，可判断此处有插入语。而通过谓语 are bolstered 得知，插入的部分至 individuals 处结束，即插入语为 such as capturing and moving at-risk or dangerous individuals，是对 Procedures 的举例说明。此句的主干实际为 Procedures are bolstered by knowledge...。

2. 从句造成的分隔结构

造成分隔结构的从句一般是状语从句或定语从句。

状语从句作为对主句的补充，可以出现在主句前、主句后或主句中。当状语从句出现在主句中时，就会形成分隔结构。

由于定语从句通常要紧接其修饰的先行词，所以句子中某一名词后接有定语从句的话，也会造成分隔结构。

[例1] It was not until the First World War, **when Britain became cut off from essential glass suppliers**, that glass became part of the scientific sector. 真

[译1] 直至第一次世界大战，英国与基本的玻璃供应商断绝了联系，玻璃才进入科学领域。

[析1] 这个句子中，when 引导的定语从句将主句 It was not until... that... 分隔，从句修饰的先行词为 the First World War。

[例2] While these artists were highly skilled, everyone—**no matter what their jobs were for the rest of the year**—was expected to contribute to communal projects. 真

[译2] 虽然这些艺术家技艺高超，但每个人——无论他们在一年中的其他时间从事什么工作——都要为公共项目做出贡献。

[析2] 本句的插入成分为让步状语从句 no matter what their jobs were for the rest of the year，从句前后有成对的破折号，是比较好判断的分隔结构，从句的作用是进一步强调公共项目的广泛参与性。

三 从句后移造成的分隔结构

有时由于从句过长，而主句较短，则会把长的从句后移，以保证主句连贯性以及避免句子结构头重脚轻，这就形成了从句后移造成的分隔结构。

遇到这种结构，只需把后移的从句，移到原本的位置即可。

[例1] A research team led by Petrie, found **early in their investigations** that many of the archaeological sites were not where they were supposed to be. 真

[译1] 由佩特里领导的一个研究小组在早期的调查中发现，许多考古遗址并不在它们理应在的地方。

[析1] 本句中，谓语 found 后面应接宾语，却出现了状语 early in their investigations，故判断 found 的宾语应是后移了。继续往后看，that 引导的从句 that many of the archaeological sites... to be 正是 found 的宾语，因此可判断 early in their investigations 作为状语造成了谓语 found 与宾语从句的分隔。句子正常的语序应为 A research team... found that... early in their investigations，意为"在早期的调查中，一个……研究团队发现了……"。

例2 During the excavation of ancient Babylon, evidence **was found** that soapmaking was known as early as 2800 BC. 真

译2 在古巴比伦的发掘过程中所发现的证据表明，早在公元前 2800 年，人们就懂得如何制作肥皂。

析2 本句的谓语部分 was found 是被动语态，主语是 evidence，故判定 found 后的从句不是它的宾语从句或主语从句。that 引导的从句实际同位语从句，解释说明 evidence，指出是什么的证据，此同位语从句由于比谓语长很多，发生了后移，形成了分隔结构，句子的正常语序应为 evidence that... was found，意为"找到了……方面的证据"。

Tips

从句后移造成的分隔结构在雅思阅读中较为常见，却不容易判别区分，它的难点在于既没有一般分隔结构的标志——逗号或破折号，又以从句的形式出现。

不过，同学们只需要掌握以下几点，即可轻松理解从句后移造成的分隔结构：

1. 找出分隔结构的典型特征：

① 状语位于从句前，造成分隔：关注介词短语，比如上述例 1 中的 early in their investigations；

② 同位语从句后移：这类句子的结构多为"表示事物的名词 + 动词 + that 引导的同位语从句"，如上述例2。判断这类句型首先要辨别句中的从句类型，如果确定从句并非宾语从句，我们就可以往同位语从句的方向思考辨析。

2. 找到主谓结构，根据从句引导词（that 最常见，还有可能出现 whether、how、when、where 等），找出后移的从句。

3. 重组句子，进行理解。

实际上，从句后移造成的分隔结构往往更符合中文句法结构和语义表达习惯，所以我们有时甚至可以不调整语序，直接按原有的句子结构翻译理解。

真题句解读·实战演练

解决分隔结构的要点是找到前后分隔的部分，把句子进行重组还原，再进行长难句的分析。利用成对出现的逗号或破折号可以快速找到插入成分。找到插入成分后，可分三种情况进行分析：

① 如果是同位语或插入语造成的分隔，可以直接去掉不看；

② 若插入的是状语从句或定语从句，可以先忽略，最后再看；

③ 若是从句后移造成的分隔，把从句还原到原来位置，再进行分析。

例 If the vehicle can do the driving, those who are challenged by existing mobility models—such as older or disabled travellers—may be able to enjoy significantly greater travel autonomy. 真

译 如果车辆能够自动驾驶，那些受到现有出行模式挑战的人——比如老年人或残障人士——也许能够拥有多得多的出行自主权。

步骤一：找分隔

根据成对出现的破折号，很容易判断破折号之间的内容为插入成分。将其去掉后，可以发现主语 those 和谓语动词 may be able to enjoy 之间仍然隔着一个 who 引导的从句，因此这个句子一共有两个插入成分。

those	who are challenged by existing mobility models	—such as older or disabled travellers—
	插入成分 1	插入成分 2

may be able to enjoy significantly greater travel autonomy.

步骤二：分析句子主干

去掉插入成分后，将被分隔的主谓结构连起来，句子很明显是一个带有条件状语从句的复合句。

If 引导的条件状语从句：**If**   the vehicle   can do   the driving,

              引导词   主语   谓语   宾语

主句：those...   may be able to enjoy   significantly greater travel autonomy

     主语   谓语   宾语

步骤三：分析插入成分

who 引导的定语从句 who are challenged by existing mobility models，修饰先行词 those，意为"那些受到现有出行模式挑战的人"。破折号之间的插入语对 those who are challenged by existing mobility models 进行举例说明。

语法点精练·小试牛刀

Exercise 1 找出以下句子中的插入成分，并划分句子成分。

1. In addition, the opening of the Suez Canal in 1869, the same year that *Cutty Sark* was launched, had a serious impact. 真

2. The lynx（猞猁）is a specialist predator（捕食者）of roe deer（狍），a species that has exploded in Britain in recent decades, holding back, by intensive browsing, attempts to re-establish forests. 真

3. She believes that oxytocin acts as a chemical spotlight that shines on social clues—a shift in posture, a flicker（闪动）of the eyes, a dip in the voice—making people more attuned（适应）to their social environment. 真

4. The products stress the values traditionally associated with the category in ways that allow consumers to oppose—or at least temporarily escape from—the aspects of trends they view as undesirable. 真

5. Trends—technological, economic, environmental, social, or political—that affect how people perceive the world around them present firms with unique opportunities for growth. 真

6. The lack of self-imagery in Harappan Civilisation（哈拉帕文明）—at a time when the Egyptians were carving and painting representations of themselves all over their temples—is only part of the mystery. 真

7. The only question is how to achieve it, and here positive psychology—a supposed science that not only identifies what makes people happy but also allows their happiness to be measured—can show the way. 真

8. In a study published in *Proceedings of the National Academy of Sciences*, a total of 57 babies from two slightly different age groups—seven months and eleven and a half months—were played a number of syllables from both their native language (English) and a non-native tongue (Spanish). 真

9. Alternative explorations—where experimentation（实验）and human instinct lead to progress and new ideas—are effectively discouraged. 真

10. They also introduced alien species—ranging from cattle, pigs, goats, rats and dogs to plants and ants—that either prey on the eggs and young tortoises or damage or destroy their habitat. 真

（答案见 pp. 176~178）

第14节 长难句解读——拆分＋简化

前面各章节已经介绍了解读长难句必需的语法知识以及常见的特殊句式，有了这些基础知识，我们就可以着手分析长难句。

拆解长难句，一般采用以下两步：第一，**拆分长句**，将其分成若干个分句；第二，**简化各分句**，寻找主干，以主干为导向捕捉句子的关键信息。

一 长难句的特点与类别

1. 长难句的特点

在学习拆分和简化长难句前，我们先来了解一下长难句的特点。长难句即长句和难句的统称，通常以并列句、复合句、并列复合句的形式出现。长难句中可以有多个分句，而且这些分句可以呈现嵌套、平行、并列等结构。除了并列分句外，长难句中常见的从属分句主要有三种：

① 名词性从句，包括主语从句、宾语从句、表语从句和同位语从句；

② 形容词性从句，即定语从句；

③ 状语从句。

长难句的一大特点是复杂，不仅结构复杂、逻辑复杂，并列成分、修饰成分也复杂。其另一个主要特点是，需要我们结合上下文以及句中的各个成分理解整个句子的意思。

2. 长难句的类别

了解长难句的特点后，我们一起来看看长难句有哪几个类别，区分不同类别的长难句有助于我们有的放矢地拆分和理解长难句。

我们可以将长难句大致分为四个类别：**倒装句、省略句、含有复杂修饰成分的句子、含有大段插入语或同位语的句子**。

• 倒装句

为了强调某些内容或避免句子头重脚轻，原本应该放在句首的成分被倒装放置句末。要理解这类句子，需要将倒装的成分找出来，并找出主谓宾，将各成分进行重新排序。

• 省略句

在某些结构中，句子中的虚词或重复部分会被省略，使句子更简练。但当句子较长、成分较多较复杂时，省略句就很容易让同学们感到迷惑。这时候更需要划分句子层次，判断所省略的属于什么成分，根据上下文推断所省略的内容。

- 含有复杂修饰成分的句子

通常，长难句中可能会同时存在多个不同的修饰成分。修饰成分包括分词、不定式、介词短语以及从句（如定语、状语从句）。

同学们可以先找出这类句子的主谓宾，理解主干句意，再逐步分析修饰成分，将其意思添加到主干中，进行整句理解。

- 含有大段插入语或同位语的句子

句子中大段的插入语或同位语会分割句子前后连贯的语义，干扰同学们把握句子主干。

遇到这类长难句，可以跳过插入成分，先抓住主干，理解句子大意。同学们需要提高自身的抗干扰能力，才能从根本上克服这类句子的理解障碍。

二 长难句的拆分

英语基础较好的同学通过速读句子，理解意思，即可把长难句拆分成若干个分句。基础薄弱的同学也不用怕，可通过以下三种手段来拆分长句。

1. 利用标点符号

逗号、分号和冒号是英语句子中最常见的连接符号，因此也是我们拆分句子的好帮手。

最常见的用来连接句子的标点是逗号，但注意逗号一般不能单独使用，还需要加上连词。

分号表示并列关系，一般前后均为完整的分句，通常情况下不需要连词。

冒号前后通常是完整的分句，一般情况下，冒号后的分句对冒号前的分句（或分句的某一内容）进行解释说明。

例1 People had become more environmentally conscious, **and** the Danish experiment had proved that bike-sharing was a real possibility. 真

译1 人们的环境意识越来越强，而且丹麦的实验证明，共享自行车是真实可行的。

析1 本句前后用逗号连接，且逗号后有并列连词and，所以此处利用逗号就可以把句子分为两个分句。（注意：有时逗号后虽然有连词，但两端不是分句，而是短语，那么句子就不能从这个地方断开。）本句的结构大致如下：

分句1	People 主语	had become 系动词	more environmentally conscious, 表语
连词		and	
分句2	the Danish experiment 主语	had proved 谓语	that... 从句作宾语

例2 Some have claimed that major glacier-fed rivers changed their course, dramatically affecting the water supply and agriculture; **and yet** others that climate change caused an environmental change that affected food and water provision. 真

译2 一些人认为，由冰川融水补给的主要河流改变了流向，严重影响了供水和农业；而其他人则认为气候变化引起环境变化，从而影响了粮食和水的供应。

析2 本句中间出现分号，分号后出现并列连词and yet，显而易见，分号前后是两个分句。本句的结构如下：

分句 1	Some 主语	have claimed 谓语	that major...; 从句作宾语
连词	and yet		
分句 2	others 主语	(have claimed) 谓语（被省略）	that climate change... 从句作宾语

例3 Soils also store water, preventing flood damage: in the UK, damage to buildings, roads and bridges from floods caused by soil degradation costs £233 million every year. 真

译3 土壤还能蓄水，避免洪水造成破坏：在英国，因为土壤退化导致的洪灾损毁了建筑物、道路和桥梁，每年带来 2.33 亿英镑的损失。

析3 本句中出现冒号，冒号前后是两个独立的句子。(注意：冒号后面也可能只有单词或短语，对冒号前的内容做简单补充说明，此时冒号后的内容就不构成分句。)本句的结构大致如下：

| 分句 1 | Soils
主语 | also store
谓语 | water,
宾语 | preventing flood damage
状语 | |
| 分句 2 | in the UK
状语 | damage to...
主语 | costs
谓语 | £233 million
宾语 | every year
状语 |

Tips

在前两个例句中，都出现了并列连词 and。并列连词经常和标点符号一起用于连接句子，也可以单独使用。因此，我们可以利用并列连词拆分句子。第 5 节提到，分句之间的逻辑关系不同，采用的并列连词也不同。此处再次列出常见的四类并列连词，供同学们参考：

逻辑关系	连词
并列、顺承、递进关系	and, both... and, not only... but (also), neither... nor
转折、对比关系	but, while, yet, whereas
因果关系	so, for
选择关系	or, either... or

2. 利用从句标志找从句始末

雅思阅读中，拆分句子最常用且最有效的方法是利用从句的引导词。从句引导词标志着从句的开始，找到引导词，就找到了从句的开头。而从句的结尾则较为隐蔽，从句的结束标志大致可分为三种：标点符号（逗号、分号、冒号等）；下一个引导词；第二个谓语动词前。

（1）从句结束于标点符号

例 But the biggest blow came **when** Postbank decided to abolish the chip card**, because** it wasn't profitable. 真

译 但最大的打击是，因为无利可图，邮政银行决定取消芯片卡。

析 本句中，首先找到两个从句的引导词 when 和 because，就找到了两个从句的开头。很明显，when 引导的从句以逗号结尾，因为逗号后的 because 之后就是另一个从句了。而 because 引导的从句则是以句号结束。本句的结构大致如下：

主句	But 连词		the biggest blow 主语		came 谓语
when 从句	when 引导词	Postbank 主语		decided 谓语	to abolish the chip card, 宾语
because 从句	because 引导词	it 主语		wasn't 系动词	profitable 表语

（2）从句结束于下一个引导词

例 Many studies have demonstrated **that** neuron activity decreases **if** outcomes become predictable. 真

译 许多研究表明，如果结果变得可预测，神经元活动就会减少。

析 本句中没有标点符号，但可发现两个引导词 that 和 if，由此可确定存在两个从句。that 引导的从句结束于下一个从句引导词 if，而 if 引导的从句则结束于标点符号(句末的句号)。本句的大致结构如下：

主句	Many studies 主语		have demonstrated 谓语		that... 从句作宾语
that 从句	that 引导词		neuron activity 主语		decreases 谓语
if 从句	if 引导词	outcomes 主语		become 系动词	predictable 表语

> **Tips**
>
> 以上两个例句的从句虽然都能单独分开，但语义上存在包含与被包含的关系，这是英语中常见的"嵌套结构"。所谓嵌套结构，就是句子中有多层次的从句，从句套从句。要弄清楚各层次的关系，要先从内而外，拆分句子，再从外而内，理解句意。上述两句的层次关系如下所示：
>
>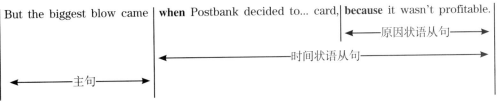

- 67 -

（3）从句结束于第二个谓语动词前

从句本身作为一个完整的分句，有且只能有一个谓语动词（除非存在并列谓语或包含另一个从句），所以从引导词数起，第一个谓语动词是从句的谓语，而第二个则不是，属于从句外的成分，所以从句要结束在第二个谓语动词前。

例 The Hamiltonian view is **that** those **who** are less intelligent need the good offices of the more intelligent to keep them in line. 真

译 汉密尔顿派别的观点是，没那么聪明的人需要聪明人的大力协助，使他们自己有章可循。

析 本句可找到两个从句的引导词that和who，两从句之间没有标点符号，that引导的表语从句一直到句号结束，那么who引导的从句到哪里结束呢？通过观察可发现，从who后开始数，第一个动词是系词are，第二个谓语动词是need，所以该从句要结束在need之前，即为who are less intelligent，修饰先行词those。

本句的结构大致如下：

主句	The Hamiltonian view 主语		is 系动词	that... 从句作表语
that 从句	that 引导词	those... 主语	need 谓语	the good offices... 宾语 to keep them in line 状语
who 从句	who 引导词		are 系动词	less intelligent 表语

3. 分析主谓结构

有时候，句子没有太多标点符号，从句的引导词也会被省略(如宾语从句、定语从句常省略引导词that)，这时就不能单靠标点或从句的引导词来拆分长难句，而需要分析主谓结构。

分析主谓结构的关键是找到谓语动词，找到**谓语动词**，它前面的成分就是主语了（但注意，完全倒装结构中，主语在谓语动词后）。

雅思阅读中，常出现以下两种特殊的主谓结构：**主谓（宾）主谓；主主谓谓**。

（1）主谓（宾）主谓，后面的"主谓"为从句

例 **They believed the scheme was** an answer to the perceived threats of air pollution and consumerism. 真

译 他们认为该计划是在回应空气污染和消费主义造成的已知威胁。

析 本句开头即出现两个主谓结构，分别是 They believed 和 the scheme was，从而判断这是"主谓（宾）主谓"结构。该结构中，后面的主谓结构为从句，即 the scheme was an answer to the perceived threats of air pollution and consumerism 为从句，结合句意，可知这是省略了 that 的宾语从句。

主句	They 主语	believed 谓语	(that) the scheme was... 从句作宾语
（that）从句	(that) 引导词（被省略）	the scheme 主语	was 系动词 an answer to... 表语

（2）主主谓谓，中间的"主谓"为从句

例 **The first thing they discovered is** that music triggers the production of dopamine. 真

译 他们的第一个发现是音乐刺激多巴胺的产生。

析 The first thing they discovered is 是"主主谓谓"结构，中间的"主谓"是从句，插入到主句中间，隔开了主句的主语和谓语。具体到本句，they discovered 是省略了引导词 that 的定语从句，修饰 the first thing，隔开了句子的主语 the first thing 和系动词 is，主句的主干是 The first thing is that...。

	The first thing	is	that...
主句	主语	系动词	从句作表语
(that) 从句	(that) 引导词（被省略）	they 主语	discovered 谓语	
that 从句	that 引导词	music 主语	triggers 谓语	the production of dopamine 宾语

三 长难句的简化

有时把长难句拆分成若干个分句（简单句的形式）后，也不一定能马上读懂意思，因为简单句也不一定很简单，会有很多限定成分、修饰成分。这个时候就需要对分句进行简化，提取主干。

简化简单句，第3节和第4节有提到相关要点，此处再次重申简化句子的方法是：先提取句子的核心部分（主要是主、谓、宾），理解大意；其他修饰成分后看，或去掉不看。在看懂句子核心内容后，再深入研究细节。

例1 As with many other species, the lynx has been able to spread as farming has left the hills and people discover that it is more lucrative to protect charismatic wildlife than to hunt it, as tourists will pay for the chance to see it. 真

译1 随着农耕活动退出山区，猞猁与许多其他物种已经能繁衍生息，并且人们也发现保护这些具有超凡魅力的野生动物比猎捕它们更有利可图，因为游客们愿意为观赏这些野生动物的机会付费。

步骤一：拆分

速读句子，发现句中出现2个逗号，将句子分成3个部分：

第一部分（As引导的状语）：As with many other species,

第二部分：the lynx has... hunt it,

第三部分（as引导的状语从句）：as tourists... see it.

第二部分 the lynx has... hunt it 中出现连词 and，and 前后各有两个谓语动词，依次是 has been able to spread、has left、discover、is，从而可以断定此处至少有四个分句，可以先在连词 and 处将第二部分分为两句：

句1: the lynx *has been able to spread*　　**as** farming *has left* the hills

　　　　　　　主句　　　　　　　　　　状语从句

这句出现了连词 as，可以以 as 为界将此句断开，the lynx has been able to spread 为主句，as farming has left the hills 为状语从句。

句2: **and**　people *discover*　**that** it *is* more lucrative to protect charismatic wildlife than to hunt it

　　连词　　　主句　　　　　　　　　　宾语从句

句2是一个"主谓（宾）主谓"的结构，因此主句的主语和谓语分别是 people 和 discover，that 从句（that it is... hunt it）作主句的宾语。

步骤二：简化

句首 As 引导的状语以及句中、句末 as 引导的状语从句并非核心内容，将其去掉后，剩下的内容就是主干：

~~As with many other species,~~ // <u>the lynx has been able to spread</u> // ~~as farming has left the hills~~ // and // <u>people discover</u> // **that** it is more lucrative to protect charismatic wildlife than to hunt it, // ~~as tourists will pay for the chance to see it.~~

步骤三：分析从句

句中两个 as 引导的从句都是原因状语从句，分别说明猞猁能繁衍生息的原因和保护野生动物更有利可图的原因。

that 引导的宾语从句同时使用了 "it is+ 形容词 +to do sth." 的结构和比较结构，表示 "做某事比做某事更……"，it 为形式主语，逻辑主语是 to protect charismatic wildlife。

- -

例2 However, more professional and better-informed boards would have been particularly appropriate for banks where the executives had access to information that part-time non-executive directors lacked, leaving the latter unable to comprehend or anticipate the 2008 crash. 真

译2 然而，更专业和更了解情况的董事会对银行来说尤其合适，因为高管们可以获取兼职非执行董事所缺乏的信息，这也是为什么后者无法理解或预测 2008 年崩盘的原因。s

步骤一：拆分

首先，可以利用标点和从句引导词来进行断句。第一个逗号前仅有一个 However，对断句作用不大，第二个逗号后是一个非谓语动词 doing 短语，而逗号前则出现了从句引导词 where 和 that，故句子可分成四部分。

主句：However, more professional and better-informed boards would have been particularly appropriate for banks

where 从句：where the executives had access to information

that 从句：that part-time non-executive directors lacked

非谓语动词 doing 短语：leaving the latter unable to comprehend or anticipate the 2008 crash

步骤二：简化主句

主句中，主语是 more professional and better-informed boards，其中心词是 boards，而 more professional and better-informed 是 boards 的修饰语；would have been 是使用了虚拟语气的系动词，表示对过去事情的假设；particularly appropriate for banks 是表语，使用了固定搭配 be appropriate for "适合……"，particularly 是 appropriate 的修饰语。因此，主句可简化为 ... boards would have been appropriate for banks，大意为 "……的董事会适合银行"。

主句：~~However,~~ // ~~more professional and better-informed~~ boards **would have been** ~~particularly~~ appropriate for banks

步骤三：分析从句及其他修饰成分

where 后的部分不仅有 "嵌套结构"，还带有一个非谓语动词 doing 短语，理解难度较大，但可以按照步骤一的拆分逐个分析。

从步骤一可知，where 从句到下一个引导词 that 前结束。该从句跟在 banks 后，将 banks 当作地点状语代入从句，从句语义通顺，表示"在银行里，高管们可以获取信息"，可知 where 从句是修饰 banks 的定语从句。

that 从句跟在 information 后，谓语是 lacked，缺宾语。information 代入从句后，语义上正是 lacked 的宾语，因此 that 引导的是修饰 information 的定语从句，补充说明银行高管们获取的是什么信息。

逗号后的非谓语动词 doing 短语作状语，修饰 that 引导的宾语从句，补充说明兼职非执行董事缺乏信息的后果。这里的 latter "后者"指代的是从句中出现的 part-time non-executive directors。

<u>**where** the executives had access to information</u> // <u>**that** part-time non-executive directors</u>
   修饰 banks 的定语从句   修饰 information 的定语从句

<u>lacked,</u> // <u>leaving the latter unable to comprehend or anticipate the 2008 crash</u>
          结果状语

例3 Without knowing anything much of Jeremy Bentham or the school of moral theory he established—since they are by education and intellectual conviction illiterate in the history of ideas—our advocates of positive psychology follow in his tracks in rejecting as outmoded and irrelevant pretty much the entirety of ethical reflection on human happiness to date. 真

译3 我们积极心理学的倡导者在不了解杰里米·边沁以及他所建立的道德理论学派的情况下——因为他们在教育和知识信念上是思想史的文盲——追随他的脚步，拒绝接受迄今为止几乎所有对于人类幸福的伦理思考，认为它们已经过时，是无关紧要的。

步骤一：拆分

这个句子很长，但我们首先发现句中出现成对的破折号，将句子分成三个部分。很明显，第一个破折号前的部分是 Without 引导的状语，两个破折号中间是 since 引导的从句（谓语动词是 are），第二个破折号后的内容是主句（谓语动词是 follow in his tracks）。由于 since 从句为插入成分，因此可以先拎出来，将 Without 引导的状语与主句合起来理解。这样，通过拆分和寻找谓语动词，句子的大致框架就出来了。

主句：Without knowing anything much of Jeremy Bentham or the school of moral theory he established, //our advocates of positive psychology **follow in his tracks** in rejecting as outmoded and irrelevant pretty much the entirety of ethical reflection on human happiness to date.

从句：since they **are** by education and intellectual conviction illiterate in the history of ideas

步骤二：简化主句

Without 引导的是一个伴随状语，可先略去不看。主句中，谓语是 follow in his tracks，这是一个固定短语，意为"步他的后尘"；谓语前的 our advocates of positive psychology 是主语，中心词是 advocates；谓语后的部分是一个较长的介宾短语作方式状语，也可先略去。因此，主句简化后为 ... advocates... follow in his tracks，意为"……的倡导者追随他的脚步"。

主句：~~Without knowing anything much of Jeremy Bentham or the school of moral theory he established,~~ // ~~our~~ advocates ~~of positive psychology~~ **follow in his tracks** // ~~in rejecting as outmoded and irrelevant pretty much the entirety of ethical reflection on human happiness to date.~~

步骤三：分析从句及其他修饰成分

Without 引导的伴随状语，逻辑主语同主句主语，即 our advocates of positive psychology，这个状语说明这些人是在什么状态下追随杰里米·边沁的脚步的。另外，通过确定谓语动词可以发现，这个状语中还包含着一个从句 he established，这是省略了关系词修饰 the school of moral theory 的定语从句。

since引导的状语从句中的主语是they，这里需要结合主句进行理解，指代的对象是主句的主语(在英语中，前置的状语经常使用代词指代主句提到的人或事物)，系动词是are，表语是illiterate。此处，by education and intellectual conviction是被前置的插入成分，将系动词和表语分隔，对句子理解造成一定的障碍。这个从句的正常语序应该是since they are illiterate in the history of ideas by education and intellectual conviction，说明这些人不了解杰里米·边沁及其理论的原因。

在主句的方式状语in rejecting... to date中，也出现了分隔结构，由于rejecting的宾语过长，as outmoded and irrelevant被前置，分隔了非谓语动词rejecting及其宾语，这部分的正常语序应为in rejecting pretty much the entirety of ethical reflection on human happiness to date as outmoded and irrelevant。reject sth. as 意为"拒绝接受某物，认为它……"。

Without 状语：Without knowing anything much of Jeremy Bentham or the school of moral theory // he **established**

since 从句：*since* they **are** <u>by education and intellectual conviction</u> illiterate in the history of ideas

方式状语：in rejecting <u>as outmoded and irrelevant</u> pretty much the entirety of ethical reflection on human happiness to date

真题句解读·实战演练

例 The chair of the remuneration committee can be an exposed and lonely role, as Alison Carnwath, chair of Barclays Bank's remuneration committee, found when she had to resign, having been roundly criticised for trying to defend the enormous bonus to be paid to the chief executive; the irony being that she was widely understood to have spoken out against it in the privacy of the committee. 真

译 薪酬委员会主席可能会是一个孤立无助的角色，巴克莱银行薪酬委员会主席艾莉森·卡瓦思在不得不辞职时就有此体会，当时她因试图为支付给首席执行官的巨额奖金进行辩护而受到了严厉批评；讽刺的是，根据很多人的说法，在委员会的内部讨论中，她对高额奖金是持反对态度的。

步骤一：拆分

首先尝试利用标点来进行断句，然后根据从句引导词和谓语动词进行拆分。可以先在分号处将句子分成两部分：

分号前：The chair of the remuneration committee **can be** an exposed and lonely role, // <u>as</u> Alison Carnwath, chair of Barclays Bank's remuneration committee, **found** // <u>when</u> she **had to resign**, // having been roundly criticised for trying to defend the enormous bonus to be paid to the chief executive;

分号前的部分出现由as引导的从句，从句中嵌套了另一个由when引导的从句，还有一个非谓语动词短语having been... 作状语。

分号后：the irony being //<u>that</u> she **was** widely **understood** to have spoken out against it in the privacy of the committee.

分号后的部分,除了that引导的从句中出现谓语动词was understood to do sth.外,that前面没有谓语动词,故判断这不是一个完整的句子,而是一个由"名词 + 非谓语动词 doing"构成的独立结构,是对分号前的部分的补充说明。

步骤二：分析并简化分号前的部分

as前的分句有谓语动词can be,没有引导词,故判断该分句为主句。主句成分清晰,为"主 + 系 + 表"结构,无须简化也较好理解。

主句：<u>The chair of the remuneration committee</u>　　　<u>can be</u>　　<u>an... role</u>
　　　　　　　　　主语　　　　　　　　　　　　　　　　　系动词　　　表语

as引导的从句比较复杂,我们一一拆解。

首先找出从句的主谓宾,主语是Alison Carnwath,谓语动词是found,found后缺少宾语,引导词as正好充当这个成分,而as指代的先行词是前面的一整句话,故as引导的是一个特殊的定语从句,从句主干是as Alison Carnwath found。紧跟Alison Carnwath后的chair of Barclays Bank's remuneration committee,为Alison Carnwath的同位语,补充说明人物的职位,可以先忽略。when she had to resign是一个时间状语从句,说明found这个动作何时发生。

第二个逗号后的非谓语动词doing短语充当伴随状语,说明艾莉森·卡瓦思是在何种背景下被迫辞职的,其逻辑主语就是Alison Carnwath。该短语可简化为having been criticised for trying to defend the enormous bonus。

as 从句：<u>as</u>　　<u>Alison Carnwath,</u>　　<s>chair of Barclays Bank's remuneration committee,</s>　　<u>found</u>
　　　　　关系词　　　主语　　　　　　　　　　　　同位语　　　　　　　　　　　　　　谓语

　　　　　<u>when she had to resign,</u>
　　　　　　　时间状语从句

<u>having been</u> ~~roundly~~ <u>criticised for trying to defend the enormous bonus</u> ~~to be paid to the chief executive~~;
　　　　　　　　　　非谓语动词 doing 短语作原因状语

步骤三：分析分号后的部分

由步骤一可知,分号后是一个独立结构,表示伴随状况,being为非谓语动词,其后that引导的从句作其表语。这个独立结构可以改写为一个独立分句,即the irony is that...。

that从句是"主 + 谓 + 宾"结构,be understood to do sth.表示"被认为在做什么"。宾语it指代前文提到的the enormous bonus to be paid to the chief executive。

<u>that</u>　　　　<u>she</u>　　　<u>was widely understood to have spoken out against</u>　　　<u>it</u>
引导词　　　主语　　　　　　　谓语（被动语态）　　　　　　　　　　宾语

<u>in the privacy of the committee</u>
　　　　状语

✏️ 语法点精练 · 小试牛刀

Exercise 1 划分以下句子的句子成分。

1. If the music is too obvious, it is annoyingly boring, like an alarm clock. 真

2. It could be argued that New Zealand is not a typical destination. 真

3. Conservationists accept that the old preservation-jar model is failing, even on its own terms. 真

4. The opportunities for free play, which I experienced almost every day of my childhood, are becoming increasingly scarce. 真

5. The Painting Fool is one of a growing number of computer programs which, so their makers claim, possess creative talents. 真

6. By contrast, the service sector, and more specifically hotels, has traditionally not extended these practices to address basic employee needs, such as good working conditions. 真

7. In the past, businesses have changed when the public came to expect and require different behaviour, and to reward businesses for behaviour that the public wanted. 真

8. She found that children with greater self-control solved problems more quickly when exploring an unfamiliar set-up requiring scientific reasoning. 真

9. Moreover, cork forests are a resource which support local biodiversity, and prevent desertification in the regions where they are planted. 真

10. When he came to write the *National Geographic* magazine article that broke the story to the world in April 1913, he knew he had to produce a big idea. 真

11. Until this discovery, the lynx—a large spotted cat with tasselled ears—was presumed to have died out in Britain at least 6,000 years ago, before the inhabitants of these islands took up farming. 真

12. Intent on securing their hold over every nutmeg-producing island, the Dutch offered a trade: if the British would give them the island of Run, they would in turn give Britain a distant and much less valuable island in North America. 真

13. Today, professors routinely treat the progressive interpretation of history and progressive public policy as the proper subject of study while portraying conservative or classical liberal ideas—such as free markets and self-reliance—as falling outside the boundaries of routine, and sometimes legitimate, intellectual investigation.

14. As a sailing ship, *Cutty Sark* depended on the strong trade winds of the southern hemisphere, and Woodget took her further south than any previous captain, bringing her dangerously close to icebergs off the southern tip of South America. 真

15. However, this is to disregard the role the human mind has in conveying remote places; and this is what interests me: how a fresh interpretation, even of a well-travelled route, can give its readers new insights. 真

（答案见 pp. 178~180）

第 3 章　雅思真题单句训练 200 句

第 1 节　基础训练 100 句

划分以下句子的成分。

Test 1

1. Certain diseases have disappeared. 真

_____

_____

2. This has happened. 真

_____

_____

3. The other crops failed. 真

_____

_____

4. The average captive animal will not die of drought. 真

_____

_____

5. No evidence exists. 真

_____

_____

词汇释义

disease /dɪˈziːz/ *n.* 疾病

crop /krɒp/ *n.* 庄稼

average /ˈævərɪdʒ/ *adj.* 典型的，正常的

drought /draʊt/ *n.* 干旱，旱灾

exist /ɪgˈzɪst/ *v.* 存在

disappear /ˌdɪsəˈpɪə(r)/ *v.* 消失

fail /feɪl/ *v.* 歉收

captive /ˈkæptɪv/ *adj.* 被关起来的

evidence /ˈevɪdəns/ *n.* 证据，证明

1 Certain diseases   have disappeared.
　　　主语　　　　　　　谓语

【参考译文】某些疾病已经消失。

【理解要点】本句的主语是Certain diseases，谓语是动词disappear的现在完成时态，意指"已经消失了"。

2 This   has happened.
　　主语　　　谓语

【参考译文】这已经发生了。

【理解要点】本句的主语是指示代词This，谓语是动词happen的现在完成时态，意指"已经发生"。

3 The other crops   failed.
　　　　主语　　　　　　谓语

【参考译文】其他作物都歉收了。

【理解要点】本句的主语是The other crops，谓语是动词fail的过去式，fail与"庄稼"连用时表示"歉收"。

4 The average captive animal   will not die   of drought.
　　　　　　主语　　　　　　　　　　谓语　　　　　状语

【参考译文】圈养动物一般不会死于旱灾。

【理解要点】本句的主语是The average captive animal，意指"普通圈养动物"；谓语will not die是将来时态，且是否定式；of drought是介宾短语作状语，表明死亡原因。

5 No evidence   exists.
　　　主语　　　　谓语

【参考译文】不存在证据。

【理解要点】本句的主语是No evidence，谓语是动词exist的第三人称单数形式。

Test ❷

1. As early as six weeks old, babies smile. 真

2. Prices rise at certain times of the year. 真

3. He retired completely from photography. 真

4. In the 1870s and 1880s Henderson travelled widely throughout Quebec and Ontario. 真

5. The US explorer and academic Hiram Bingham arrived in South America in 1911. 真

词汇释义

rise /raɪz/ *v.* 增加，增长

completely /kəmˈpliːtli/ *adv.* 彻底地，完全地

widely /ˈwaɪdli/ *adv.* 广泛地，范围广地

explorer /ɪkˈsplɔːrə(r)/ *n.* 探险家

retire /rɪˈtaɪə(r)/ *v.* 退休

photography /fəˈtɒɡrəfi/ *n.* 摄影业

throughout /θruːˈaʊt/ *prep.* 各处，遍及

academic /ˌækəˈdemɪk/ *n.* 大学教师

1 As early as six weeks old,   babies   smile.
           状语   主语   谓语

【参考译文】早在六周大的时候，婴儿就会微笑。

【理解要点】本句的主语是babies，谓语是不及物动词smile，而As early as six weeks old是状语，修饰smile。

2 Prices   rise   at certain times of the year.
  主语   谓语   状语

【参考译文】价格在一年中的某些时候上涨。

【理解要点】本句的主语是Prices，谓语是不及物动词rise，而at certain times of the year是状语，说明rise的时间。

3 He   retired   completely from photography.
 主语   谓语   状语

【参考译文】他彻底从摄影业退休了。

【理解要点】本句的主语是He，谓语是动词retire的过去式，completely是副词，修饰谓语动词retired。from photography是状语，补充说明是从哪个领域退休。

4 In the 1870s and 1880s   Henderson   travelled   widely throughout Quebec and Ontario.
     时间状语   主语   谓语   状语

【参考译文】在19世纪70和80年代，亨德森在魁北克省和安大略省四处旅行。

【理解要点】本句的主语是Henderson，谓语是动词travel的过去式，widely是副词，修饰谓语动词travelled。throughout Quebec and Ontario是地点状语，句首的In the 1870s and 1880s是时间状语。

5 The US explorer and academic   Hiram Bingham   arrived   in South America   in 1911.
      同位语   主语   谓语   地点状语   时间状语

【参考译文】美国探险家兼大学老师海勒姆·宾厄姆于1911年抵达南美洲。

【理解要点】本句的主语是Hiram Bingham，而The US explorer and academic是Hiram Bingham的同位语，说明其身份。谓语是动词arrive的过去式，in South America和in 1911分别作地点状语和时间状语。

Test ③

1. Of course, all hobbies give pleasure. 真

2. People have two major types of needs. 真

3. The students then completed a task requiring persistence. 真

4. We need radical changes, to make it healthier, more enjoyable, and less environmentally damaging to travel around cities. 真

5. Alongside the instruction he received at the Royal College of Art, Moore visited many of the London museums, particularly the British Museum. 真

pleasure /ˈpleʒə(r)/ *n.* 乐趣

radical /ˈrædɪkl/ *adj.* 根本的，彻底的

environmentally /ɪnˌvaɪrənˈmentəli/ *adv.* 与环境有关地

alongside /əˌlɒŋˈsaɪd/ *prep.* 伴随，与……同时

particularly /pəˈtɪkjələli/ *adv.* 尤其

persistence /pəˈsɪstəns/ *n.* 坚持不懈，毅力

enjoyable /ɪnˈdʒɔɪəbl/ *adj.* 愉快的

damaging /ˈdæmɪdʒɪŋ/ *adj.* 造成破坏的

instruction /ɪnˈstrʌkʃn/ *n.* 教导，指导，训练

1 Of course,   all hobbies   give   pleasure.
　　　插入语 　　　　　主语 　　　　谓语 　　　宾语

【参考译文】当然，所有的爱好都能带来乐趣。

【理解要点】本句的主语是all hobbies，谓语是及物动词give，故直接跟宾语pleasure，句首的Of course作为插入语，表示一种必然的可能性。

2 People   have   two major types of needs.
　　主语 　　　谓语 　　　　　　宾语

【参考译文】人们主要有两种需求。

【理解要点】本句的主语是People，谓语是及物动词have，因此后接宾语two major types of needs，意指"两种主要的需求"。

3 The students   then   completed   a task   requiring persistence.
　　主语 　　　　　状语 　　　谓语 　　　宾语 　　　　后置定语

【参考译文】然后，学生们完成了一项需要毅力的任务。

【理解要点】本句的主语是The students，谓语是及物动词complete的过去式，后接宾语a task requiring persistence，其中requiring persistence是现在分词短语作后置定语，修饰task。

4 We   need   radical changes,   to make it healthier, more enjoyable, and less
主语 　谓语 　　　宾语 　　　　　　　　　　　　状语

environmentally damaging to travel around cities.

【参考译文】我们需要彻底的改变，使城市出行更健康、更愉快，并减少对环境的破坏。

【理解要点】本句的主干是We need radical changes，主语是We，谓语是及物动词need，宾语是radical changes。to make it... to travel around cities是不定式短语充当目的状语，表示改变的目的，其中it为to make的形式宾语，真正的宾语是不定式to travel around cities。

5 Alongside the instruction he received at the Royal College of Art,   Moore   visited
　　　　　　　　　　状语 　　　　　　　　　　　　　　　　　　主语 　　　　谓语

many of the London museums,   particularly the British Museum.
　　　宾语 　　　　　　　　　　　　　　插入语

【参考译文】除了在皇家艺术学院接受指导外，摩尔还参观了伦敦的许多博物馆，尤其是大英博物馆。

【理解要点】本句的主干是Moore visited many of the London museums。句首的Alongside the instruction he received at the Royal College of Art是介词短语作状语，其中instruction后的部分是它的定语从句，该从句省略了关系词，instruction在从句中充当宾语。particularly the British Museum则是插入语，对主干的宾语many of the London museums进行补充说明。

Test ❹

1. Goetz's group has one suggestion. 真

2. This grass growth would reduce temperatures. 真

3. The classic cork stopper does have several advantages. 真

4. Participants then discussed the incident with their partner for 10 minutes. 真

5. The Massachusetts Institute of Technology investigated automated mobility in Singapore. 真

1 Goetz's group　　has　　one suggestion.
　　主语　　　　谓语　　　宾语

【参考译文】戈茨的小组有一个建议。

【理解要点】本句的主语是Goetz's group，谓语是have的第三人称单数形式，后接宾语one suggestion。

2 This grass growth　　would reduce　　temperatures.
　　　主语　　　　　　谓语　　　　　宾语

【参考译文】草的生长会降低温度。

【理解要点】本句的主语是This grass growth，谓语的主要动词是reduce，与情态动词would一起组成过去将来时的形式，表示从过去的角度说将来会发生的事情，后接宾语temperatures。

3 The classic cork stopper　　does　　have　　several advantages.
　　　主语　　　　　　　　助动词　谓语　　　宾语

【参考译文】传统的软木塞确实有几个优点。

【理解要点】本句以"do+谓语动词原形"的结构，强调了谓语动词have，表示"确实有……"。因为主语为第三人称单数，所以助动词do也相应用第三人称单数形式的does。

4 Participants　　then　　discussed　　the incident　　with their partner for 10 minutes.
　　主语　　　　状语　　谓语　　　　宾语　　　　　　状语

【参考译文】然后参与者与他们的伴侣一起讨论了该事件十分钟。

【理解要点】本句的主语是Participants，谓语是discuss的过去式，后接宾语the incident。with their partner以及for 10 minutes都是作状语，分别说明和谁讨论、讨论的时长。

5 The Massachusetts Institute of Technology　　investigated　　automated mobility　　in Singapore.
　　　　　　主语　　　　　　　　　　　　谓语　　　　　宾语　　　　　　后置定语

【参考译文】麻省理工学院研究了新加坡的自动化出行情况。

【理解要点】本句的主语是The Massachusetts Institute of Technology，谓语是investigate的过去式，后接宾语automated mobility in Singapore，其中in Singapore是automated mobility的后置定语，说明是哪里的自动化出行情况。

Test ⑤

1. The scientists played the subjects the music. 真

_____

_____

2. This gives the work an eerie, ghostlike quality. 真

_____

_____

3. The British would give them the island of Run. 真

_____

_____

4. This gives us insight into the types of interactive networks. 真

_____

_____

5. Observing children at play can give us important clues about their well-being. 真

_____

_____

1	The scientists	played	the subjects	the music.
	主语	谓语	间接宾语	直接宾语

【参考译文】科学家给实验对象播放音乐。

【理解要点】本句的主语是The scientists，谓语是play的过去式。played的直接宾语是the music，表示播放什么；间接宾语是the subjects，表示为谁播放。

2	This	gives	the work	an eerie, ghostlike quality.
	主语	谓语	间接宾语	直接宾语

【参考译文】这给了这部作品一种诡异、鬼魅般的感觉。

【理解要点】本句的主语是指示代词This，谓语是give的第三人称单数形式。gives的直接宾语是an eerie, ghost-like quality，表示给予的东西；间接宾语是the work，表示给予的对象。

3	The British	would give	them	the island of Run.
	主语	谓语	间接宾语	直接宾语

【参考译文】英国人会把伦岛交给他们。

【理解要点】本句的主语是The British，谓语的主要动词是give，与情态动词would连用，表示过去将来时。give的直接宾语是the island of Run，间接宾语是them。

4	This	gives	us	insight	into the types of interactive networks.
	主语	谓语	间接宾语	直接宾语	后置定语

【参考译文】这使我们能够深入了解交往网络的类型。

【理解要点】本句主语是指示代词This，谓语gives后接了两个宾语，一是直接宾语insight into the types of interactive networks(其中into... networks是介词短语作insight的后置定语)，二是间接宾语us。

5	Observing children at play	can give	us	important clues	about their well-being.
	主语		谓语	间接宾语	直接宾语	后置定语

【参考译文】观察孩子们玩耍可以为我们提供有关他们健康状况的重要线索。

【理解要点】本句主语是动名词短语Observing children at play，即"观察孩子们玩耍"这件事；谓语的主要动词是give，与情态动词can连用，意指"能够给予"，后接两个宾语，一是直接宾语important clues about their well-being(其中about their well-being是介词短语作clues的后置定语)，二是间接宾语us。

1. That will give them a greater appreciation for wildlife. 真

_____

_____

2. The supercomputer was simply telling them what they already knew. 真

_____

_____

3. Playful experiences do facilitate this aspect of development. 真

_____

_____

4. Someone could use the very same knowledge of means to achieve a much less noble end. 真

_____

_____

5. None of that tells us how many birds or fish or sea turtles could die from plastic pollution. 真

_____

_____

词汇释义

appreciation /əˌpriːʃiˈeɪʃn/ *n.* 欣赏

supercomputer /ˈsuːpəkəmpjuːtə(r)/ *n.* 超级计算机

playful /ˈpleɪfl/ *adj.* 嬉戏的

means /miːnz/ *n.* 手段，方法

end /end/ *n.* 目的

pollution /pəˈluːʃn/ *n.* 污染

wildlife /ˈwaɪldlaɪf/ *n.* 野生动物

simply /ˈsɪmpli/ *adv.* 仅仅，只，不过

facilitate /fəˈsɪlɪteɪt/ *v.* 促进

noble /ˈnəʊbl/ *adj.* 高尚的，崇高的

plastic /ˈplæstɪk/ *n.* 塑料

1 That   will give   them   a greater appreciation for wildlife.

主语   谓语   间接宾语   直接宾语

【参考译文】这将使他们更加欣赏野生动物。

【理解要点】本句的主语是指示代词That, 谓语的主要动词是give, 与情态动词will连用, 意指"将给", 后接两个宾语, 一是间接宾语them, 二是直接宾语a greater appreciation for wildlife。appreciation for sth. 表示"对某物的欣赏"。

2 The supercomputer   was simply telling   them   *what* they already knew.

主语   谓语   间接宾语   直接宾语

【参考译文】这个超级计算机只是告诉他们已知的东西。

【理解要点】本句的主语是The supercomputer, 谓语是tell的过去进行时形式, 后面有两个宾语, 一是间接宾语them, 二是由从句充当的直接宾语what they already knew, 意为"他们已经知道的东西"。

3 Playful experiences   do   facilitate   this aspect of development.

主语   助动词   谓语   宾语

【参考译文】玩乐的体验确实有助于这方面的发展。

【理解要点】本句以"do+谓语动词原形"的结构, 强调了谓语动词facilitate, 表示"的确促进"。

4 Someone   could use   the very same knowledge of means   to achieve a much less noble end.

主语   谓语   宾语   状语

【参考译文】有人会用同样的关于"手段"的知识来达到一个不那么高尚的目的。

【理解要点】本句的谓语为could use。宾语中的means作名词, 表示"手段, 方法"。句末的不定式短语为目的状语。

5 None of that   tells   us   *how many* birds or fish or sea turtles could die from

主语   谓语   间接宾语   直接宾语

plastic pollution.

【参考译文】这些都不能告诉我们有多少鸟、鱼或海龟会死于塑料污染。

【理解要点】本句主语是短语None of that, 意指"没有一个", 谓语tells接两个宾语, 一个是直接宾语how many birds or fish or sea turtles could die from plastic pollution, 这是一个宾语从句, 意为"有多少鸟、鱼或海龟会死于塑料污染", 是tells的内容, 而间接宾语则为tells的对象us, 即"我们"。

Test ⑦

1. We consider insects to be everywhere. 真

2. It allowed local people to withstand years of drought. 真

3. This can make it difficult to obtain sufficient quantities of the compound for subsequent testing. 真

4. Many primary school children find writing difficult. 真

5. The arrival of whaling ships in the 1790s saw this exploitation grow exponentially. 真

词汇释义

consider /kənˈsɪdə(r)/ **v.** 认为，觉得

withstand /wɪðˈstænd/ **v.** 承受

obtain /əbˈteɪn/ **v.** 获得

quantity /ˈkwɒntəti/ **n.** 数量

subsequent /ˈsʌbsɪkwənt/ **adj.** 后来的

whaling ship 捕鲸船

exponentially /ˌekspəˈnenʃəli/ **adv.** 以指数方式

insect /ˈɪnsekt/ **n.** 昆虫

drought /draʊt/ **n.** 干旱，旱灾

sufficient /səˈfɪʃnt/ **adj.** 足够的

compound /ˈkɒmpaʊnd/ **n.** 复合物

arrival /əˈraɪvl/ **n.** 到达

exploitation /ˌeksplɔɪˈteɪʃn/ **n.** 开发

1 | We | consider | insects | to be everywhere.
主语 | 谓语 | 宾语 | 宾语补语

【参考译文】我们认为昆虫无处不在。

【理解要点】当句子的主谓宾完整，但句意残缺时，需要加上补充说明的内容，也就是宾语补语(即宾补)。本句的主谓宾是We consider insects，意为"我们认为昆虫"，意义不完整，故有宾补to be everywhere，意指"无处不在"，补充说明insects的情况。

2 | It | allowed | local people | to withstand years of drought.
主语 | 谓语 | 宾语 | 宾语补语

【参考译文】它使当地人能够熬过多年的干旱。

【理解要点】本句的主谓宾It allowed local people是完整的，但意义残缺，故有不定式to withstand years of drought充当宾补，意为"熬过多年的干旱"，对宾语local people做补充说明。

3 | This | can make | it | difficult | to obtain sufficient quantities of the
主语 | 谓语 | 形式宾语 | 宾语补语 | 真正宾语

compound for subsequent testing.

【参考译文】这会导致很难获得足够数量的化合物用于后续测试。

【理解要点】本句的宾补是形容词difficult，其后的不定式并不属于宾补的一部分，而是真正的逻辑宾语，也就是说，困难的事情是to obtain sufficient quantities of the compound for subsequent testing。

4 | Many primary school children | find | writing | difficult.
主语 | 谓语 | 宾语 | 宾语补语

【参考译文】许多小学生发现写作很难。

【理解要点】本句的宾补是形容词difficult，是对宾语writing的补充说明。

5 | The arrival of whaling ships in the 1790s | saw | this exploitation | grow exponentially.
主语 | 谓语 | 宾语 | 宾语补语

【参考译文】18世纪90年代捕鲸船的到来让这种开发利用呈指数级增长。

【理解要点】本句的宾补是省略了to的不定式grow，对宾语this exploitation做补充说明，而exponentially是副词，修饰动词grow，说明增长的程度。

Test ⑧

1. I find it fascinating. 真

_____

_____

2. A fast-food company encouraged the government to introduce legislation. 真

_____

_____

3. Boredom may encourage us to avoid an unpleasant experience. 真

_____

_____

4. Oxytocin（催产素）drives people to care for those in their social circles. 真

_____

_____

5. A track down the valley canyon enabled rubber to be brought up by mules from the jungle. 真

_____

_____

词汇释义

fascinating /ˈfæsɪneɪtɪŋ/ *adj.* 极有吸引力的

government /ˈɡʌvənmənt/ *n.* 政府

legislation /ˌledʒɪsˈleɪʃn/ *n.* 法规

avoid /əˈvɔɪd/ *v.* 避免

drive /draɪv/ *v.* 促使

track /træk/ *n.* 小道，小路

rubber /ˈrʌbə(r)/ *n.* 橡胶

jungle /ˈdʒʌŋɡl/ *n.* 丛林

encourage /ɪnˈkʌrɪdʒ/ *v.* 鼓励

introduce /ˌɪntrəˈdjuːs/ *v.* 推行，实施

boredom /ˈbɔːdəm/ *n.* 无聊，厌倦

unpleasant /ʌnˈpleznt/ *adj.* 不愉快的

social circle 社交圈

canyon /ˈkænjən/ *n.* 峡谷

mule /mjuːl/ *n.* 骡子

1 | I | find | it | fascinating.
主语　谓语　宾语　宾语补语

【参考译文】我觉得它很迷人。

【理解要点】本句的宾补是形容词fascinating，是对宾语it的补充说明。

2 | A fast-food company | encouraged | the government | to introduce legislation.
　　　　主语　　　　　　　谓语　　　　　宾语　　　　　　宾语补语

【参考译文】一家快餐公司鼓励政府立法。

【理解要点】本句的宾补是不定式to introduce legislation，意为"去立法"。

3 | Boredom | may encourage | us | to avoid an unpleasant experience.
　　　主语　　　　谓语　　　宾语　　　　宾语补语

【参考译文】厌倦感可能促使我们避免不愉快的经历。

【理解要点】本句的宾补是不定式to avoid an unpleasant experience，意为"去避免不愉快的经历"。

4 | Oxytocin | drives | people | to care for those in their social circles.
　　主语　　谓语　　宾语　　　　　宾语补语

【参考译文】催产素促使人们关心他们社交圈中的人。

【理解要点】本句的宾补是不定式to care for those in their social circles，对宾语people做补充说明。

5 | A track down the valley canyon | enabled | rubber | to be brought up by mules from the jungle.
　　　　　　主语　　　　　　　　　　谓语　　宾语　　　　　　宾语补语

【参考译文】峡谷底部的一条小路使得骡子能够把丛林里的橡胶运上去。

【理解要点】本句的宾补是包含被动态的不定式，表示橡胶被运上去。enable sb. to do sth.表示"使某人能够做某事"。

Test 9

1. The passenger pigeon was a legendary species. 真

2. The project's goal is to return mammoths（猛犸）, or a mammoth-like species, to the area. 真

3. That was the founder's motto for Cornell University. 真

4. In my view, by definition boredom is an undesirable state. 真

5. The problem was also a pressing one. 真

词汇释义

legendary /ˈledʒəndri/ *adj.* 传奇的

return /rɪˈtɜːn/ *v.* 送回，把……放回原处

motto /ˈmɒtəʊ/ *n.* 座右铭

undesirable /ˌʌndɪˈzaɪərəbl/ *adj.* 不好的，讨厌的

pressing /ˈpresɪŋ/ *adj.* 紧迫的

species /ˈspiːʃiːz/ *n.* 物种

founder /ˈfaʊndə(r)/ *n.* 创始人

definition /ˌdefɪˈnɪʃn/ *n.* 释义，定义

state /steɪt/ *n.* 状态

1 The passenger pigeon　　was　　a legendary species.
　　　　　主语　　　　　　系动词　　　　表语

【参考译文】旅鸽是一种传奇的物种。

【理解要点】本句的系动词是was,表语是a legendary species,是对主语The passenger pigeon的描述。

2 The project's goal　　is　　to return mammoths, or a mammoth-like species, to the area.
　　　　主语　　　　　系动词　　　　　　　　　　表语

【参考译文】该项目的目标是将猛犸或类似猛犸的物种送回该地区。

【理解要点】本句的系动词是is,表语是不定式to return mammoths, or a mammoth-like species, to the area, 说明目标的内容。

3 That　　was　　the founder's motto for Cornell University.
　　主语　系动词　　　　　　表语

【参考译文】那是康奈尔大学创始人的座右铭。

【理解要点】本句的系动词是was,表语是the founder's motto for Cornell University,具体说明主语That是什么。

4 In my view,　　by definition　　boredom　　is　　an undesirable state.
　　状语　　　　　　状语　　　　主语　　系动词　　　　表语

【参考译文】在我看来,根据定义,无聊是一种讨厌的状态。

【理解要点】本句的系动词是is,表语an undesirable state说明主语boredom的性质。by definition是前置的状语, 对主句做补充说明。

5 The problem　　was　　also　　a pressing one.
　　主语　　　系动词　　状语　　表语

【参考译文】这也是一个紧迫的问题。

【理解要点】本句的系动词是was,表语是a pressing one,其中one为代词,泛指problem。

Test ⑩

1. He seems to have said little about his discovery. 真

2. The origins of Silbo Gomero（戈梅拉岛口哨语）remain obscure. 真

3. The new glass proved invaluable to the optical industry. 真

4. The future of this ancient material looks promising. 真

5. The Uffington White Horse is a unique, stylised representation of a horse consisting of a long, sleek back, thin disjointed legs, a streaming tail, and a bird-like beaked head. 真

词汇释义

discovery /dɪˈskʌvəri/ *n.* 发现

remain /rɪˈmeɪn/ *v.* 保持

invaluable /ɪnˈvæljuəbl/ *adj.* 极有价值的，极有用的

ancient /ˈeɪnʃənt/ *adj.* 古老的

unique /juˈniːk/ *adj.* 独一无二的

representation /ˌreprɪzenˈteɪʃn/ *n.* 描绘

sleek /sliːk/ *adj.* 线条流畅的

stream /striːm/ *v.* 飘动，飘扬

origin /ˈɒrɪdʒɪn/ *n.* 起源

obscure /əbˈskjʊə(r)/ *adj.* 模糊的

optical /ˈɒptɪkl/ *adj.* 光学的

promising /ˈprɒmɪsɪŋ/ *adj.* 有前景的

stylised /ˈstaɪlaɪzd/ *adj.* 非写实的，风格化的

consist of 由……构成

disjointed /dɪsˈdʒɔɪntɪd/ *adj.* 脱节的

beaked /biːkt/ *adj.* 有喙的

1 He   seems to have said   little   about his discovery.

     主语   谓语   宾语   状语

【参考译文】他似乎很少谈到他的发现。

【理解要点】此句中，系动词seems和不定式to have said一起构成谓语动词。seem to do sth.是固定搭配，表示"似乎……"。

2 The origins of Silbo Gomero   remain   obscure.

          主语   系动词   表语

【参考译文】戈梅拉岛口哨语的起源仍不清楚。

【理解要点】本句的系动词是持续系动词remain，表语是形容词obscure，形容戈梅拉岛口哨语的起源是"不清楚的，模糊的"。

3 The new glass   proved   invaluable to the optical industry.

     主语   系动词   表语

【参考译文】这种新型玻璃后来被证明对光学行业极有价值。

【理解要点】本句的系动词proved是终止系动词，意为"证明是，这发现是"，表语是invaluable to the optical industry。(be) invaluable to sth.表示"对某物极有用"。

4 The future of this ancient material   looks   promising.

          主语   系动词   表语

【参考译文】这种古老材料的未来看起来一片光明。

【理解要点】本句的系动词是感官动词look的第三人称单数形式looks，表语是形容词promising，形容主语The future。

5 The Uffington White Horse   is   a unique, stylised representation of a horse consisting of a

        主语   系动词   表语

long, sleek back, thin disjointed legs, a streaming tail, and a bird-like beaked head.

【参考译文】乌芬顿白马描绘了一匹风格独特的马，它拥有长而光滑的背部、细长而不连贯的腿、流线型的尾巴和鸟喙状的头部。

【理解要点】本句的表语中，consisting of... head是现在分词短语作horse的后置定语。该短语又包含了由连词and连接的并列结构，并列成分包括多个名词短语a long, sleek back、thin disjointed legs、a streaming tail和a bird-like beaked head。

1. Initiatives for car-sharing become much more viable, particularly in urban areas with significant travel demand. 真

_____

_____

2. The carving has been placed in such a way as to make it extremely difficult to see from close quarters, and like many geoglyphs（地质印痕）is best appreciated from the air. 真

_____

_____

3. These giant carvings are a fascinating glimpse into the minds of their creators and how they viewed the landscape in which they lived. 真

_____

_____

4. 'White Horse Hill' is mentioned in documents from the nearby Abbey of Abingdon, and the first reference to the horse itself is soon after, in 1190 CE. 真

_____

_____

5. Old worker ants can do everything just as well as the youngsters, and their brains appear just as sharp. 真

_____

_____

词汇释义

initiative /ɪˈnɪʃətɪv/ **n.** 倡议

particularly /pəˈtɪkjələli/ **adv.** 尤其

significant /sɪɡˈnɪfɪkənt/ **adj.** 数量相当的

carving /ˈkɑːvɪŋ/ **n.** 雕刻图案

appreciate /əˈpriːʃieɪt/ **v.** 欣赏

creator /kriˈeɪtə(r)/ **n.** 创造者

youngster /ˈjʌŋstə(r)/ **n.** 年轻人

viable /ˈvaɪəbl/ **adj.** 可行的

urban /ˈɜːbən/ **adj.** 城市的

demand /dɪˈmɑːnd/ **n.** 需要

extremely /ɪkˈstriːmli/ **adv.** 极其

glimpse /ɡlɪmps/ **n.** 一瞥

reference /ˈrefrəns/ **n.** 提及，谈到

1 Initiatives for car-sharing | become | much more viable, | particularly in urban areas with
主语 | 系动词 | 表语 | 状语
significant travel demand.

【参考译文】汽车共享计划变得更加可行，尤其是在有大量出行需求的城市地区。

【理解要点】本句的系动词是变化动词become，表语是much more viable，意指汽车共享计划"更加可行"。

2 The carving | has been placed | in such a way as to make it extremely difficult to see from
主语 | 谓语1 | 状语
close quarters, | *and* | like many geoglyphs | is best appreciated | from the air.
| 连词 | 状语 | 谓语2 | 状语

【参考译文】这个雕刻图案的位置使它很难从近处看到，像许多地质印痕一样，它最好从空中欣赏。

【理解要点】本句的连词and连接了两个并列谓语，都是被动态，动作的承受者都是The carving。

3 These giant carvings | are | a fascinating glimpse into the minds of their creators and *how*
主语 | 系动词 | 表语（含宾语从句、定语从句）
they viewed the landscape *in which* they lived.

【参考译文】透过这些巨大的雕刻图案，我们得以一瞥其创造者的思想以及他们如何看待他们生活的地区，这令人着迷。

【理解要点】本句的表语很长，中心词是a fascinating glimpse，介词into后的内容都是其后置定语。介词into有两个并列宾语，一个是the minds of their creators，另一个是宾语从句how they viewed the landscape。该宾语从句中的the landscape还带有一个定语从句in which they lived。

4 'White Horse Hill' is mentioned in documents from the nearby Abbey of Abingdon, | *and* | the
分句1 | 连词 |
first reference to the horse itself is soon after, in 1190 CE.
分句2

分句1 'White Horse Hill' | is mentioned | in documents from the nearby Abbey of Abingdon
主语 | 谓语 | 状语
分句2 the first reference to the horse itself | is | soon after, in 1190 CE
主语 | 系动词 | 表语

【参考译文】附近阿宾顿修道院的文件中提到了"白马山"，不久之后，即公元1190年，人们第一次提到马本身。

【理解要点】本句的两个分句由表示顺承的并列连词and连接，两个分句是平行关系，分别表述"白马山"在哪本文献中出现和"马"本身何时被提及这两个逻辑存在延伸的事件。

5 Old worker ants can do everything just as well as the youngsters, | *and* | their brains appear
分句1 | 连词 | 分句2
just as sharp.

分句1 Old worker ants | can do | everything | just as well as the youngsters
主语 | 谓语 | 宾语 | 状语
分句2 their brains | appear | just as sharp
主语 | 系动词 | 表语

【参考译文】老工蚁能像年轻蚂蚁一样做任何事情，它们的大脑看起来也一样敏锐。

【理解要点】本句的两个分句由并列连词and连接，分别阐述了老工蚁和年轻蚂蚁的两个共同点，两个分句没有从属关系，而是平行关系。

1. Let us apply both the terms 'means' and 'end' to marketing. 真

_____

_____

2. It has both functional and artistic value. 真

_____

_____

3. Both free and guided play are essential elements in a child-centred approach to playful learning. 真

_____

_____

4. We possess both the science and the technology to identify and redress the changes. 真

_____

_____

5. Janssen saw that there was a need for a sustainable way to clean water in both the developing and the developed countries. 真

_____

_____

词汇释义

apply /əˈplaɪ/ *v.* 应用，运用

marketing /ˈmɑːkɪtɪŋ/ *n.* 市场营销

artistic /ɑːˈtɪstɪk/ *adj.* 艺术的

element /ˈelɪmənt/ *n.* 要素

playful /ˈpleɪfl/ *adj.* 有趣的

identify /aɪˈdentɪfaɪ/ *v.* 识别

sustainable /səˈsteɪnəbl/ *adj.* 可持续的

term /tɜːm/ *n.* 术语

functional /ˈfʌŋkʃənl/ *adj.* 实用的

essential /ɪˈsenʃl/ *adj.* 必需的

approach /əˈprəʊtʃ/ *n.* 方法

possess /pəˈzes/ *v.* 拥有

redress /rɪˈdres/ *v.* 修正，矫正

1 Let　us　apply both the terms 'means' and 'end' to marketing.

　　谓语　宾语　　　　　　宾语补语

【参考译文】让我们把"手段"和"目的"这两个术语应用到市场营销上。

【理解要点】本句是一个祈使句。宾补由省略了to的不定式充当。apply sth. to表示"把某物应用到……上"。apply后有两个并列宾语，由both... and连接。

2 It　has　both functional and artistic value.

主语　谓语　　　　宾语

【参考译文】它兼具实用性和艺术价值。

【理解要点】本句的宾语中使用了both... and连接两个并列的形容词functional和artistic，修饰value。

3 Both free and guided play　are　essential elements in a child-centred approach to

　　　　主语　　　　系动词　　　　　　表语

playful learning.

【参考译文】在以儿童为中心的乐趣学习中，自由游戏和引导式游戏都是必不可少的要素。

【理解要点】本句的两个并列主语由both... and连接，这个并列结构中free and guided play的完整写法是free play and guided play，即"自由游戏和引导式游戏"。

4 We　possess　both the science and the technology　to identify and redress the changes.

主语　谓语　　　　　宾语　　　　　　　　　　　状语

【参考译文】我们拥有科学和技术识别、修正变化。

【理解要点】本句出现连词both... and，连接两个并列宾语the science和the technology。

5 Janssen　saw　*that* there was a need for a sustainable way to clean water in both the

主语　谓语　　　　　宾语从句

developing and the developed countries.

宾语从句　*that*　there was　a need　for a sustainable way to clean water in both the

　　　引导词　There be 句型　主语　　　　后置定语

　　　developing and the developed countries

【参考译文】杨森认为，发展中国家和发达国家都需要一种可持续的清洁水的方式。

【理解要点】宾语从句的主干为there was a need，之后的内容都是need的后置定语。本句最后的介词短语in both the developing and the developed countries中包含并列结构，由both... and连接，并列成分为名词短语the developing (countries)和the developed countries，分别指"发展中国家"和"发达国家"。

Test ⑬

1. It met the needs of neither group. 真

_____

_____

2. We'd like feedback on whether people are satisfied, dissatisfied or neither satisfied nor dissatisfied. 真

_____

_____

3. Using this approach, none of the donors has a stake in his idea, nor does he have any debt. 真

_____

_____

4. Neither approach guarantees continuous improvement. 真

_____

_____

5. Neither of these attitudes captures the significance of the end to the means for marketing. 真

_____

_____

词汇释义

feedback /ˈfiːdbæk/ *n.* 反馈

dissatisfied /dɪsˈsætɪsfaɪd/ *adj.* 不满意的

donor /ˈdəʊnə(r)/ *n.* 捐赠者

guarantee /ˌɡærənˈtiː/ *v.* 保证

improvement /ɪmˈpruːvmənt/ *n.* 改善，改进

significance /sɪɡˈnɪfɪkəns/ *n.* 意义，重要性

means /miːnz/ *n.* 手段，方法

satisfied /ˈsætɪsfaɪd/ *adj.* 满意的

approach /əˈprəʊtʃ/ *n.* 方法

stake /steɪk/ *n.* 重大利害关系

continuous /kənˈtɪnjuəs/ *adj.* 不断的，持续的

capture /ˈkæptʃə(r)/ *v.* 俘获，捕获

end /end/ *n.* 目的

1 | It | met | the needs of neither group.
主语　谓语　　　宾语

【参考译文】这两个群体的需求它都没有满足。

【理解要点】本句中的neither为代词，neither group表示"两个组别都不"。

2 | We | 'd like | feedback on *whether* people are satisfied, dissatisfied or neither satisfied
主语　谓语　　　　　　　　　宾语（含宾语从句）

nor dissatisfied.

宾语从句 *whether* | people | are | satisfied, dissatisfied or neither satisfied nor dissatisfied
　　　　　引导词　　主语　系动词　　　　　　　表语

【参考译文】我们希望得到关于人们满意、不满意或两者皆不是的反馈。

【理解要点】本句的从句中出现并列连词neither... nor，连接的并列成分为satisfied和dissatisfied，表示两者皆不是。

3 | Using this approach, | none of the donors has a stake in his idea, | *nor* | does he have any debt.
　　　状语　　　　　　　　　分句1　　　　　　　　连词　　分句2

【参考译文】使用这种方法，没有一个捐款人与他的想法产生利害关系，他也没有任何债务。

【理解要点】分句1和分句2都含有否定意味，因此分句2由nor连接，又由于nor放在句首，所以分句2使用了部分倒装结构，助动词does置于主语he之前。句首的Using this approach为现在分词短语作方式状语。

4 | Neither approach | guarantees | continuous improvement.
　　主语　　　　　　谓语　　　　宾语

【参考译文】这两种方法都不能保证持续的改进。

【理解要点】本句的句首出现代词Neither，表示"两者都不"，Neither approach指"两种方法都不……"。

5 | Neither of these attitudes | captures | the significance of the end to the means for marketing.
　　　主语　　　　　　　谓语　　　　　宾语

【参考译文】这两种态度都没有抓住营销目的对于营销手段的意义。

【理解要点】本句的代词Neither位于句首，Neither of these attitudes表示"这两种态度都没有……"。

Test ⑭

1. Dancing not only makes us feel good, it's also extremely good for our health. 真

_____

_____

2. We suggest that humour is not only enjoyable but more importantly, energising. 真

_____

_____

3. This would mean not only the loss of potential breakthroughs in human medicine, but the disappearance of an intelligent animal. 真

_____

_____

4. These microbes vary not only between species but also between individuals. 真

_____

_____

5. The Jacksonian view is that all people are equal, not only as human beings but in terms of their competencies.

_____

_____

词汇释义

humour /ˈhjuːmə(r)/ *n.* 幽默

energising /ˈenədʒaɪzɪŋ/ *adj.* 令人振奋的，给人力量的

breakthrough /ˈbreɪkθruː/ *n.* 突破

microbe /ˈmaɪkrəʊb/ *n.* 微生物

competency /ˈkɒmpɪtənsi/ *n.* 能力

enjoyable /ɪnˈdʒɔɪəbl/ *adj.* 使人愉快的

potential /pəˈtenʃl/ *adj.* 潜在的

disappearance /ˌdɪsəˈpɪərəns/ *n.* 消失

vary /ˈveərɪ/ *v.* 相异，不同

1 <u>Dancing **not only** makes us feel good,</u>　<u>it's **also** extremely good for our health.</u>

　　分句 1（含连词 not only）　　　　　　分句 2（含连词 also）

【参考译文】跳舞不仅让我们感觉良好，而且对我们的健康也非常有益。

【理解要点】本句是由 not only... but also 连接的并列句，其中 but 被省略了。分句1为"主＋谓＋宾＋宾补"结构；分句2为"主＋系＋表"结构。

2 <u>We</u>　<u>suggest</u>　<u>**that** humour is not only enjoyable but more importantly, energising.</u>

主语　谓语　　　　　　　　　　　宾语从句

【参考译文】我们认为，幽默不仅令人愉快，更重要的是，它能带给人力量。

【理解要点】本句的宾语从句是"主＋系＋表"结构，其中表语有一个由 not only... but (also) 连接的并列结构，两个并列成分分别是 enjoyable 和 energising。more importantly 作状语，表示"更重要的是"。

3 <u>This</u>　<u>would mean</u>　<u>not only the loss of potential breakthroughs in human medicine, but the</u>

主语　　谓语　　　　　　　　　　　宾语

<u>disappearance of an intelligent animal.</u>

【参考译文】这不仅意味着人类医学会失去潜在的突破，也意味着一种聪明的动物会消失。

【理解要点】由 not only... but (also) 连接两个并列宾语，即 the loss of potential breakthroughs in human medicine 和 the disappearance of an intelligent animal。

4 <u>These microbes</u>　<u>vary</u>　<u>not only between species but also between individuals.</u>

主语　　　　谓语　　　　　　状语

【参考译文】这些微生物不仅在物种之间存在差异，而且在个体之间也存在差异。

【理解要点】本句由 not only... but also 连接的并列结构出现在状语中，两个并列成分分别是 between species 和 between individuals。

5 <u>The Jacksonian view</u>　<u>is</u>　<u>**that** all people are equal, not only as human beings but in</u>

主语　　　　系动词　　　　　　表语从句

<u>terms of their competencies.</u>

【参考译文】杰克逊派的观点是，所有人都是平等的，不仅作为人而言，而且在能力方面也是相同的。

【理解要点】本句的表语从句是"主＋系＋表"结构，not only 后的内容为状语，其中有连词 not only... but (also) 连接两个并列成分，分别是 as human beings 和 in terms of their competencies。

1. To continue the project we would have needed to set up another system, but the business partner had lost interest. 真

_____

_____

2. It is regarded as one of the two most cycle-friendly capitals in the world—but the city never got another Witte Fietsenplan. 真

_____

_____

3. By 1921, the football team were regularly attracting crowds in the tens of thousands, but the year ended in catastrophe for them. 真

_____

_____

4. These models are necessary, but they are built on specific world views. 真

_____

_____

5. After leaving school, Moore hoped to become a sculptor, but instead he complied with his father's wish. 真

_____

_____

词汇释义

set up 建立

regularly /ˈreɡjələli/ *adv.* 经常

necessary /ˈnesəsəri/ *adj.* 必要的

sculptor /ˈskʌlptə(r)/ *n.* 雕塑家

capital /ˈkæpɪtl/ *n.* 首都

catastrophe /kəˈtæstrəfi/ *n.* 灾难

specific /spəˈsɪfɪk/ *adj.* 具体的

comply with 遵从，服从

1 To continue the project we would have needed to set up another system,　*but*　the business
　　　　　　　　　　　　　　　分句1　　　　　　　　　　　　　　　　　　　　　　连词　　　分句2

partner had lost interest.

【参考译文】为继续这个项目，我们需要建立另一个系统，但业务合作伙伴已经失去了兴趣。

【理解要点】本句出现表示转折的并列连词but，连接了两个简单句。分句1为"主+谓+宾"结构，不定式短语To
　　　　　continue the project表目的，为分句1的状语。分句2也是"主+谓+宾"结构。

2 It is regarded as one of the two most cycle-friendly capitals in the world—*but*　the city never
　　　　　　　　　　　　　　　分句1　　　　　　　　　　　　　　　　　　　　连词　　　　分句2

got another Witte Fietsenplan.

【参考译文】它被认为是世界上对自行车最友好的两个首都城市之一，但这座城市再未出现过另一个维特·费
　　　　　森普兰。

【理解要点】本句中but前后两个分句是简单句，分句1为"主+谓"结构（被动态），分句2为"主+谓+宾"结构，
　　　　　but在中间起转折作用。两个分句之间有时不用逗号隔开，而是用分号或破折号等，本句的两个分句
　　　　　就是用破折号隔开的。

3 By 1921, the football team were regularly attracting crowds in the tens of thousands,　*but*
　　　　　　　　　　　　　　　　分句1　　　　　　　　　　　　　　　　　　　　　　　　连词

the year ended in catastrophe for them.
　　分句2

【参考译文】到1921年，这支足球队经常吸引到数以万计的观众，但这一年对她们来说以灾难告终。

【理解要点】本句由两个简单句构成，两个分句的逻辑关系是转折关系，故用but连接。分句1是"主+谓+宾"结构，
　　　　　分句2是"主+谓"结构。

4 These models are necessary,　*but*　they are built on specific world views.
　　　　分句1　　　　　　　连词　　　　　　分句2

【参考译文】这些模型是必要的，但它们是建立在特定的世界观之上的。

【理解要点】本句是并列句，由转折并列连词but连接。分句1是"主+系+表"结构，分句2是"主+谓"结构，分
　　　　　句2中出现了被动语态are built。

5 After leaving school,　Moore hoped to become a sculptor,　*but*　instead he complied with his
　　　状语　　　　　　　分句1　　　　　　　　　　　连词　　　　分句2

father's wish.

【参考译文】离开学校后，摩尔本希望成为一名雕塑家，但相反他遵从了父亲的愿望。

【理解要点】本句是一个but连接的并列句，but前后是两个简单句。句首After leaving school是状语，说明时间。

1. The result has been a gradual yet steady move first towards plastic stoppers. 真

_____

_____

2. The Harappan Civilisation was a sophisticated Bronze Age society, and yet seemed to have left almost no depictions of themselves. 真

_____

_____

3. Humans with comparative levels of adipose tissue (脂肪组织) would be likely to suffer from diabetes and heart disease, yet the polar bear experiences no such consequences.

_____

_____

4. We do not generally associate feathers with the military in Europe, yet history shows that in fact feathers have played an intriguing role in European military clothing. 真

_____

_____

5. We tend to see the dangers posed by bacteria, yet at the same time we are sold yoghurts and drinks that supposedly nurture 'friendly' bacteria. 真

_____

_____

词汇释义

gradual /ˈɡrædʒuəl/ *adj.* 逐渐的

sophisticated /səˈfɪstɪkeɪtɪd/ *adj.* 复杂的

comparative /kəmˈpærətɪv/ *adj.* 相对的

experience /ɪkˈspɪəriəns/ *v.* 经历

feather /ˈfeðə(r)/ *n.* 羽毛

clothing /ˈkləʊðɪŋ/ *n.* 服装

yoghurt /ˈjəʊɡət/ *n.* 酸奶

nurture /ˈnɜːtʃə(r)/ *v.* 培养

steady /ˈstedi/ *adj.* 稳步的

depiction /dɪˈpɪkʃn/ *n.* 描绘

diabetes /ˌdaɪəˈbiːtiːz/ *n.* 糖尿病

consequence /ˈkɒnsɪkwəns/ *n.* 后果

intriguing /ɪnˈtriːɡɪŋ/ *adj.* 有趣的

bacteria /bækˈtɪəriə/ *n.* 细菌

supposedly /səˈpəʊzɪdli/ *adv.* 据说，据称

1 The result　has been　a gradual yet steady move first towards plastic stoppers.
　　　主语　　系动词　　　　　　　　表语

【参考译文】其结果是人们逐渐稳步地开始使用塑料瓶塞。

【理解要点】本句出现转折连词yet, 连接的是两个形容词gradual和steady, 修饰名词move。

2 The Harappan Civilisation　was　a sophisticated Bronze Age society,　**and yet**
　　　主语　　　系动词　　　　　　表语　　　　　　连词

seemed to have left　almost no depictions of themselves.
　　谓语　　　　　　　宾语

【参考译文】哈拉帕文明是一个复杂的青铜时代社会, 但似乎没有留下任何关于自己的描述。

【理解要点】需要注意, yet有时会和and连用, 但仍然表示转折关系。本句由and yet连接两个并列的谓语。

3 Humans with comparative levels of adipose tissue would be likely to suffer from diabetes and
　　　　　　　　　　　　　　　　分句1

heart disease,　**yet**　the polar bear experiences no such consequences.
　　　　　　　连词　　　　　　　分句2

分句1　Humans　with comparative levels of adipose tissue　would be likely to suffer
　　　主语　　　　　后置定语　　　　　　　　　　　谓语

from diabetes and heart disease
　　　状语

分句2　the polar bear　experiences　no such consequences
　　　主语　　　　　谓语　　　　　宾语

【参考译文】脂肪组织水平相对较高的人可能会患糖尿病和心脏病, 然而北极熊不会有这种问题。

【理解要点】分句2实则与前面分句1的意思相反, 所以连词用表转折的yet。

4 We do not generally associate feathers with the military in Europe,　**yet**　history shows **that**
　　　　　　　　　　分句1　　　　　　　　　　　连词

in fact feathers have played an intriguing role in European military clothing.
　　　　　　　分句2（含宾语从句）

宾语从句　**that**　in fact　feathers　have played an intriguing role in European military clothing
　　　引导词　状语　主语　　　谓语（play a role in sth. 结构）

【参考译文】我们通常不会把羽毛和欧洲的军事联系起来, 但历史表明, 事实上, 羽毛在欧洲的军事服装中扮演了一个有趣的角色。

【理解要点】本句是一个并列句, 由表示转折的并列连词yet连接, 分述观点与事实。分句1中的动词短语associate... with表示"把……和……联系起来", 分句2为"主+谓+宾"结构, 宾语为从句。

5 We tend to see the dangers posed by bacteria,　**yet**　at the same time we are sold yoghurts
　　　　　　　分句1　　　　　　　　连词　　　　分句2（含定语从句）

and drinks **that** supposedly nurture 'friendly' bacteria.

定语从句　yoghurts and drinks　**that**　supposedly　nurture　'friendly' bacteria
　　　先行词　　　　关系词　状语　谓语　宾语

【参考译文】我们倾向于看到细菌带来的危险, 但与此同时, 市面上在销售那些据说培养"友好"细菌的酸奶和饮料。

【理解要点】本句是由转折并列连词yet连接的并列句, 两个分句描述了事实与看法的相悖。分句1中的posed by bacteria是过去分词短语作定语, 修饰the dangers, 意指"细菌带来的危险"。分句2中的are sold是sell sb. sth.的被动语态, 而that引导的则是一个定语从句, 修饰yoghurts and drinks, 关系词在从句中作主语。

Test ⑰

1. The movement of glaciers tends to destroy anything at their bases, so the team focused on stationary patches of ice. 真

_____

_____

2. The boots aren't very warm in cold winter weather so they're best for country walks in spring and summer. 真

_____

_____

3. The people dancing in a group reported feeling happier, whereas those dancing alone did not. 真

_____

_____

4. While many historians are convinced the figure is prehistoric（史前的）, others believe that it was the work of an artistic monk from a nearby priory and was created between the 11th and 15th centuries. 真

_____

_____

5. Oak trees rely much more on temperature, whereas ash trees rely on measuring day length to determine their seasonal timing. 真

_____

_____

词汇释义

movement /ˈmuːvmənt/ *n.* 移动，运动

destroy /dɪˈstrɔɪ/ *v.* 破坏

patch /pætʃ/ *n.* 小块，小片

convinced /kənˈvɪnst/ *adj.* 确信的

artistic /ɑːˈtɪstɪk/ *adj.* 艺术的

priory /ˈpraɪəri/ *n.* 小修道院

determine /dɪˈtɜːmɪn/ *v.* 决定

glacier /ˈɡlæsiə(r)/ *n.* 冰川

stationary /ˈsteɪʃənri/ *adj.* 静止的，不动的

historian /hɪˈstɔːriən/ *n.* 历史学家

figure /ˈfɪɡə(r)/ *n.* 图案

monk /mʌŋk/ *n.* 僧侣

day length 日长，昼长

seasonal /ˈsiːzənl/ *adj.* 季节性的

1 The movement of glaciers tends to destroy anything at their bases,   *so*   the team focused on
分句 1   连词   分句 2
stationary patches of ice.

【参考译文】冰川的运动往往会毁坏其底部的东西, 因此该团队主要研究静止的冰层。

【理解要点】本句是由表结果的并列连词 so 连接的并列句, 两个分句之间是因果关系。分句 1 的谓语使用了 tend to do sth. "往往会发生某事" 的表达, 分句 2 则使用了 focus on "集中注意力于"。

2 The boots aren't very warm in cold winter weather   *so*   they're best for country walks in
分句 1   连词   分句 2
spring and summer.

【参考译文】这双靴子在寒冷的冬天不够温暖, 所以它最适合在春夏去乡村散步时穿着。

【理解要点】本句是由表结果的并列连词 so 引导的并列句, 两个分句都是 "主 + 系 + 表" 结构。be best for (doing) sth. 表示 "最适合做某事"。

3 The people dancing in a group reported feeling happier,   *whereas*   those dancing alone did not.
分句 1   连词   分句 2

【参考译文】在集体中跳舞的人称感觉更快乐, 而单独跳舞的人则没有这样说。

【理解要点】本句中 whereas 连接了两个简单句, 分述不同人的感受。分句 1、2 都是 "主 + 谓 + 宾" 结构, 只是分句 2 省略了和分句 1 重复的部分 report feeling happier。report doing sth. 表示 "声称做某事"。两个分句中, dancing in a group 和 dancing alone 都是现在分词短语作后置定语, 分别修饰 The people 和 those。

4 *While*   many historians are convinced the figure is prehistoric,   others believe *that* it was the
连词   分句 1 (含宾语从句 1)   分句 2 (含宾语从句 2)
work of an artistic monk from a nearby priory and was created between the 11th and 15th centuries.

分句 1	many historians	are	convinced	the figure is prehistoric	
	主语	系动词	表语	宾语从句 1	
宾语从句 2	*that*	it	was	the work of an artistic monk from a nearby priory	and
	引导词	主语	系动词	表语	连词
	was created		between the 11th and 15th centuries		
	谓语		状语		

【参考译文】虽然许多历史学家相信这个图案属于史前时期, 但其他人认为这是附近一座修道院的一位有艺术才能的僧侣的作品, 创作于 11 世纪到 15 世纪之间。

【理解要点】本句是由转折并列连词 while 引导的并列句, 两个分句说明了关于图案创作时间不同的观点。分句 1 的谓语使用了 be convinced (that) 的固定表达, 表示 "确信", 有一类特殊的形容词后能跟宾语从句, convinced 就是其中之一, 可以理解为 convinced 后省略了介词 of。此处宾语从句 1 是 "主 + 系 + 表" 结构。分句 2 包含了一个 that 引导的宾语从句 2, 该从句中又有并列谓语 was 和 was created。

5 Oak trees rely much more on temperature,   *whereas*   ash trees rely on measuring day length
分句 1   连词   分句 2
to determine their seasonal timing.

【参考译文】橡树更多依赖于温度, 而灰树则依靠测量白天长度来确定季节的节点。

【理解要点】本句的转折并列连词是 whereas, 前后两个分句有明显对比, 说明橡树与灰树不同的特征。两个分句中都使用了 rely on sth. 的表达, 表示 "依赖于某物"。两个分句皆为 "主 + 谓 + 宾" 结构。

Test 18

1. Knowledge about implicit theories of intelligence is important, for this knowledge is so often used by people to make judgments. 真

_____

_____

2. Sometimes a load has to be held away from the body, for there is a large obstacle in the area and the person lifting needs to be able to see where their feet are going. 真

_____

_____

3. This type of activity increases the stress on the lower back, for the back muscles have to support the weight of the upper body. 真

_____

_____

4. Many people are simply not familiar with many instances of AI actually working, for it often happens in the background. 真

_____

_____

5. Watson wouldn't be able to explain why its treatment was plausible, for its machine-learning algorithms (算法) were too complex to be fully understood by humans. 真

_____

_____

词汇释义

implicit /ɪmˈplɪsɪt/ *adj.* 不言明的，含蓄的

judgment /ˈdʒʌdʒmənt/ *n.* 评价，判断

obstacle /ˈɒbstəkl/ *n.* 障碍

muscle /ˈmʌsl/ *n.* 肌肉

instance /ˈɪnstəns/ *n.* 例子

plausible /ˈplɔːzəbl/ *adj.* 看似合理的，有道理的

intelligence /ɪnˈtelɪdʒəns/ *n.* 智力

load /ləʊd/ *n.* 负载，负荷

lift /lɪft/ *v.* 举起，抬起

be familiar with 熟悉

treatment /ˈtriːtmənt/ *n.* 疗法，诊治

1 Knowledge about implicit theories of intelligence is important, *for* this knowledge is so
　　　　　　　　　　分句1　　　　　　　　　　　　　　　　　　　　连词　　　　　　分句2

often used by people to make judgments.

【参考译文】关于智力的内隐理论的知识很重要,因为人们经常使用这些知识来做出判断。

【理解要点】本句使用表原因的并列连词for连接两个分句,分句2是分句1的原因。分句1是"主+系+表"结构,
　　　　　　分句2是"主+谓"结构,使用了被动语态is used。

2 Sometimes a load has to be held away from the body, *for* there is a large obstacle in the
　　　　　　　　分句1　　　　　　　　　　　　　　　　连词1　　　　　　分句2

area *and* the person lifting needs to be able to see where their feet are going.
连词2　　　　　　　　　　　　分句3 (含宾语从句)

分句1　Sometimes　　a load　　has to be held　　away from the body
　　　　　状语　　　　主语　　　谓语　　　　　状语

分句3　the person　　lifting　　needs to be able to see　　*where* their feet are going
　　　　　主语　　　后置定语　　　谓语　　　　　　宾语从句

【参考译文】有时,由于附近区域有很大的障碍物,而举着重物的人需要能够看到自己的脚走的地方,所以必
　　　　　　须将重物从身体上抱开。

【理解要点】本句一共有三个分句,其中分句2和分句3由and连接,一起表示分句1的原因。分句3中,现在分词
　　　　　　lifting是person的后置定语,see的宾语是where引导的从句where their feet are going。

3 This type of activity increases the stress on the lower back, *for* the back muscles have to
　　　　　　　　　　分句1　　　　　　　　　　　　　　连词　　　　　分句2

support the weight of the upper body.

【参考译文】这种类型的活动增加了下背部的压力,因为背部肌肉必须支撑上半身的重量。

【理解要点】本句是由表原因的并列连词for连接的并列句,两个分句都是"主+谓+宾"结构。

4 Many people are simply not familiar with many instances of AI actually working, *for*
　　　　　　　　　　　　　　　分句1　　　　　　　　　　　　　　　　　　连词

it often happens in the background.
　　　　分句2

【参考译文】许多人根本不熟悉人工智能实际上起到作用的许多实例,因为这经常发生在后台。

【理解要点】本句由表原因的并列连词for连接两个分句,分句1是"主+系+表"结构,分句2是"主+谓"结构。

5 Watson wouldn't be able to explain *why* its treatment was plausible, *for*
　　　　　　　　　　分句1 (含宾语从句)　　　　　　　　　　　　连词

its machine-learning algorithms were too complex to be fully understood by humans.
　　　　　　　　　　　　　　分句2

【参考译文】沃森无法解释为什么它给出的治疗方案是合理的,因为它的机器学习算法太复杂,人类无法完
　　　　　　全理解。

【理解要点】本句由表原因的并列连词for连接两个分句。分句1是"主+谓+宾"结构,其中宾语是why引导的从
　　　　　　句why its treatment was plausible。分句2是"主+系+表"结构,too... to表示"太……以致不能……"。

Test ⑲

1. Places are strictly limited so please do book early to avoid disappointment. 真

_____

_____

2. First impressions really do last, so it's important you perform well on your first day in the new job. 真

_____

_____

3. You've probably already been into the office for an interview, so you'll have some idea of what the dress code is. 真

_____

_____

4. Whereas medieval builders improvised through their intimate knowledge of materials and personal experience of the conditions on a site, building designs are now conceived and stored in media technologies. 真

_____

_____

5. Band-tailed pigeons scatter and make maybe one or two nests per hectare, whereas passenger pigeons were very social and would make 10,000 or more nests in one hectare. 真

_____

_____

词汇释义

strictly /ˈstrɪktli/ *adv.* 完全地，确切地

disappointment /ˌdɪsəˈpɔɪntmənt/ *n.* 失望；沮丧

perform well 表现良好

dress code 着装要求，着装规定

improvise /ˈɪmprəvaɪz/ *v.* 即兴创作

conceive /kənˈsiːv/ *v.* 想出

hectare /ˈhekteə(r)/ *n.* 公顷

limited /ˈlɪmɪtɪd/ *adj.* 有限的

impression /ɪmˈpreʃn/ *n.* 印象

interview /ˈɪntəvjuː/ *n.* 面试

medieval /ˌmediˈiːvl/ *adj.* 中世纪的

intimate knowledge of 精通

scatter /ˈskætə(r)/ *v.* 分散

1 Places are strictly limited <u>*so*</u> please do book early to avoid disappointment.
　　　分句1　　　　　　　　　连词　　　　　　　　　分句2

【参考译文】名额非常有限，因此请尽早预订，以免落空。

【理解要点】本句是由表结果的并列连词so引导的并列句，分句2是分句1的结果。分句2是祈使句，助动词do表示强调，谓语动词中心词是book"预订"。

2 First impressions really do last, <u>*so*</u> it's important you perform well on your first day in
　　　　分句1　　　　　　　　连词　　　　　　分句2（含主语从句）
the new job.

分句2	it	's	important	you perform well on your first day in the new job
	形式主语	系动词	表语	主语从句

【参考译文】第一印象真的会一直留存，所以你在新工作的第一天表现出色很重要。

【理解要点】本句中，连词so引导的分句2是分句1的结果。分句2中，真正的主语是句末省略了that的从句，正常语序为that you perform well on your first day in the new job is important。

3 You've probably already been into the office for an interview, <u>*so*</u> you'll have some idea of
　　　　　　　分句1　　　　　　　　　　　　　　连词　　分句2（含宾语从句）
what the dress code is.

【参考译文】你可能已经到过办公室面试了，所以你会对着装要求有所了解。

【理解要点】本句是由表结果的并列连词so连接两个分句，分句1是"主+系+表"结构(表语为介词短语into the office)，分句2是"主+谓+宾"结构。分句2中，介词of的宾语为从句what the dress code is，此介词短语作idea的后置定语。

4 *Whereas* medieval builders improvised through their intimate knowledge of materials and
　连词　　　　　　　　　　　　　　分句1
personal experience of the conditions on a site, building designs are now conceived and stored
　　　　　　　　　　　　　　　　　　　　　　　　分句2
in media technologies.

【参考译文】中世纪的建造者们根据对材料的透彻了解和对现场环境的个人体验即兴发挥，现在建筑设计则通过媒体技术进行构思和存档。

【理解要点】本句是由转折并列连词whereas引导的并列句，两个分句描述了不同时期的不同建造方式。Whereas连接并列句可以放在开头。分句1和分句2都是"主+谓"结构，分句1的主干是medieval builders improvised，分句2的主干是building designs are conceived and stored，其余部分都是状语。

5 Band-tailed pigeons... per hectare, *whereas* passenger pigeons were... in one hectare.
　　　　　分句1　　　　　　　　　连词　　　　　分句2

分句1	Band-tailed pigeons	scatter	and	make	maybe one or two nests	per hectare
	主语	谓语1	连词	谓语2	宾语	状语
分句2	passenger pigeons	were	very social	and	would make	10,000 or more nests
	主语	系动词	表语	连词	谓语	宾语
	in one hectare					
	状语					

【参考译文】斑尾鸽分散而居，每公顷可能筑巢一到两个，而旅鸽群居性很强，每公顷可以筑巢10,000多个。

【理解要点】whereas连接的并列句通常强调两个分句的对比。本句对比了斑尾鸽与旅鸽的生活习性。两个分句各带有两个并列谓语。

1. Although the majority of these geoglyphs（地质印痕）date within the last 300 years or so, there are one or two that are much older. 真

2. One of the two axes（轴）measures how positive or negative the feeling is. 真

3. Play is regarded as something trivial, or even as something negative that contrasts with "work". 真

4. There isn't even agreement over whether boredom is always a low-energy, flat kind of emotion or whether feeling agitated and restless counts as boredom, too. 真

5. They played repeating vowel sounds made by a special synthesizing device（合成器）that mimicked sounds made by either an adult woman or another baby. 真

词汇释义

majority /məˈdʒɒrəti/ *n.* 大部分

negative /ˈnegətɪv/ *adj.* 消极的

contrast /ˈkɒntrɑːst/ *v.* 对比

emotion /ɪˈməʊʃn/ *n.* 情绪

restless /ˈrestləs/ *adj.* 焦躁不安的

mimic /ˈmɪmɪk/ *v.* 模仿

date /deɪt/ *v.* 追溯

trivial /ˈtrɪviəl/ *adj.* 不重要的

agreement /əˈɡriːmənt/ *n.* （意见的）一致

agitated /ˈædʒɪteɪtɪd/ *adj.* 紧张不安的

vowel sound 元音

1 *Although* the majority of these geoglyphs date within the last 300 years or so, | there are one or
　　　　　　　　　让步状语从句 | 主句（含定语从句）

two *that* are much older.

让步状语从句	*Although*	the majority of these geoglyphs	date within	the last 300 years or so
	引导词	主语	谓语	宾语

主句	there are	one or two	*that* are much older
	There be 句型	主语	定语从句

【参考译文】虽然大多数这些地质印痕都是在大概过去300年里绘制的, 但也有一两个更为古老。

【理解要点】本句是一个复合句, 含有两个从句。主句中的one or two代表one or two geoglyphs, 定语从句修饰先行词one or two, 关系词that在从句中作主语, 定语从句为"主＋系＋表"结构。

2 One of the two axes | measures | *how* positive or negative the feeling is.
　　主语　　　　　　　　　谓语　　　　　　宾语从句

【参考译文】两条轴线的其中一条衡量这种感觉的积极或消极程度。

【理解要点】宾语从句是"主＋系＋表"结构, 并且有一个or连接的并列结构, 并列成分是一对反义词——positive和negative。

3 Play | is regarded | as something trivial, or even as something negative *that* contrasts with "work".
　主语　　谓语　　　　　　　　　　状语（含定语从句）

【参考译文】玩耍被视为无关紧要的事情, 甚至是与"工作"相对的消极的事情。

【理解要点】本句使用了be regarded as"被视作"的表达。状语中, that引导的定语从句修饰先行词something negative, 关系词that在从句中作主语。contrast with表示"与……形成对比"。

4 There isn't | even agreement | over *whether* boredom is always a low-energy, flat kind of
There be 句型　　主语　　　　　　后置定语（含两个并列的**宾语从句**）

emotion or *whether* feeling agitated and restless counts as boredom, too.

宾语从句 1	*whether*	boredom	is	always a low-energy, flat kind of emotion
	引导词	主语	系动词	表语

宾语从句 2	*whether*	feeling agitated and restless	counts	as boredom, too
	引导词	主语	谓语	状语

【参考译文】无聊是否总是一种低能量、平淡的情绪, 以及感到焦虑不安是否也算无聊, 在这两个问题上人们甚至没有一致的意见。

【理解要点】本句的主干是There isn't even agreement, 之后的介词短语都是agreement的后置定语。介词over的宾语是两个并列的从句, 由于主句有否定词isn't, 因此从句的并列连词要用or。宾语从句2的主语由动名词短语充当, count as表示"算作, 看作"。

5 They | played | repeating vowel sounds | made by a special synthesizing device *that*
　主语　谓语　　　宾语　　　　　　　　后置定语（含定语从句）

mimicked sounds made by either an adult woman or another baby.

定语从句	device	*that*	mimicked	sounds	made by either an adult woman or another baby
	先行词	关系词	谓语	宾语	后置定语

【参考译文】他们播放由特殊合成器发出的重复元音, 该设备能模仿成年女性或其他婴儿发出的声音。

【理解要点】主句和定语从句中, 都出现了过去分词短语made by...作后置定语, 分别修饰repeating vowel sounds和sounds。that引导的定语从句, 修饰device, 说明该设备的功能, 关系词在从句中充当主语。

第 2 节　提高训练 100 句

划分以下句子的成分。

Test **1**

1. We should remember that *Lost City of the Incas* is a work of hindsight. 真

_____

_____

2. Researchers have also found that different types of laughter serve as codes to complex human social hierarchies. 真

_____

_____

3. Richard Sennett argues that urban design has suffered from a separation between mind and body since the introduction of the architectural blueprint. 真

_____

_____

4. We now know that Vilcabamba（维尔卡班巴古城）actually lies in the depths of the jungle. 真

_____

_____

5. We are aware that the product we have envisioned is mainly finding application in the developing world and humanitarian sector and that this is the way we will proceed. 真

_____

_____

词汇释义

hindsight /ˈhaɪndsaɪt/ **n.** 后见之明，马后炮

laughter /ˈlɑːftə(r)/ **n.** 笑声

architectural /ˌɑːkɪˈtektʃərəl/ **adj.** 建筑的

aware /əˈweə(r)/ **adj.** 意识到的，明白的

humanitarian /hjuːˌmænɪˈteəriən/ **adj.** 人道主义的

researcher /rɪˈsɜːtʃə(r)/ **n.** 研究人员

hierarchy /ˈhaɪərɑːki/ **n.** 等级制度（尤指社会或组织）

blueprint /ˈbluːprɪnt/ **n.** 蓝图

envision /ɪnˈvɪʒn/ **v.** 设想，想象

proceed /prəˈsiːd/ **v.** 继续进行，继续做

1 We | should remember | *that* Lost City of the Incas is a work of hindsight.
主语 | 谓语 | 宾语从句

【参考译文】我们应该记住,《印加失落之城》这部作品是事后才写成的。

【理解要点】本句的谓语后接了一个由 that 引导的宾语从句,该从句是"主+系+表"结构。

2 Researchers | have also found | *that* different types of laughter serve as codes to complex
主语 | 谓语 | 宾语从句
human social hierarchies.

【参考译文】研究人员还发现,不同类型的笑声是复杂的人类社会等级的密码。

【理解要点】that 引导的宾语从句中, as codes to complex human social hierarchies 作谓语 serve 的状语, serve as 意为"起到……作用"。

3 Richard Sennett | argues | *that* urban design has suffered... blueprint.
主语 | 谓语 | 宾语从句

宾语从句 | *that* | urban design | has suffered | from a separation between mind and body
| 引导词 | 主语 | 谓语 | 状语
since the introduction of the architectural blueprint
状语

【参考译文】理查德·桑内特认为,自从建筑蓝图问世以来,城市设计一直受到思想与肉体相分离的困扰。

【理解要点】宾语从句使用了 suffer from 表示"受……折磨"。从句中的 since 是一个介词,意为"自……以来", 常接一个表示时间或事件的名词,作时间状语。

4 We | now know | *that* Vilcabamba actually lies in the depths of the jungle.
主语 | 谓语 | 宾语从句

【参考译文】我们现在知道维尔卡班巴古城实际上位于丛林深处。

【理解要点】本句的宾语从句由 that 引导,从句是"主+谓"结构,谓语 lies 后接地点状语 in the depths of the jungle,说明古城的位置。

5 We | are | aware | *that* the product... humanitarian sector | *and*
主语 | 系动词 | 表语 | 宾语从句 1(含定语从句 1) | 连词
that this is the way we will proceed.
宾语从句 2(含定语从句 2)

宾语从句 1 | *that* | the product | we have envisioned | is mainly finding | application
| 引导词 | 主语 | 定语从句 1 | 谓语 | 宾语
in the developing world and humanitarian sector
状语
宾语从句 2 | *that* | this | is | the way | we will proceed
| 引导词 | 主语 | 系动词 | 表语 | 定语从句 2

【参考译文】我们意识到,我们所设想的产品将主要在发展中国家和慈善领域中寻求应用,这也是我们会继续前进的道路。

【理解要点】本句的主干属于"系动词+形容词+宾语从句"的结构,形容词 aware 后的介词被省略。此句的两个宾语从句为并列关系,两个宾语从句中又各含有一个定语从句。宾语从句 1 中, we have envisioned 是一个省略了 that 的定语从句,修饰主语 the product,关系词在从句中作宾语。宾语从句 2 中,定语从句 we will proceed 也省略了关系词 that,修饰的先行词是 the way,关系词在从句中作状语。

Test ②

1. The result is that less attention will be allocated to reading processes. 真

---

2. A strong possibility is that play supports the early development of children's self-control. 真

---

3. The result is that businesses and people spend time and money organising themselves for the sake of organising. 真

---

4. The mistake was that the two parts of the tunnel failed to meet. 真

---

5. The idea of de-extinction（反灭绝）is that we can reverse this process, bringing species that no longer exist back to life. 真

词汇释义

attention /əˈtenʃn/ *n.* 注意力

process /ˈprəʊses/ *n.* 过程

self-control *n.* 自制力，自我控制

for the sake of sth. 因为某事的缘故

reverse /rɪˈvɜːs/ *v.* 反转，使完全相反

allocate /ˈæləkeɪt/ *v.* 分配

possibility /ˌpɒsəˈbɪləti/ *n.* 可能，可能性

organise /ˈɔːgənaɪz/ *v.* 规划，管理

tunnel /ˈtʌnl/ *n.* 隧道

1 The result is *that* less attention will be allocated to reading processes.
    主语   系动词   表语从句

表语从句   *that*   less attention   will be allocated to   reading processes
        引导词   主语   谓语   宾语

【参考译文】结果是更少的注意力被分配到阅读过程中。

【理解要点】本句是"主+系+表"结构，表语是由that引导的从句。be allocated to表示"分配给"。

2 A strong possibility is *that* play supports the early development of children's self-control.
    主语   系动词   表语从句

表语从句 *that*   play   supports   the early development of children's self-control
      引导词 主语   谓语   宾语

【参考译文】玩游戏很可能有助于儿童自我控制力的早期发展。

【理解要点】本句中，that引导的是表语从句，从句的主干play supports the development是"主+谓+宾"结构。

3 The result is *that* businesses and people... for the sake of organising.
    主语   系动词   表语从句

表语从句 *that* businesses and people   spend   time and money   organising themselves
      引导词   主语   谓语   宾语   状语

        for the sake of organising

【参考译文】结果是，企业和人们为了管理而花费时间和金钱来管理自己。

【理解要点】本句中，that引导的表语从句使用了spend time/money doing sth.的固定表达，表示"花费时间/金钱做某事"。

4 The mistake was *that* the two parts of the tunnel failed to meet.
    主语   系动词   表语从句

表语从句 *that*   the two parts of the tunnel   failed to meet
       引导词   主语   谓语

【参考译文】错误在于隧道的两个部分未能接到一起。

【理解要点】在由that引导的表语从句中，fail to do sth.表示"未做成某事"。

5 The idea of de-extinction is *that* we can reverse... back to life.
    主语   系动词   表语从句

表语从句 *that*   we   can reverse   this process,   bringing species *that* no longer exist
      引导词 主语   谓语   宾语   状语（含定语从句）

        back to life

【参考译文】反灭绝的想法是，我们可以逆转这一过程，使灭绝的物种复活。

【理解要点】表语从句中，bringing species that... back to life是现在分词短语作目的状语，说明reverse this process的目的。其中，that no longer exist是一个定语从句，修饰先行词species，关系词在从句中作主语。bring sth./sb. back to life表示"使某物/某人复活"。

Test ③

1. What is amazing is that the number of microbial ones is higher. 真

_____

_____

2. We know that what we are doing today is not enough, and we have to be willing to take some calculated and measured risks. 真

_____

_____

3. It is possible that using antibacterial products in the home fails to have the desired effect. 真

_____

_____

4. It is advisable that you involve employees in this process. 真

_____

_____

5. It is important that you make sure these boots are done up tightly before starting a walk. 真

_____

_____

词汇释义

amazing /əˈmeɪzɪŋ/ *adj.* 令人惊奇的

a calculated risk 预料到的风险

antibacterial /ˌæntibækˈtɪəriəl/ *adj.* 抗菌的

advisable /ədˈvaɪzəbl/ *adj.* 明智的，可取的

employee /ɪmˈplɔɪiː/ *n.* 雇员

tightly /ˈtaɪtli/ *adv.* 紧紧地

microbial /maɪˈkrəʊbɪəl/ *adj.* 微生物的

measured /ˈmeʒəd/ *adj.* 慎重的，几经斟酌的

desired /dɪˈzaɪə(r)d/ *adj.* 渴望的，理想的

involve /ɪnˈvɒlv/ *v.* 使参与

do up 系上，扣上

1 | **_What_ is amazing** | **is** | **_that_ the number of microbial ones is higher.**
主语从句 | 系动词 | 表语从句

表语从句 | **_that_** | **the number of microbial ones** | **is** | **higher**
引导词 | 主语 | 系动词 | 表语

【参考译文】令人惊讶的是，微生物的数量更高。

【理解要点】本句的主干、主语从句、表语从句皆为"主+系+表"结构。the number of表示"……的数量"。

2 | **We** | **know** | **_that what_ we are doing today is not enough,** | **_and_** | **we** | **have to be willing**
主语1 | 谓语1 | 宾语从句（含主语从句） | 连词 | 主语2 | 谓语2

to take | **some calculated and measured risks.**
宾语

宾语从句 | **_that_** | **_what_ we are doing today** | **is** | **not enough**
引导词 | 主语从句 | 系动词 | 表语

【参考译文】我们知道，我们今天所做的还不够，我们必须愿意承担一些经过权衡考虑的审慎的风险。

【理解要点】本句有两个分句，由并列连词and连接，分句1的宾语是由that引导的宾语从句，宾语从句中又含有一个由what引导的主语从句，主语从句为"主+谓+宾"结构。分句2中使用了be willing to do sth."愿意做某事"的表达。

3 | **It** | **is** | **possible** | **_that_ using... desired effect.**
形式主语 | 系动词 | 表语 | 主语从句

主语从句 | **_that_** | **using antibacterial products in the home** | **fails to have the desired effect**
引导词 | 主语 | 谓语（fail to do sth.结构）

【参考译文】在家中使用抗菌产品可能达不到预期效果。

【理解要点】本句中，It是形式主语，真正的主语是that引导的主语从句。该从句的主语为动名词短语，所以谓语动词要用第三人称单数形式fails。

4 | **It** | **is** | **advisable** | **_that_ you involve employees in this process.**
形式主语 | 系动词 | 表语 | 主语从句

主语从句 | **_that_** | **you** | **involve** | **employees** | **in this process**
引导词 | 主语 | 谓语 | 宾语 | 状语

【参考译文】建议您让员工参与此过程。

【理解要点】本句的It是形式主语，真正的主语是that引导的主语从句。involve sb. in sth.表示"允许/邀请某人参与某事"。

5 | **It** | **is** | **important** | **_that_ you make sure... starting a walk.**
形式主语 | 系动词 | 表语 | 主语从句（含宾语从句）

主语从句 | **_that_** | **you** | **make sure** | **these boots are done up tightly** | **before starting a walk**
引导词 | 主语 | 谓语 | 宾语从句 | 状语

【参考译文】重要的是，在开始散步之前，你要确保靴子系紧了。

【理解要点】本句的主语从句中包含了一个宾语从句，该宾语从句使用了被动语态，为"主+谓"结构。before starting a walk为"介词+动名词"构成的时间状语，动作的逻辑主语是主语从句的主语you，此状语也可以写为before you start a walk。

Test ❹

1. Never mind the fact that the water bottles feel out-of-date to anyone over the age of 40. 真

_____

_____

2. Surprisingly, Davies does not discuss the fact that Bentham meant his Panopticon（全景敞视建筑） not just as a model prison but also as an instrument of control. 真

_____

_____

3. My views may seem to ignore the belief that businesses should act in accordance with moral principles even if this leads to a reduction in their profits. 真

_____

_____

4. Evidence that polar bears have good problem-solving abilities challenges those assumptions. 真

_____

_____

5. These problems have led to the intriguing suggestion that coconuts originated on coral islands（珊瑚岛） in the Pacific and were dispersed from there. 真

_____

_____

词汇释义

out-of-date _adj._ 过时的

prison /ˈprɪzn/ _n._ 监狱，牢狱

in accordance with 依照，遵照

reduction /rɪˈdʌkʃn/ _n._ 减少，缩小，降低

challenge /ˈtʃælɪndʒ/ _v._ 质疑

intriguing /ɪnˈtriːgɪŋ/ _adj._ 非常有趣的

disperse /dɪˈspɜːs/ _v._ 传播，散布

surprisingly /səˈpraɪzɪŋli/ _adv._ 令人惊讶地

instrument /ˈɪnstrəmənt/ _n._ 手段，方法；工具

moral principles 道德准则

profit /ˈprɒfɪt/ _n._ 利润

assumption /əˈsʌmpʃn/ _n._ 假定，假设

originate /əˈrɪdʒɪneɪt/ _v._ 发源，起源

1 Never mind | the fact | *that* the water bottles feel out-of-date to anyone over the age of 40.
　谓语　　　　宾语　　　　　　　　　　　　　　同位语从句

同位语从句　*that*　the water bottles　feel　out-of-date　to anyone over the age of 40
　　　　　　引导词　　　主语　　　系动词　　表语　　　　　　状语

【参考译文】别在意40岁以上的人认为这些水瓶过时了。

【理解要点】本句的主干是祈使句。that引导的是同位语从句,补充说明fact的内容,从句是"主+系+表"结构,此处feel意为"给人……感觉"。over the age of 40是anyone的后置定语。

2 Surprisingly, | Davies | does not discuss | the fact | *that* Bentham meant... of control.
　状语　　　　主语　　　　谓语　　　　　宾语　　　　　　　同位语从句

同位语从句　*that*　Bentham　meant　his Panopticon　not just as a model prison
　　　　　引导词　　主语　　谓语　　　宾语　　　　　　宾语补语

but also as an instrument of control

【参考译文】令人惊讶的是,戴维斯并没有讨论这样一个事实,即边沁设想的全景敞视建筑并不仅是一个监狱模型,还是一个控制手段。

【理解要点】主句的主干是Davies does not discuss the fact,后接that引导的同位语从句,说明宾语fact的内容。mean sth. as表示"计划某物成为……"。

3 My views | may seem to ignore | the belief | *that* businesses should... their profits.
　主语　　　　谓语　　　　　　宾语　　　　　　同位语从句(含状语从句)

同位语从句　*that*　businesses　should act　in accordance with moral principles
　　　　　引导词　　主语　　　谓语　　　　　　　状语

even if this leads to a reduction in their profits
　　　　　　状语从句

【参考译文】我的观点似乎忽视了这样一种信念,即企业应该按照道德准则行事,即使这会导致利润减少。

【理解要点】主句是My views may seem to ignore the belief,后接that引导的同位语从句,是对belief的补充说明。从句中的in accordance with表示"依照"。另外,同位语从句中又含有一个由even if引导的让步状语从句,句中的谓语动词leads to表示"导致"。

4 Evidence | *that* polar bears have good problem-solving abilities | challenges | those assumptions.
　主语　　　　　　　　　同位语从句　　　　　　　　　　　　谓语　　　　宾语

同位语从句　*that*　polar bears　have　good problem-solving abilities
　　　　　引导词　　主语　　谓语　　　　宾语

【参考译文】有证据表明北极熊有很好的解决问题的能力,使得这些假设遭到质疑。

【理解要点】本句的主句为Evidence challenges those assumptions,主语Evidence后接由that引导的同位语从句,对Evidence的内容做补充说明。

5 These problems | have led to | the intriguing suggestion | *that* coconuts... from there.
　主语　　　　　谓语　　　　　　宾语　　　　　　　　　同位语从句

同位语从句　*that*　coconuts　originated　on coral islands in the Pacific　and
　　　　　引导词　　主语　　　谓语1　　　　　　状语　　　　　　　　连词

were dispersed　from there.
　谓语2　　　　　状语

【参考译文】这些问题产生了一种有趣的暗示,即椰子起源于太平洋的珊瑚岛,并从那里传播开来。

【理解要点】本句的主句是"主+谓+宾"结构,宾语suggestion后接同位语从句,补充说明suggestion的内容。该从句中,有两个并列谓语由and连接,分别是originated和were dispersed,后者是被动语态。

Test ⑤

1. In their hats, British fusiliers（火枪手）have a clipped feather plume whose colour varies according to their regiment. 真

_____

_____

2. EMI created replicas which still rely completely on the original artist's creative impulses. 真

_____

_____

3. We move to a model where consumers are tending not to own a single vehicle. 真

_____

_____

4. Truly great baristas（咖啡师）take the time to develop the key skills that will enable them to deliver the highest possible quality of coffee-based beverage and service. 真

_____

_____

5. Individuals should avoid things such as humour that may distract them from the accomplishment of task goals. 真

_____

_____

词汇释义

clipped /klɪpt/ *adj.* 剪短的，整齐的

vary /'veərɪ/ *v.* 变化，变更

replica /'replɪkə/ *n.* 复制品，仿制品

creative /kri'eɪtɪv/ *adj.* 创作的，创造（性）的

consumer /kən'sjuːmə(r)/ *n.* 消费者，用户

beverage /'bevərɪdʒ/ *n.* 饮料

accomplishment /ə'kʌmplɪʃmənt/ *n.* 完成，实现

plume /pluːm/ *n.* 羽毛，羽饰

regiment /'redʒɪmənt/ *n.* （军队的）团

completely /kəm'pliːtli/ *adv.* 彻底地，完全地

impulse /'ɪmpʌls/ *n.* 冲动

vehicle /'viːəkl/ *n.* 车辆

distract /dɪ'strækt/ *v.* 使分心，分散（注意力）

1
In their hats,	British fusiliers	have	a clipped feather plume	*whose* colour... regiment.
状语	主语	谓语	宾语	定语从句

定语从句	a clipped feather plume	*whose*	colour	varies	according to their regiment
	先行词	关系词	主语	谓语	状语

【参考译文】英国的火枪手帽子上有一根剪短的羽毛,颜色因兵团而异。

【理解要点】本句的定语从句为"主+谓"结构,先行词feather plume与从句主语colour为所属关系,故关系词用whose。

2
EMI	created	replicas	*which* still rely completely on the original artist's creative impulses.
主语	谓语	宾语	定语从句

定语从句	replicas	*which*	still rely completely on	the original artist's creative impulses
	先行词	关系词	谓语	宾语

【参考译文】EMI创造的仿制品仍然完全依赖于原艺术家的创作冲动。

【理解要点】主句是EMI created replicas,后接由关系词which引导的定语从句,修饰先行词replicas,关系词which在从句中充当主语。

3
We	move to	a model	*where* consumers are tending not to own a single vehicle.
主语	谓语	宾语	定语从句

定语从句	a model	*where*	consumers	are tending not to own	a single vehicle
	先行词	关系词	主语	谓语	宾语

【参考译文】我们转向这样一种模式,即消费者不倾向于拥有单部车辆。

【理解要点】主句是We move to a model,后接由关系词where引导的定语从句,修饰先行词a model,关系词where在从句中作状语,指代的成分为in the model。

4
Truly great baristas	take	the time	to develop the key skills	*that* will... and service.
主语	谓语	宾语	状语	定语从句

定语从句	the key skills	*that*	will enable	them	to deliver the highest possible quality
	先行词	关系词	谓语	宾语	宾语补语
	of coffee-based beverage and service				

【参考译文】真正优秀的咖啡师会花时间培养关键技能,使他们能够提供最高质量的咖啡饮料和服务。

【理解要点】主句使用了take time to do sth.的表达,表示"花时间做某事"。关系词that引导的定语从句,修饰先行词the key skills,关系词that在从句中充当主语,从句使用了enable sb. to do sth."使某人能够做某事"的表达。

5
Individuals	should avoid	things	such as humour	*that* may... task goals.
主语	谓语	宾语	插入语	定语从句

定语从句	things	*that*	may distract	them	from the accomplishment of task goals
	先行词	关系词	谓语	宾语	状语

【参考译文】人们应避免幽默等可能使他们无法专心完成任务目标的东西。

【理解要点】主句主干是Individuals should avoid things,其后的such as humour是插入语,举例说明things。that引导的定语从句所修饰的先行词是插入语前的things,关系词that在从句中充当主语。distract sb. from sth. 表示"使某人不能专心做某事"。

1. They are uniquely adapted to the extreme conditions of the Arctic Circle, where temperatures can reach -40°C. 真

_____

_____

2. This has left forests stagnant and therefore unwelcoming to the plants and animals which evolved to help regenerate the forest after a disturbance. 真

_____

_____

3. One of the reasons why the enthusiasm for rewilding is spreading so quickly in Britain is that it helps to create a more inspiring vision. 真

_____

_____

4. Those children who listened to a lot of baby talk were talking more than the babies that listened to more adult talk or standard speech. 真

_____

_____

5. Provo, the organisation that came up with the idea, was a group of Dutch activists who wanted to change society. 真

_____

_____

词汇释义

uniquely /juˈniːkli/ *adv.* 独特地，唯一地

temperature /ˈtemprətʃə(r)/ *n.* 温度

unwelcoming /ʌnˈwelkəmɪŋ/ *adj.* 不适合居住的，不惬意的

regenerate /rɪˈdʒenəreɪt/ *v.* 使恢复

enthusiasm /ɪnˈθjuːziæzəm/ *n.* 热情，热忱

inspiring /ɪnˈspaɪərɪŋ/ *adj.* 鼓舞人心的

come up with 提出，想出

the Arctic Circle 北极圈

stagnant /ˈstægnənt/ *adj.* 停滞的，无变化的

evolve /iˈvɒlv/ *v.* 进化

disturbance /dɪˈstɜːbəns/ *n.* 打扰，干扰

rewilding /ˌriːˈwaɪldɪŋ/ *n.* 再野化

vision /ˈvɪʒn/ *n.* 构想，设想

activist /ˈæktɪvɪst/ *n.* 活动家，积极分子

1 | They | are uniquely adapted to | the extreme conditions of the Arctic Circle, | *where*
主语 | 谓语 | 宾语 | 定语从句
temperatures can reach -40℃.

【参考译文】它们独特地适应了北极圈的极端条件，那里的温度可以达到 –40℃。

【理解要点】where引导的非限制性定语从句修饰the Arctic Circle，对北极圈的极端条件做了进一步的说明。关系词在从句中作地点状语，从句为"主+谓+宾"结构。

2 | This | has left | forests | stagnant and therefore unwelcoming to the plants and animals
主语 | 谓语 | 宾语 | 宾语补语
which evolved to help regenerate the forest after a disturbance.
定语从句

定语从句 | plants and animals | *which* | evolved | to help regenerate the forest after a disturbance
先行词 | 关系词 | 谓语 | 状语

【参考译文】这使得森林无法发展，并因此不适合动植物生存，这些动植物已进化到能帮助森林在受到干扰后恢复。

【理解要点】主句的主干是This has left forests stagnant and unwelcoming，其中，"leave sb./sth. +宾语补语"的结构表示"使某人或某物处于某种状态"。宾语补语中包含一个由which引导的定语从句，修饰先行词plants and animals。关系词which在从句中充当主语。

3 | One of the reasons | *why* the enthusiasm for rewilding is spreading so quickly in Britain | is
主语 | 定语从句 | 系动词
that it helps to create a more inspiring vision.
表语从句

定语从句 | reasons | *why* | the enthusiasm for rewilding | is spreading | so quickly in Britain
先行词 | 关系词 | 主语 | 谓语 | 状语
表语从句 | *that* | it | helps | to create a more inspiring vision
引导词 | 主语 | 谓语 | 宾语

【参考译文】对再野化的狂热在英国迅速蔓延的原因之一是，它有助于创造一个更加鼓舞人心的愿景。

【理解要点】本句含有一个定语从句和一个表语从句。定语从句修饰的先行词是reasons，说明是什么的原因。表语从句则由that引导，说明主语One of the reasons的内容。

4 | Those children | *who* listened to a lot of baby talk | were talking | more than the babies
主语 | 定语从句1 | 谓语 | 状语
that listened to more adult talk or standard speech.
定语从句2

【参考译文】那些听了很多模仿儿语的孩子比那些听了更多成人谈话或标准用语的孩子说话更多。

【理解要点】主句的主干是Those children were talking more than the babies。定语从句1中，关系词who指代的是先行词Those children；在定语从句2中，关系词that指代先行词the babies。两个定语从句都是"主+谓+宾"结构，关系词都充当主语。

5 | Provo, | the organisation | *that* came up with the idea, | was | a group of Dutch activists
主语 | 同位语 | 定语从句1 | 系动词 | 表语
who wanted to change society.
定语从句2

【参考译文】提出这一想法的组织Provo是由一群希望改变社会的荷兰活动家组成的。

【理解要点】主句的主干是Provo was a group of Dutch activist。the organisation是Provo的同位语，而同位语后又有一个定语从句，由关系词that引导，修饰先行词the organisation。主句的表语后又接有另一个定语从句，由who引导，修饰先行词activists。两个定语从句皆为"主+谓+宾"结构，关系词都充当主语。

Test ⑦

1. It does not exceed its budget, which is currently around £1m a year. 真

---

2. He designed a number of principles to improve the efficiency of the work process, which have since become widespread in modern companies. 真

---

3. This unprecedented effort was made possible by the owners of the 67-metre yacht *White Cloud*, who provided the Galapagos National Park with free use of their helicopter and its experienced pilot, as well as the logistical support of the yacht. 真

---

4. Sadly, the passenger pigeon's existence came to an end on 1 September 1914, when the last living specimen died at Cincinnati Zoo. 真

---

5. The Hamiltonian view, which is similar to the Platonic view, is that people are born with different levels of intelligence. 真

词汇释义

exceed /ɪkˈsiːd/ *v.* 超过，超出

efficiency /ɪˈfɪʃnsi/ *n.* 效率

unprecedented /ʌnˈpresɪdentɪd/ *adj.* 前所未有的，没有先例的

yacht /jɒt/ *n.* 游艇

experienced /ɪkˈspɪəriənst/ *adj.* 有经验的，熟练的

logistical /ləˈdʒɪstɪk(ə)l/ *adj.* 后勤的

specimen /ˈspesɪmən/ *n.* 单一实例

be born with 生来就有

currently /ˈkʌrəntli/ *adv.* 现时，当前

widespread /ˈwaɪdspred/ *adj.* 分布广的，广泛流传的

helicopter /ˈhelɪkɒptə(r)/ *n.* 直升机

pilot /ˈpaɪlət/ *n.* 飞行员

existence /ɪgˈzɪstəns/ *n.* 存在

be similar to 与……相似

intelligence /ɪnˈtelɪdʒəns/ *n.* 智力水平，才智

1 | It | does not exceed | its budget, | *which* is currently around £1m a year.
主语 | 谓语 | 宾语 | 定语从句

定语从句 | budget | *which* | is | currently around £1m | a year
先行词 | 关系词 | 系动词 | 表语 | 状语

【参考译文】它没有超过目前每年约100万英镑的预算。

【理解要点】本句的主干是It does not exceed its budget, 关系词which引导的定语从句补充说明预算有多少。

2 | He | designed | a number of principles | to improve the efficiency of the work process,
主语 | 谓语 | 宾语 | 状语

which have since become widespread in modern companies.
定语从句

定语从句 | principles | *which* | have since become | widespread | in modern companies
先行词 | 关系词 | 系动词 | 表语 | 状语

【参考译文】他设计了许多原则来提高工作流程的效率, 之后这些原则在现代公司中得到了广泛应用。

【理解要点】定语从句的先行词是principles, 关系词是which, 要注意状语to improve the efficiency of the work process表作用和目的, work process不是从句的先行词。

3 | This unprecedented effort | was made | possible | by the owners of the 67-metre yacht
主语 | 谓语 | 主语补语 | 状语

White Cloud, | *who* provided... of the yacht.
定语从句

定语从句 | the owners | *who* | provided | the Galapagos National Park | with free use of
先行词 | 关系词 | 谓语 | 宾语 | 状语

their helicopter and its experienced pilot, as well as the logistical support of the yacht

【参考译文】这一创举是由游艇"白云号"(长67米)所有者促成的, 他们向加拉帕戈斯国家公园免费提供了他们的直升机和经验丰富的飞行员, 还有游艇的后勤支持。

【理解要点】主句主干是This effort was made possible, 为被动语态。who引导的非限制性定语从句, 对先行词the owners of the 67-metre yacht *White Cloud* 进行补充说明。

4 | Sadly, | the passenger pigeon's existence | came to an end | on 1 September 1914,
状语 | 主语 | 谓语 | 状语

when the last living specimen died at Cincinnati Zoo.
定语从句

定语从句 | 1 September 1914 | *when* | the last living specimen | died | at Cincinnati Zoo
先行词 | 关系词 | 主语 | 谓语 | 状语

【参考译文】不幸的是, 当最后一只存活的旅鸽于1914年9月1日在辛辛那提动物园死亡时, 旅鸽就不复存在了。

【理解要点】本句的定语从句关系词是when, 对表示日期的先行词1 September 1914进行补充说明, 1 September 1914在主句和从句中皆作时间状语。

5 | The Hamiltonian view, | *which* is similar to the Platonic view, | is | *that* people are born with
主语 | 定语从句 | 系动词 | 表语从句

different levels of intelligence.

【参考译文】汉密尔顿派别的观点与柏拉图派别的观点相似, 认为人们生来就有不同的智力水平。

【理解要点】本句出现两个从句, 分别是非限制性定语从句和表语从句。其中, 定语从句由which引导, 为"主+系+表"结构, 关系词which在从句中作主语。定语从句对主句的主语The Hamiltonian view做补充说明。而表语从句则是由that引导, 说明主语的内容。

1. With that in mind, Tesco introduced its Greener Living programme, which demonstrates the company's commitment to protecting the environment. 真

2. "This is the first time anyone has looked at both behavioural and neural changes in these ants so thoroughly," says Giraldo, who recently published the findings in the *Proceedings of the Royal Society B*. 真

3. Glass making has become a modern, hi-tech industry operating in a fiercely competitive global market where quality, design and service levels are critical to maintaining market share. 真

4. He became interested in the paintings of the Spanish artist Pablo Picasso, whose work inspired him to distort the human body in a radical way. 真

5. Djoser's main official, whose name was Imhotep, conceived of building a taller, more impressive tomb for his king. 真

词汇释义

demonstrate /ˈdemənstreɪt/ *v.* 展示，表露

behavioural /bɪˈheɪvjərəl/ *adj.* 关于行为的

thoroughly /ˈθʌrəli/ *adv.* 彻底地，详尽地

fiercely competitive 竞争激烈的

maintain /meɪnˈteɪn/ *v.* 维持，保持

distort /dɪˈstɔːt/ *v.* 扭曲，使变形

conceive of 设想

commitment /kəˈmɪtmənt/ *n.* 投入，奉献

neural /ˈnjʊərəl/ *adj.* 神经的，神经系统的

finding /ˈfaɪndɪŋ/ *n.* 发现

critical /ˈkrɪtɪkl/ *adj.* 关键的，极重要的

inspire /ɪnˈspaɪə(r)/ *v.* 鼓舞，启迪

radical /ˈrædɪkl/ *adj.* 激进的，极端的

tomb /tuːm/ *n.* 坟墓，冢

1 | With that in mind, | Tesco | introduced | its Greener Living programme, | *which* demonstrates
状语 | 主语 | 谓语 | 宾语 | 定语从句

the company's commitment to protecting the environment.

定语从句 | *which* | demonstrates | the company's commitment | to protecting the environment
关系词 | 谓语 | 宾语 | 后置定语

【参考译文】考虑到这一点，乐购推出了"绿色生活"计划，表明公司致力于保护环境。

【理解要点】本句的主句是Tesco introduced its Greener Living programme, 后接的非限制性定语从句由which引导，是对主句的补充说明，关系词which指代主句的内容。

2 | "This is... so thoroughly," | says | Giraldo, | *who* recently published the findings in the
直接引语（含定语从句1） | 谓语 | 主语 | 定语从句2

Proceedings of the Royal Society B.

直接引语 | This | is | the first time | anyone... so thoroughly
主语 | 系动词 | 表语 | 定语从句1

定语从句1 | the first time | *(when)* | anyone | has looked at | both behavioural and
先行词 | 关系词（被省略） | 主语 | 谓语 | 宾语

neural changes in these ants | so thoroughly
状语

【参考译文】"这是人们首次对这些蚂蚁的行为和神经变化进行如此彻底的研究。"吉拉尔多说，他最近在《英国皇家学会会刊B辑》上发表了这些发现。

【理解要点】主句是包含直接引语的倒装句，直接引语中含有一个定语从句，修饰先行词the first time。主句后的非限制性定语从句由who引导，为"主+谓+宾"结构，修饰先行词Giraldo, 对人物进行补充说明。

3 | Glass making | has become | a modern, hi-tech industry | operating in a fiercely
主语 | 系动词 | 表语 | 后置定语

competitive global market | *where* quality... market share.
定语从句

定语从句 | global market | *where* | quality, design and service levels | are | critical to
先行词 | 关系词 | 主语 | 系动词 | 表语

maintaining market share

【参考译文】玻璃制造已成为一个在竞争激烈的全球市场上运作的高科技现代行业，质量、设计和服务水平对保持市场份额至关重要。

【理解要点】主句主干是Glass making has become a... industry, 现在分词短语operating in a fiercely competitive global market是industry的后置定语。定语从句所修饰的先行词global market在从句中作地点状语，故关系词用where, 也可用in which。定语从句相当于quality... are critical to... market share in a fiercely competitive global market。

4 | He | became | interested | in the paintings of the Spanish artist Pablo Picasso, | *whose* work
主语 | 系动词 | 表语 | 状语 | 定语从句

inspired him to distort the human body in a radical way.

定语从句 | Pablo Picasso | *whose* | work | inspired | him | to distort... radical way
先行词 | 关系词 | 主语 | 谓语 | 宾语 | 宾语补语

【参考译文】他对西班牙画家巴勃罗·毕加索的画作产生了兴趣，毕加索的作品启发他以激进的方式扭曲人类形体。

【理解要点】主句主干是He became interested in the paintings, 介词短语of the Spanish artist Pablo Picasso是paintings的后置定语。inspire sb. to do sth.表示"激励某人做某事"。

5 | Djoser's main official, | *whose* name was Imhotep, | conceived of | building a taller, more
主语 | 定语从句 | 谓语 | 宾语

impressive tomb for his king.

【参考译文】左塞尔的主要官员伊姆霍特普打算为他的国王建造一座更高、更令人印象深刻的陵墓。

【理解要点】定语从句的先行词是Djoser's main official, 先行词与从句主语name之间为所属关系，所以关系词用whose。从句为"主+系+表"结构。

1. The first commercial versions of the Desolenator（海水淡化器）are expected to be in operation in India early next year, after field tests are carried out. 真

_____

_____

2. Nothing of any importance had been thought on the subject until it came to their attention. 真

_____

_____

3. The really big surprise came when he looked at the cautionary elements of the story. 真

_____

_____

4. Once his phylogenetic analysis（演化发展分析）had established that they were indeed related, he used the same methods to explore how they have developed and altered over time. 真

_____

_____

5. When Bingham and his team set off down the Urubamba（乌鲁班巴河）in late July, they had an advantage over travellers who had preceded them. 真

_____

_____

词汇释义

commercial /kəˈmɜːʃl/ **adj.** 商业的
in operation 使用中，工作中
carry out 实施，执行
cautionary /ˈkɔːʃənəri/ **adj.** 告诫的，警告的
establish /ɪˈstæblɪʃ/ **v.** 证实，确定
set off 动身，启程
precede /prɪˈsiːd/ **v.** 处在……之前

version /ˈvɜːʃn/ **n.** 版本
field test 实地试验
subject /ˈsʌbdʒɪkt/ **n.** 主题，话题
element /ˈelɪmənt/ **n.** 要素，基本部分
alter /ˈɔːltə(r)/ **v.** 改变，变化
advantage /ədˈvɑːntɪdʒ/ **n.** 有利条件，优势

1 | The first commercial versions of the Desolenator | are expected | to be in operation
主语 | 谓语 | 主语补语

in India early next year, | *after* field tests are carried out.
状语 | 状语从句

【参考译文】在进行实地测试后，第一批商用的海水淡化器预计将于明年年初在印度投入使用。

【理解要点】本句的状语从句中，从属连词是after，表示"在……之后"，后接一个完整的陈述句，说明主句发生的时间。从句是"主+谓"结构，谓语are carried out为被动态。

2 | Nothing of any importance | had been thought | on the subject | *until* it came to their attention.
主语 | 谓语 | 状语 | 状语从句

【参考译文】在他们注意到这个问题之前，人们从未认真思考过它。

【理解要点】本句含有until引导的时间状语从句，until表示"在……之前"。状语从句的主语it指代主句中的subject。come to one's attention为固定表达，意为"吸引某人的注意力"。

3 | The really big surprise | came | *when* he looked at the cautionary elements of the story.
主语 | 谓语 | 状语从句

状语从句 | *when* | he | looked at | the cautionary elements of the story
引导词 | 主语 | 谓语 | 宾语

【参考译文】他在研究了故事中的警示性内容后，发现了真正的大惊喜。

【理解要点】本句的时间状语从句位于主句之后，由从属连词when引导，表示"当……的时候"。

4 | *Once* his phylogenetic analysis had established *that* they were indeed related, | he | used
状语从句（含宾语从句1） | 主语 | 谓语

the same methods | to explore *how* they have developed and altered over time.
宾语 | 状语（含宾语从句2）

状语从句 | *Once* | his phylogenetic analysis | had established | *that* they were indeed related
引导词 | 主语 | 谓语 | 宾语从句1

宾语从句2 | *how* | they | have developed and altered | over time
引导词 | 主语 | 谓语 | 状语

【参考译文】一旦他的演化发展分析法证实它们之间确实相关联，他就用同样的方法来探讨它们是如何随着时间的推移而发展和改变的。

【理解要点】本句的状语从句位于主句前面，从属连词Once表示"一旦"，从句中的宾语为宾语从句，引导词是that，后接"主+系+表"结构的陈述句，related意为"相关的"。而主句中也含有一个宾语从句，在句末的状语中，由how引导，作不定式to explore的宾语。

5 | *When* Bingham and his team set off down the Urubamba in late July, | they | had
状语从句 | 主语 | 谓语

an advantage | over travellers *who* had preceded them.
宾语 | 状语（含定语从句）

状语从句 | *When* | Bingham and his team | set off | down the Urubamba in late July
引导词 | 主语 | 谓语 | 状语

【参考译文】当宾厄姆和他的团队在七月下旬动身沿着乌鲁班巴河下山时，他们比他们之前的旅行者具备一个有利条件。

【理解要点】状语从句中的down为介词，意为"沿着，顺着"。have an advantage over sb.为常用表达，意为"比某人具有优势"。主句的状语中含有一个修饰travellers的定语从句，关系词在从句中作主语，从句为"主+谓+宾"结构。

1. Since soil grows 95% of our food, and sustains human life in other more surprising ways, that is a huge problem. 真

_____

_____

2. Ferrando's story is fascinating because it seems like an indicator of something unexpected. 真

_____

_____

3. In the 60s we didn't stand a chance because people were prepared to give their lives to keep cars in the city. 真

_____

_____

4. Now that lots of books have been digitalised, people can access them from their own computers at home. 真

_____

_____

5. People find these boots useful when travelling as they are not heavy. 真

_____

_____

sustain /səˈsteɪn/ *v.* 维持（生命，生存）

surprising /səˈpraɪzɪŋ/ *adj.* 令人惊讶的，令人吃惊的

fascinating /ˈfæsɪneɪtɪŋ/ *adj.* 极有吸引力的

indicator /ˈɪndɪkeɪtə(r)/ *n.* 标志，迹象

unexpected /ˌʌnɪkˈspektɪd/ *adj.* 出乎意料的，意外的

stand a chance 有机会，有希望

digitalise /ˈdɪdʒɪtəlaɪz/ *v.* （使）数字化

access /ˈækses/ *v.* 取得，获取

boot /buːt/ *n.* 靴子

1 | *Since* soil... surprising ways, | that | is | a huge problem.
状语从句 | 主语 | 系动词 | 表语

状语从句	*Since*	soil	grows	95% of our food,	and	sustains	human life
	引导词	主语	谓语1	宾语1	连词	谓语2	宾语2

in other more surprising ways
状语

【参考译文】由于土壤种植了我们95%的食物，并以其他更令人惊讶的方式维持着人类的生命，因此这是一个巨大的问题。

【理解要点】本句的状语从句的从属连词是Since，表原因，从句中的并列连词and连接了两个并列谓语，主语同是soil。

2 Ferrando's story | is | fascinating | *because* it seems like an indicator of something unexpected.
主语 | 系动词 | 表语 | 状语从句

状语从句	*because*	it	seems	like an indicator of something unexpected
	引导词	主语	系动词	表语

【参考译文】费兰多的故事令人着迷，因为它似乎预示着一些意想不到的事情。

【理解要点】本句的原因状语从句位于主句后，由从属连词because引导，说明主句的原因。

3 In the 60s | we | didn't stand a chance | *because* people... in the city.
时间状语 | 主语 | 谓语 | 状语从句

状语从句	*because*	people	were prepared to give	their lives	to keep cars in the city
	引导词	主语	谓语	宾语	状语

【参考译文】在60年代，我们没有机会，因为人们为了让汽车留在城市里愿意赌上自己的性命。

【理解要点】主句的谓语stand a chance为固定表达，意为"有机会，有希望"。从属连词because引导的原因状语从句，位于主句后，从句中were prepared to do sth.表示"愿意做某事"，to keep cars in the city为目的的状语。

4 *Now that* lots of books have been digitalised, | people | can access | them | from their own
状语从句 | 主语 | 谓语 | 宾语 | 状语

computers at home.

状语从句	*Now that*	lots of books	have been digitalised
	引导词	主语	谓语

【参考译文】由于很多书都被数字化了，人们可以在家里用自己的计算机阅读。

【理解要点】本句中，状语从句由从属连词Now that引导，表示"既然，由于"，从句的谓语为现在完成时的被动语态。

5 People | find | these boots | useful | when travelling | *as* they are not heavy.
主语 | 谓语 | 宾语 | 宾语补语 | 状语 | 状语从句

【参考译文】人们发现这些靴子在旅行时很实用，因为它们不重。

【理解要点】本句出现一个由"从属连词+现在分词"构成的时间状语when travelling，因为travel与主句主语People是主动关系，所以用doing形式。这个状语也可以理解为省略了主语people和be动词的从句，补充完整后为when people are travelling。句末的状语从句由as引导，表原因，they指代these boots，从句为"主+系+表"结构。

Test ⑪

1. If you hear 'can', you will likely activate words like 'candy' and 'candle' as well, at least during the earlier stages of word recognition. 真

_____

_____

2. If a plant finds itself in shade, phytochromes（植物光敏素）are quickly inactivated—enabling it to grow faster to find sunlight again. 真

_____

_____

3. Although some of the steps in the puzzle of how and why play is important have been looked at, there is very little data on its impact on the child's later life. 真

_____

_____

4. While earlier theories of music focused on the way a sound can refer to the real world of images and experiences, Meyer argued that the emotions we find in music come from the unfolding events of the music itself. 真

_____

_____

5. Even if boredom has evolved to help us survive, it can still be toxic. 真

_____

_____

词汇释义

activate /ˈæktɪveɪt/ v. 激活，启动

inactivate /ɪnˈæktɪveɪt/ v. 使不活跃

puzzle /ˈpʌzl/ n. 难题，疑问

refer to 关系到，涉及

evolve /iˈvɒlv/ v. 逐步发展，逐渐演变

recognition /ˌrekəgˈnɪʃn/ n. 识别

enable /ɪˈneɪbl/ v. 使能够

impact /ˈɪmpækt/ n. 作用，影响

unfold /ʌnˈfəʊld/ v. 展开，展现

toxic /ˈtɒksɪk/ adj. 有毒的

1 *If* you hear 'can', | you | will likely activate | words like 'candy' and 'candle' as well,
状语从句 | 主语 | 谓语 | 宾语

at least during the earlier stages of word recognition.
状语

【参考译文】如果你听到can这个音，你可能也会激活像candy、candle这样的词，至少在单词识别的早期阶段是这样。

【理解要点】句首是If引导的条件状语从句，为"主+谓+宾"结构。

2 *If* a plant finds itself in shade, | phytochromes | are quickly inactivated—enabling it to grow
状语从句 | 主语 | 谓语 | 状语

faster to find sunlight again.

【参考译文】如果植物发现自己处于阴暗处，植物光敏素就会迅速失活，植物就能够更快地生长，重新找到阳光。

【理解要点】本句的主句是"主+谓"结构，谓语are inactivated是被动语态，enabling... sunlight again是现在分词短语作状语，表明主句的结果。句首的状语从句是"主+谓+宾+宾补"结构，宾补为介词短语in shade。

3 *Although* some of the steps in the puzzle of *how* and *why* play is important have been looked at,
状语从句（含宾语从句）

there is | very little data | on its impact on the child's later life.
There be 句型 | 主语 | 后置定语

状语从句 | *Although* | some of the steps | in the puzzle of *how* and *why* play is important
| | 引导词 | 主语 | 后置定语

have been looked at,
谓语

【参考译文】对于玩耍如何起作用以及它为何重要这一难题已经有了阶段性的研究，但尽管如此，关于玩耍对儿童未来人生的影响的数据非常少。

【理解要点】Although引导的让步状语从句中，主语中心词为steps，谓语动词have been looked at使用了现在完成时被动态，主语的后置定语中包含了一个how and why引导的宾语从句，作介词of的宾语，说明puzzle的内容。

4 *While* earlier theories... and experiences, | Meyer | argued | *that* the emotions... the music itself.
状语从句（含定语从句1）| 主语 | 谓语 | 宾语从句（含定语从句2）

状语从句 | *While* | earlier theories of music | focused on | the way | a sound can refer to the
| | 引导词 | 主语 | 谓语 | 宾语 | 定语从句1

real world of images and experiences

宾语从句 | *that* | the emotions | we find in music | come from | the unfolding events of the
| | 引导词 | 主语 | 定语从句2 | 谓语 | 宾语

music itself

【参考译文】早期的音乐理论侧重于关注声音如何反映真实世界中的图像和体验，而迈耶认为，我们在音乐中体会到的情感来自音乐本身的展开。

【理解要点】While引导的让步状语从句中，有一个定语从句，修饰the way，定语从句的关系词that被省略，the way在定语从句中作状语。主句的宾语是宾语从句，由that引导，其中也包含一个省略了关系词的定语从句we find in music，先行词是emotions，它在定语从句中作find的宾语。

5 *Even if* boredom has evolved to help us survive, | it | can still be | toxic.
状语从句 | 主语 | 系动词 | 表语

【参考译文】即使厌倦感已经演变成帮助我们生存的东西，它仍可能是有害的。

【理解要点】本句中的让步状语从句由 Even if 引导，该从句是"主+谓"结构，谓语has evolved是现在完成时，to help us survive为结果状语。

1. Any visitors who had not been invited were cleverly prevented from entering the pyramid grounds unless they knew the real entrance. 真

---

2. Just imagine a neonatal (新生儿的) hospital ward coated in a specially mixed cocktail of microbes so that babies get the best start in life. 真

---

3. However, the software was programmed such that it was nearly impossible to achieve 10 consecutive correct answers. 真

---

4. Many decisions in our lives require a good forecast, and AI is almost always better at forecasting than we are. 真

---

5. We think back to a golden age, as if exploration peaked somehow in the 19th century. 真

词汇释义

cleverly /ˈklevəli/ *adv.* 巧妙地

entrance /ˈentrəns/ *n.* 入口

coat /kəʊt/ *v.* 覆盖，在……上涂

microbe /ˈmaɪkrəʊb/ *n.* 微生物

consecutive /kənˈsekjətɪv/ *adj.* 连续的

exploration /ˌekspləˈreɪʃn/ *n.* 探索

pyramid /ˈpɪrəmɪd/ *n.* 金字塔

ward /wɔːd/ *n.* 病房

cocktail /ˈkɒkteɪl/ *n.* 混合物

programme /ˈprəʊɡræm/ *v.* 编写程序

forecast /ˈfɔːkɑːst/ *n./v.* 预测，预料

peak /piːk/ *v.* 达到高峰

1 Any visitors | *who* had not been invited | were cleverly prevented | from entering the pyramid
主语 | 定语从句 | 谓语 | 状语
grounds | *unless* they knew the real entrance.
| 状语从句

【参考译文】任何未被邀请的访客都被巧妙地阻止进入金字塔，除非他们知道真正的入口。

【理解要点】本句中，主句的谓语使用了prevent sb. from doing sth. "阻止某人做某事"这一固定表达的被动态。who had not been invited是定语从句，修饰Any visitors，表示"未被邀请的访客"。句末是unless引导的条件状语从句，为"主+谓+宾"结构。

2 Just imagine | a neonatal hospital ward | coated in a specially mixed cocktail of microbes
谓语 | 宾语 | 后置定语
so that babies get the best start in life.
状语从句

【参考译文】试想一下，新生儿医院的病房涂有一层特别调制的微生物混合物，使得婴儿的生命有一个最好的开始。

【理解要点】主句是祈使句，省略了主语you，句中coated in a specially mixed cocktail of microbes是过去分词短语作定语，修饰a neonatal hospital ward。句末由so that引导的目的状语从句修饰该后置定语，说明病房涂一层特制混合物的目的。

3 However, | the software | was programmed | *such that* it was... correct answers.
副词 | 主语 | 谓语 | 状语从句
状语从句 *such that* | it | was | nearly impossible | to achieve 10 consecutive
引导词 | 形式主语 | 系动词 | 表语 | 主语
correct answers

【参考译文】然而，软件所编写的方式，使得其几乎不可能连续获得10个正确的答案。

【理解要点】主句的谓语was programmed是一般过去时的被动语态。状语从句则由such that引导，是主句导致的结果，从句中含有"it+be+形容词+to do sth."的句型。

4 Many decisions in our lives require a good forecast, | *and* | AI is almost always better
分句1 | 连词 | 分句2（含状语从句）
at forecasting *than* we are.

【参考译文】我们生活中的许多决策都需要准确的预测，而且人工智能几乎总是比我们更善于预测。

【理解要点】本句中，并列连词and连接两个分句，分句1是"主+谓+宾"结构，分句2则是"主+系+表"结构。分句2中的than we are为比较状语从句，从句省略了与主句相同的部分，即good at forecasting。

5 We | think back to | a golden age, | *as if* exploration peaked somehow in the 19th century.
主语 | 谓语 | 宾语 | 状语从句
状语从句 *as if* | exploration | peaked | somehow in the 19th century
引导词 | 主语 | 谓语 | 状语

【参考译文】我们回想起黄金时代，似乎探索就那样在19世纪达到顶峰。

【理解要点】主句的谓语为短语动词think back to，意为"回想，追忆"。从句的谓语peaked为不及物动词，意为"达到顶峰"。

Test ⑬

1. But there were also more complex reasons. 真

---

2. There is little likelihood of the city having another bike-sharing scheme. 真

---

3. Not only can you upset your schedule, but also other people's too. 真

---

4. Not only do customers keep giving you their custom, but they also tell their friends about you. 真

---

5. Neither did his analysis support the theory that the central section of a story is the most conserved part. 真

词汇释义

complex /ˈkɒmpleks/ *adj.* 复杂的

scheme /skiːm/ *n.* 计划，方案

schedule /ˈskedʒuːl/ *n.* 日程安排

section /ˈsekʃn/ *n.* 部分，段，节

likelihood /ˈlaɪklihʊd/ *n.* 可能，可能性

upset /ʌpˈset/ *v.* 打乱，搅乱

custom /ˈkʌstəm/ *n.* 惠顾，光顾

conserve /kənˈsɜːv/ *v.* 保护，保存

1 | But | there were | also | more complex reasons.
连词 | There be 句型 | 状语 | 主语

【参考译文】但还有更复杂的原因。

【理解要点】本句是There be句型，属于完全倒装句的一种，句子的谓语是were，主语是more complex reasons。

2 | There is | little likelihood | of the city having another bike-sharing scheme.
There be 句型 | 主语 | 后置定语

【参考译文】这座城市几乎不可能有另一个自行车共享计划。

【理解要点】本句是There be句型，属于完全倒装句的一种，句子的谓语是is，主语中心词是likelihood，介词of后的内容为主语的后置定语。介词of的宾语the city having another bike-sharing scheme是一个动名词复合结构，动名词having前的名词the city为其逻辑主语。

3 | Not only | can | you | upset | your schedule, | but also | other people's | too.
连词 | 情态动词 | 主语 | 谓语 | 宾语1 | 连词 | 宾语2 | 状语

【参考译文】你不仅会打乱你的日程，还会打乱别人的日程。

【理解要点】含有否定意义的短语Not only置于句首，因此需要把情态动词can提前至主语前，形成部分倒装。句子的两个并列宾语由not only... but also连接，宾语2省略了重复的schedule。调整为正常语序的完整句子应为"You can upset not only your schedule, but also other people's schedule too."。

4 | *Not only* | do customers keep giving you their custom, | *but* | they also tell their friends about you.
连词 | 分句1 | 连词 | 分句2

【参考译文】客户不仅自己不断光顾你，而且还会让他们的朋友来光顾。

【理解要点】由于Not only置于句首，分句1为部分倒装结构，助动词do提前至主语customers前，谓语使用了keep doing sth."保持做某事"的表达。句子的正常语序为"Customers not only keep giving you their custom but also tell their friends about you."。

5 | Neither | did | his analysis | support | the theory | *that* the central section of a story is
副词 | 助动词 | 主语 | 谓语 | 宾语 | 同位语从句

the most conserved part.

同位语从句 *that* | the central section of a story | is | the most conserved part
引导词 | 主语 | 系动词 | 表语

【参考译文】他的分析也不支持故事的中心部分保存得最好这一理论。

【理解要点】含有否定意义的副词Neither位于句首，因此助动词did提前至主语前，形成部分倒装结构。that引导的是同位语从句，解释说明theory的内容。

Test 14

1. Also unclear is what has gone wrong. 真

_____

_____

2. Contentedly in the human gut sits microbes.

_____

_____

3. Little resemblance did the abstract sculptures bear to the human form, and the pages of his sketchbooks from this period show this idea. 真

_____

_____

4. Not until 1966 did serious efforts to revive the women's game begin. 真

_____

_____

5. Not until the early twentieth century did mathematics and physics become part of meteorology (气象学). 真

_____

_____

词汇释义

unclear /ˌʌnˈklɪə(r)/ *adj.* 不清楚的，不确定的

contentedly /kənˈtentɪdli/ *adv.* 满足地，满意地

resemblance /rɪˈzembləns/ *n.* 相似，相像

sculpture /ˈskʌlptʃə(r)/ *n.* 雕塑，雕像

sketchbook /ˈsketʃbʊk/ *n.* 素描簿，速写册，写生本

mathematics /ˌmæθəˈmætɪks/ *n.* 数学

go wrong 出现问题，出错

gut /gʌt/ *n.* 肠胃，肠道

abstract /ˈæbstrækt/ *adj.* 抽象的

bear /beə(r)/ *v.* 带有

revive /rɪˈvaɪv/ *v.* 重新使用，使重新流行

1 Also unclear　　is　　***what*** has gone wrong.
　　表语　　　系动词　　　　主语从句

【参考译文】也不清楚是什么出了问题。

【理解要点】本句把形容词unclear提前至句首，主语放在系动词is后，构成了"表＋系＋主"的完全倒装结构。本句的正常语序是"What has gone wrong is also unclear."。

2 Contentedly in the human gut　　sits　　microbes.
　　　　状语　　　　　　　谓语　　　主语

【参考译文】在人类的肠道里心满意足地坐着微生物。

【理解要点】本句把介词短语前置形成了倒装句，句子的正常语序为"Microbes sits contentedly in the human gut."。

3 Little resemblance did the abstract sculptures bear to the human form,　　***and***　　the pages of
　　　　　　　　　　分句1　　　　　　　　　　　　　　　　　连词　　　分句2

his sketchbooks from this period show this idea.

　分句1　Little resemblance　　did　　the abstract sculptures　　bear　　to the human form
　　　　　　宾语　　　　　助动词　　　　主语　　　　　谓语　　　后置定语
　分句2　the pages　　of his sketchbooks from this period　　show　　this idea
　　　　　主语　　　　　　后置定语　　　　　　　　　谓语　　宾语

【参考译文】这些抽象雕塑与人类形态相去甚远，而他在这一时期的速写本展示了这一思想。

【理解要点】分句1中，否定词Little置于句首，句子要部分倒装，故did提前至主语前。该分句的正常语序应为the abstract sculptures bore little resemblance to the human form。bear little resemblance to sth.为常见表达，意为"与某物几乎没有相似之处"。

4 Not until 1966　　did　　serious efforts to revive the women's game　　begin.
　　　状语　　　助动词　　　　　　　　主语　　　　　　　　　谓语

【参考译文】直到1966年，人们才开始认真努力恢复女子比赛。

【理解要点】Not until置于句首时，句子要部分倒装，因此助动词did提前至主语前。句子的正常语序应为"Serious efforts to revive the women's game didn't begin until 1966."。本句的主语中心词为efforts，其后的不定式短语为其后置定语，说明努力做什么。

5 Not until the early twentieth century　　did　　mathematics and physics　　become
　　　　　　状语　　　　　　　　　助动词　　　　主语　　　　系动词

part of meteorology.
　表语

【参考译文】直到二十世纪初，数学和物理学才成为气象学的一部分。

【理解要点】本句同样是因为Not until引导的时间状语位于句首而引起的部分倒装，句子的正常语序应为"Mathematics and physics didn't become part of meteorology until the early twentieth century."。

Test ⑮

1. It was in 1944 that Harlow, a town near London, offered Moore a commission for a sculpture depicting a family. 真

---

2. It is only in recent years that the end of the virtual monopoly of cork as the material for bottle stoppers have been seen. 真

---

3. It was Moore who held an exhibition at the Leicester Galleries in London in 1931. 真

---

4. It is the zoos that play a key role in research. 真

---

5. It is those objects that are of interest to archaeologists.

词汇释义

commission /kəˈmɪʃn/ *n.* 制作委托，创作委托

depict /dɪˈpɪkt/ *v.* 描绘，描画

monopoly /məˈnɒpəli/ *n.* 垄断

exhibition /ˌeksɪˈbɪʃn/ *n.* 展览

archaeologist /ˌɑːkiˈɒlədʒɪst/ *n.* 考古学家

sculpture /ˈskʌlptʃə(r)/ *n.* 雕像，雕塑

virtual /ˈvɜːtʃuəl/ *adj.* 事实上的，很接近的

stopper /ˈstɒpə(r)/ *n.* 瓶塞

research /rɪˈsɜːtʃ/ *n.* 研究，调查

1 | *It was* | in 1944 | *that* | Harlow, | a town near London, | offered | Moore

状语   主语   同位语   谓语   间接宾语

a commission | for a sculpture depicting a family.

直接宾语   后置定语

【参考译文】是在1944年,伦敦附近的一个小镇哈洛委托摩尔做一个家庭雕像。

【理解要点】本句强调时间状语in 1944。主语Harlow后的名词短语a town near London为其同位语,动词offered后接双宾语,直接宾语为a commission,介词短语for a sculpture是commission的后置定语,而sculpture本身也带有一个后置定语,即现在分词短语depicting a family。

2 | *It is* | only in recent years | *that* | the end of the virtual monopoly of cork as the material for

状语   主语

bottle stoppers | have been seen.

谓语

【参考译文】直到最近几年,几乎只用软木制作瓶塞的状况才被打破。

【理解要点】本句强调时间状语only in recent years。句子的主语很长,中心词是the end,句子主干是the end have been seen。

3 | *It was* | Moore | *who* | held | an exhibition | at the Leicester Galleries in London in 1931.

主语   谓语   宾语   状语

【参考译文】1931年,是摩尔在伦敦莱斯特画廊举办了一场展览。

【理解要点】本句强调的成分是主语Moore,指人,所以引导词用who。

4 | *It is* | the zoos | *that* | play a key role | in research.

主语   谓语   状语

【参考译文】动物园在研究中起着关键作用。

【理解要点】本句强调的是主语the zoos,谓语使用了固定表达play a key role in sth.表示"在某方面起关键作用"。

5 | *It is* | those objects | *that* | are | of interest to archaeologists.

主语   系动词   表语

【参考译文】考古学家感兴趣的是那些物品。

【理解要点】本句强调的是主语those objects。be of interest to sb.表示"某人有兴趣"。

1. If we didn't have physical pain, bad things would happen to us. 真

---

2. If they had known of its existence so close to Cusco（库斯科）, they would certainly have come in search of gold. 真

---

3. If a significant proportion of the population had chosen to use shared automated vehicles, mobility demand might have been met by far fewer vehicles.

---

4. If you became distracted by the conversation that is going on nearby, you might ultimately miss the mark from a service perspective. 真

---

5. If we are to survive climate change, we must adopt policies that let peasants diversify the plant and animal species. 真

---

certainly /ˈsɜ:tnli/ *adv.* 无疑，确定

significant /sɪgˈnɪfɪkənt/ *adj.* 数量相当的

automated /ˈɔ:təmeɪtɪd/ *adj.* 自动化的

distracted /dɪˈstræktɪd/ *adj.* 注意力分散的

miss the mark 达不到目的，失败

survive /səˈvaɪv/ *v.* 从（困难）中挺过来

diversify /daɪˈvɜ:sɪfaɪ/ *v.* （使）多样化

in search of 寻找

proportion /prəˈpɔ:ʃn/ *n.* 部分，份额

mobility /məʊˈbɪləti/ *n.* 出行

ultimately /ˈʌltɪmətli/ *adv.* 最后，最终

perspective /pəˈspektɪv/ *n.* 角度

peasant /ˈpeznt/ *n.* 农民

1 **If** we didn't have physical pain,   bad things   would happen to   us.
状语从句   主语   谓语   宾语

【参考译文】如果我们的身体感受不到疼痛，那么不好的事情就会发生在我们身上。

【理解要点】条件状语从句的谓语是一般过去时的否定式 didn't have，主句的谓语是 would do 的形式，所以此句的虚拟语气是对现在情况的假设，是非真实的条件，事实上我们的确能感觉到痛。

2 **If** they had known of its existence so close to Cusco,   they   would certainly have come
状语从句   主语   谓语
in search of gold.
状语

状语从句   **If**   they   had known of   its existence   so close to Cusco
           引导词   主语   谓语   宾语   后置定语

【参考译文】如果他们知道它的存在离库斯科这么近，他们肯定会来寻找黄金。

【理解要点】条件状语从句的谓语是 had known of，主句的谓语 would have come，由此判断 If 引导的为非真实条件句，句子是对过去情况的假设。

3 **If** a significant proportion of the population had chosen to use shared automated vehicles,
状语从句
mobility demand   might have been met   by far fewer vehicles.
   主语   谓语   状语

状语从句   **If**   a significant proportion of the population   had chosen to use   shared
          引导词   主语   谓语   宾语
automated vehicles

【参考译文】如果很大一部分人选择使用共享的自动驾驶车辆，那么或许只需更少的车辆就能满足出行需求。

【理解要点】条件状语从句的谓语是 had done 的形式，主句的谓语是 might have done 的形式，因此此句的虚拟语气是对过去情况的假设。

4 **If** you became distracted by the conversation *that* is going on nearby,   you
状语从句（含定语从句）   主语
might ultimately miss   the mark   from a service perspective.
    谓语   宾语   状语

状语从句   **If**   you   became   distracted   by the conversation   *that* is going on nearby
          引导词   主语   系动词   表语   状语   定语从句

【参考译文】如果你被附近的谈话分心，从服务的角度看，你最终可能会出错。

【理解要点】条件状语从句的谓语是过去式 became，主句的谓语是 might do 的形式，因此此句的虚拟语气是对现在情况的假设。状语从句中还包含一个修饰 conversation 的定语从句，关系词 that 在定语从句中作主语。

5 **If** we are to survive climate change,   we   must adopt   policies   *that* let peasants
状语从句   主语   谓语   宾语   定语从句
diversify the plant and animal species.

【参考译文】如果我们要顺利渡过气候变化危机，我们必须采取让农民种植多样化作物和养殖多样化牲畜的政策。

【理解要点】本句的条件状语从句所用时态为一般将来时（be to do），主句时态为一般现在时，所以 if 引导的为真实条件句。that 引导的定语从句修饰 policies，关系词在从句中作主语，从句为"主＋谓＋宾＋宾补"结构。

1. The reviewer suggests that happiness should not be the main goal of humans. 真

2. They would rather they were tested over a period of time. 真

3. It is essential that we find the right builder for the job.

4. The US government's Food and Drug Administration demanded that the meat industry should abandon practices associated with the risk of the disease spreading.

5. It's necessary that we should wait a further 15 or 20 years. 真

词汇释义

reviewer /rɪˈvjuːə(r)/ *n.* 评论家

essential /ɪˈsenʃl/ *adj.* 必需的

administration /ədˌmɪnɪˈstreɪʃn/ *n.* 管理部门，行政部门

practice /ˈpræktɪs/ *n.* 做法

further /ˈfɜːðə(r)/ *adj.* 更多的，附加的

happiness /ˈhæpinəs/ *n.* 幸福

builder /ˈbɪldə(r)/ *n.* 建筑商，建造者

abandon /əˈbændən/ *v.* 舍弃，停止

be associated with 与……有关

1 | The reviewer | suggests | *that* happiness should not be the main goal of humans.
主语 | 谓语 | 宾语从句

【参考译文】评论家提出幸福不应该是人类的主要目标。

【理解要点】本句主句的谓语动词是suggests，因此宾语从句中使用了"should+动词原形"的虚拟语气。宾语从句为"主+系+表"结构。

2 | They | would rather | they were tested over a period of time.
主语 | 谓语 | 宾语从句

【参考译文】他们宁愿经过一段时间才接受测试。

【理解要点】would rather后的宾语从句需要用虚拟语气，此处宾语从句的谓语were tested是一般过去时的被动语态，表示与现在事实相反的愿望。

3 | It | is | essential | *that* we find the right builder for the job.
形式主语 | 系动词 | 表语 | 主语从句

【参考译文】我们必须为这项工作找到合适的建筑商。

【理解要点】主句的表语为essential"必需的"，因此主语从句需要用虚拟语气。此处，主语从句的谓语省略了情态动词should。

4 | The US government's Food and Drug Administration | demanded | *that* the meat industry
主语 | 谓语 | 宾语从句

should abandon practices associated with the risk of the disease spreading.

宾语从句 *that* | the meat industry | should abandon | practices | associated with the risk of
引导词 | 主语 | 谓语 | 宾语 | 后置定语

the disease spreading

【参考译文】美国政府的食品和药物管理局要求肉类行业放弃存在疾病传播风险的做法。

【理解要点】主句的谓语动词demanded意为"要求"，因此宾语从句要用虚拟语气"should+动词原形"。从句中，associated with...是过去分词短语作定语，修饰practices，意指"与……相关的做法"。

5 | It | 's | necessary | *that* we should wait a further 15 or 20 years.
形式主语 | 系动词 | 表语 | 主语从句

主语从句 *that* | we | should wait | a further 15 or 20 years
引导词 | 主语 | 谓语 | 状语

【参考译文】我们有必要再等15年或20年。

【理解要点】主句的表语为necessary"必要的"，因此主语从句需要用虚拟语气"should+动词原形"。

1. They then asked the subjects to bring in their playlist of favourite songs—virtually every genre was represented, from techno to tango—and played them the music. 真

_____

_____

2. Music triggers the production of dopamine（多巴胺）—a chemical with a key role in setting people's moods—by the neurons（神经元）. 真

_____

_____

3. The name of the 'Great Pacific Garbage Patch'—a collection of marine debris in the northern Pacific Ocean—might conjure up a vast, floating trash island. 真

_____

_____

4. In all sorts of professions—whether artist, marine biologist or astronomer—borders of the unknown are being tested each day. 真

_____

_____

5. Automation—or 'embodied artificial intelligence'—is one aspect of the disruptive effects of technology on the labour market. 真

_____

_____

词汇释义

subject /ˈsʌbdʒɪkt/ *n.* 实验对象

genre /ˈʒɒnrə/ *n.* （音乐的）类型

trigger /ˈtrɪɡə(r)/ *v.* 触发，引起

debris /ˈdebriː/ *n.* 垃圾，废弃物

vast /vɑːst/ *adj.* 巨大的，辽阔的

automation /ˌɔːtəˈmeɪʃn/ *n.* 自动化

disruptive /dɪsˈrʌptɪv/ *adj.* 扰乱性的、破坏性的

virtually /ˈvɜːtʃuəli/ *adv.* 实际上，几乎

represent /ˌreprɪˈzent/ *v.* 代表

marine /məˈriːn/ *adj.* 海的，海洋的

conjure up 使在脑海中出现

profession /prəˈfeʃn/ *n.* 职业，行业

embody /ɪmˈbɒdi/ *v.* 使实体化

1 | They | then asked | the subjects | to bring in their playlist of favourite songs—virtually
主语 | 谓语1 | 宾语1 | 宾语补语 | **插入成分**

every genre was represented, from techno to tango—*and* | played | them | the music.
连词 | 谓语2 | 间接宾语 | 直接宾语

插入成分 virtually | every genre | was represented, | from techno to tango
状语 | 主语 | 谓语 | 状语

【参考译文】然后，他们要求受访对象展示他们最喜欢的歌曲的播放列表——几乎涵盖了每种类型，从电子舞曲到探戈——并向受访对象播放这些音乐。

【理解要点】本句中，连词and连接了两个并列谓语asked以及played。破折号之间的插入成分是一个完整的句子，对playlist进行补充说明。

2 | Music | triggers | the production of dopamine—a chemical with a key role in setting
主语 | 谓语 | 宾语 | 插入成分（同位语）

people's moods—by the neurons.
状语

【参考译文】音乐刺激神经元产生多巴胺，多巴胺是一种在调节人们情绪方面起关键作用的化学物质。

【理解要点】本句主干是Music triggers the production of dopamine by the neurons，插入成分将句子的主谓宾和状语分隔开，插入成分为dopamine的同位语，对其做解释说明。

3 | The name of the 'Great Pacific Garbage Patch'—a collection of marine debris in the
主语 | 插入成分（同位语）

northern Pacific Ocean—might conjure up | a vast, floating trash island.
谓语 | 宾语

【参考译文】"大太平洋垃圾区"——指北太平洋聚集的海洋垃圾——这样的名字可能会让人联想到一个巨大的漂浮垃圾岛。

【理解要点】本句的主干是The name of... might conjure up a... trash island。名词短语a collection of marine debris in the northern Pacific Ocean为Great Pacific Garbage Patch的同位语，将句子的主语和谓语分隔开。

4 | In all sorts of professions—whether artist, marine biologist or astronomer—borders of the
状语 | 插入成分 | 主语

unknown | are being tested | each day.
谓语 | 状语

【参考译文】各行各业的人，无论是艺术家、海洋生物学家还是天文学家，每天都在探索未知的边界。

【理解要点】本句的主干是borders of... are being tested，使用了现在进行时的被动语态。插入成分对all sorts of professions进行补充说明，将句首的状语In all sorts of professions与句子其他成分分隔开。

5 | Automation—or 'embodied artificial intelligence'— | is | one aspect of the disruptive
主语 | 插入成分 | 系动词 | 表语

effects of technology | on the labour market.
后置定语

【参考译文】自动化——亦称为"实体化人工智能"——是技术对劳动力市场产生破坏性影响的一个体现。

【理解要点】插入成分or 'embodied artificial intelligence'与主语Automation可视为并列关系，表示其别称。插入成分将主语和系动词分隔开。句末的on the labour market为effects的后置定语。

Test ⑲

1. Disorder, much like order, also seems to have diminishing utility. 真

_____

_____

2. Numerous studies, after all, have demonstrated that dopamine neurons quickly adapt to predictable rewards. 真

_____

_____

3. After a number of serious failures of governance, companies in Britain, as well as elsewhere, should consider radical changes to their directors' roles. 真

_____

_____

4. Nothing seemed to fit, until 2006, when an animal bone, dating from around 598 AD, was found in northern England. 真

_____

_____

5. Mediterranean shipbuilders shifted to another shipbuilding method, still in use today, which consisted of building the frame first and then proceeding with the hull（船体）and the other components of the ship. 真

_____

_____

词汇释义

disorder /dɪsˈɔːdə(r)/ *n.* 无秩序

utility /juːˈtɪləti/ *n.* 效用，实用

demonstrate /ˈdemənstreɪt/ *v.* 证明，证实

governance /ˈɡʌvənəns/ *n.* 统治，管理

radical /ˈrædɪkl/ *adj.* 根本的，彻底的

Mediterranean /ˌmedɪtəˈreɪniən/ *adj.* 地中海的

shift /ʃɪft/ *v.* 转向，变更

component /kəmˈpəʊnənt/ *n.* 部件

diminish /dɪˈmɪnɪʃ/ *v.* 减弱，降低

numerous /ˈnjuːmərəs/ *adj.* 很多的，众多的

predictable /prɪˈdɪktəbl/ *adj.* 可预测的，可预见的

elsewhere /ˌelsˈweə(r)/ *adv.* 在别处

fit /fɪt/ *v.* 匹配，符合

shipbuilder /ˈʃɪpbɪldə(r)/ *n.* 造船工人，造船厂

proceed /prəˈsiːd/ *v.* 继续进行，继续做

1 | Disorder, | much like order, | also seems to have | diminishing utility.
主语 | 插入成分（状语） | 谓语 | 宾语

【参考译文】去秩序，和有秩序一样，其效用似乎也会递减。

【理解要点】句中成对的逗号间的much like order是本句的插入成分，作为句子的状语，将主语和谓语分隔开。

2 | Numerous studies, | after all, | have demonstrated | *that* dopamine neurons quickly
主语 | 插入成分（状语） | 谓语 | 宾语从句
adapt to predictable rewards.

宾语从句 | *that* | dopamine neurons | quickly adapt to | predictable rewards
引导词 | 主语 | 谓语 | 宾语

【参考译文】毕竟，大量的研究表明，多巴胺神经元会迅速适应可预测的奖励。

【理解要点】本句的插入成分是成对逗号间的状语after all，插入成分将主语和谓语分隔，本句主干是Numerous studies have demonstrated that...，而that引导的是一个宾语从句。

3 | After a number of serious failures of governance, | companies in Britain, | as well as elsewhere,
状语 | 主语 | 插入成分（状语）
should consider | radical changes to their directors' roles.
谓语 | 宾语

【参考译文】在经过一系列严重失败的管理之后，英国和其他地方的公司都应该考虑彻底改变董事的角色。

【理解要点】本句的插入成分as well as elsewhere是状语，对前文的地点状语in Britain进行补充，表示除了英国的公司，其他地方的公司也应该考虑改变管理方式。此插入成分将主语和谓语分隔开。

4 | Nothing | seemed to fit, | until 2006, | *when* an animal bone, dating from around 598 AD,
主语 | 谓语 | 状语 | 定语从句
was found in northern England.

定语从句 | 2006 | *when* | an animal bone, | dating from around 598 AD, | was found
先行词 | 关系词 | 主语 | 插入成分（后置定语） | 谓语
in northern England
状语

【参考译文】似乎没有东西能与之匹配，直到2006年，在英格兰北部发现了一块追溯到公元598年左右的动物骨头。

【理解要点】本句中的until 2006虽然前后有逗号，但严格来说并不算插入成分，因为其后when引导的是修饰2006的定语从句，而不是修饰主句谓语的状语从句。定语从句中，现在分词短语dating from around 598 AD为an animal bone的后置定语，将它和谓语was found分隔开。

5 | Mediterranean shipbuilders | shifted to | another shipbuilding method, | still in use today,
主语 | 谓语 | 宾语 | 插入成分（定语）
which consisted of... of the ship.
定语从句

定语从句 | another shipbuilding method | *which* | consisted of | building the frame first
先行词 | 关系词 | 谓语 | 宾语
and then proceeding with the hull and the other components of the ship

【参考译文】地中海地区的造船者转而采用另一种造船方法，这种方法至今仍在使用，就是先建造框架，然后再进行船体和其他部件的建造。

【理解要点】本句中，插入成分still in use today为another shipbuilding method的定语，其后which引导的定语从句修饰的先行词也是another shipbuilding method。定语从句中，宾语是两个并列的动名词短语building... first和proceeding... ship。

1. The very fact that species have been saved or reintroduced proves the value of such initiatives. 真

_____

_____

2. Sadly, his vision of the site as both the beginning and end of the Inca civilisation, while a magnificent one, is inaccurate 真

_____

_____

3. As a result, the constant juggling of two languages creates a need to control how much a person accesses a language at any given time. 真

_____

_____

4. Cash transfers to poor families do not necessarily translate into increased food security, as these programmes do not always strengthen food production or raise incomes. 真

_____

_____

5. Sophia Murphy, senior advisor to the Institute for Agriculture and Trade Policy, suggested that the procurement and holding of stocks by governments can also help mitigate wild swings in food prices by alleviating uncertainties about market supply. 真

_____

_____

_____

词汇释义

reintroduce /ˌriːɪntrəˈdjuːs/ *v.* 将……放归自然栖息地

vision /ˈvɪʒn/ *n.* 构想，设想

inaccurate /ɪnˈækjərət/ *adj.* 不准确的

access /ˈækses/ *v.* 使用

translate into 导致，造成

advisor /ədˈvaɪzə(r)/ *n.* 顾问

stock /stɒk/ *n.* 储备物

swing /swɪŋ/ *n.* 摆动

initiative /ɪˈnɪʃətɪv/ *n.* 计划，措施

magnificent /mægˈnɪfɪsnt/ *adj.* 令人印象深刻的

juggling /ˈdʒʌɡlɪŋ/ *n.* 同时兼顾几件事情

transfer /trænsˈfɜː(r)/ *n.* （财产的）转让

strengthen /ˈstreŋθn/ *v.* 增强，改善

procurement /prəˈkjʊəmənt/ *n.* 购买

mitigate /ˈmɪtɪɡeɪt/ *v.* 减轻，缓和

alleviate /əˈliːvieɪt/ *v.* 减轻，缓解

1 The very fact   *that* species have been saved or reintroduced   proves
    主语   同位语从句   谓语

the value of such initiatives.
    宾语

【参考译文】物种得到拯救或被放生，这一事实证明了这些举措的价值。

【理解要点】本句中的 very 为形容词，意为"正是那一个的"，用于强调名词 fact。主语 The very fact 后接一个 that 引导的同位语从句，补充说明 fact 的内容。该从句为"主 + 谓"结构，用 or 连接两个被动态的并列谓语。

2 Sadly,   his vision   of the site as both the beginning and end of the Inca civilisation,
状语   主语   后置定语

while a magnificent one,   is   inaccurate.
   插入语   系动词   表语

【参考译文】不幸的是，尽管他把这座遗址看作是印加文明兴起与终结之地的设想很了不起，然而这是不准确的。

【理解要点】本句主语很长，其结构为 vision of sth. as，表示"把某物看作……"。while a magnificent one 是由连词 while 引导的插入语，作 his vision 的同位语，将主语与系动词分隔开。while 表示让步，意为"尽管"，这个插入语可以还原为一个让步状语从句 while it is a magnificent one，代词 one 指代 vision。

3 As a result,   the constant juggling of two languages   creates   a need   to control *how*
状语   主语   谓语   宾语   后置定语

much a person accesses a language at any given time.

【参考译文】结果是，不停在两种语言之间切换使得人们需要控制在任意特定时间使用其中一种语言的程度。

【理解要点】句末的不定式 to control... 为 need 的后置定语，说明是什么需求。to control 的宾语由从句充当，该从句由 how much 引导，为"主 + 谓 + 宾"结构。

4 Cash transfers to poor families   do not necessarily translate into   increased food security,
       主语   谓语   宾语

as these programmes do not always strengthen food production or raise incomes.
                     状语从句

状语从句	*as*	these programmes	do not always strengthen	food production	or
	引导词	主语	谓语1	宾语1	连词
	raise	incomes			
	谓语2	宾语2			

【参考译文】给贫困家庭打款并不必然能增加粮食安全性，因为这些项目并不总能提高粮食产量或提高收入。

【理解要点】主句的宾语中的 increased 为形容词，意为"增加的"，修饰 food security。as 引导的是原因状语从句。

5 Sophia Murphy, senior advisor to the Institute for Agriculture and Trade Policy, suggested
主语   同位语   谓语

that the procurement and holding of stocks by governments can also help mitigate wild swings in
food prices by alleviating uncertainties about market supply.
　　　　宾语从句

宾语从句 *that*　the procurement and holding of stocks by governments　can also help
　　　　引导词　　　　　　　　　主语　　　　　　　　　　　　　　谓语
mitigate wild swings in food prices　　by alleviating uncertainties about market supply.
　　　宾语　　　　　　　　　　　　　　　　状语

【参考译文】农业与贸易政策研究院的高级顾问索菲娅·墨菲建议,政府通过购买和持有(粮食)储备能减轻市场供应的不确定性,从而也能帮助缓解粮食价格的剧烈波动。

【理解要点】宾语从句中,谓语can help的宾语是省略了to的不定式mitigate...,而该不定式也带有宾语,为swings,其后的in food prices是后置定语,说明是什么的波动。

练习参考答案

第1章 英语语法基本概念

第1节 单词、短语、分句与句子

Exercise 1

1. The <u>spice</u> then <u>travelled</u> from that <u>great</u> trading city to markets all around Europe.
   　　　 n. 香料 　　 ***v.*** 传播 　　 ***adj.*** 伟大的
   【译文】香料随后从这个伟大的贸易城市传到了欧洲各地的市场。

2. Before Europeans arrived <u>on</u> the island, the <u>state</u> <u>had</u> <u>organised</u> the cultivation of cinnamon.
   　　　　　　　　　　　　 prep. 在(某地)　 ***n.*** 国家 　　 ***v.*** 组织
   【译文】在欧洲人到达该岛之前，该国已经在组织肉桂的种植。

3. The <u>original</u> idea for <u>an</u> urban bike-sharing scheme dates back <u>to</u> a summer's day in Amsterdam
   　　 adj. 最初的 　　 ***art.*** 一个　　　　　　　　　　 ***prep.*** 到
   in 1965.
   【译文】城市自行车共享计划的最初想法要追溯到1965年阿姆斯特丹的某个夏日。

4. <u>However</u>, Tehrani found no <u>significant</u> difference in the rate <u>of</u> evolution of incidents compared
   　 adv. 然而 　　　　　 ***adj.*** 重要的, 显著的 　　　　 ***prep.*** ……的
   with that of characters.
   【译文】然而, Tehrani发现, 与人物角色相比, 事件的演变率没有显著差异。

5. <u>One</u> way to <u>answer</u> the question is to look at the music <u>and</u> not the neurons.
   　 num. 一个 　 ***v.*** 回答 　　　　　　　　　　　　　 ***conj.*** 而
   【译文】回答这个问题的一种方法是关注音乐, 而不是神经元。

Exercise 2

1. the same health concerns——名词短语; who lives in a different geographical region——从属分句
   【译文】你不会和生活在不同地理区域的人有同样的健康问题。
   【解析】该从属分句的主语为who, 谓语为lives, 但由从属连词who开头, 语义不完整。

2. Bilingual people often excel at tasks such as this——独立分句
   【译文】双语者通常擅长这类任务, 这类任务会用到忽略矛盾的知觉信息的能力。
   【解析】该独立分句的主语为Bilingual people, 谓语为excel, 语义完整。

3. When people experience art——从属分句; might have been thinking——动词短语
   【译文】人们体验艺术时, 想知道艺术家在想什么。
   【解析】该从属分句的主语为people, 谓语为experience, 但由从属连词When开头, 语义不完整。

4. ecosystems without large predators——名词短语; in completely different ways——介词短语
   【译文】其中一个发现是, 没有大型捕食性动物的生态系统以完全不同的方式运行。

5. The prominent historian would say exploration was a thing of the past.——独立分句
   【译文】著名的历史学家会说探索是过去的事了。
   【解析】该独立分句的主语为The prominent historian, 谓语为would say。这个句子虽然包含了一个省略 that的从属分句exploration was a thing of the past, 但作为一个整体表达了完整的意思, 所以整个句子是 一个独立分句。

1. <u>Happiness</u>　　　<u>is</u>　　　　the ultimate goal.
　　主语　　　　系动词(谓语)

【译文】幸福是终极目标。

【解析】本句只有一个主谓结构,为简单句。

2. If　　<u>we</u>　　<u>didn't have</u>　　physical pain,　　<u>bad things</u>　　<u>would happen</u>　　to us.
　　　　主语1　　　谓语1　　　　　　　　　　　　　主语2　　　　　谓语2

【译文】如果我们的身体感受不到疼痛,那么不好的事情就会发生在我们身上。

【解析】本句包含If引导的条件状语从句,为复合句。

3. <u>We</u>　　<u>can predict</u>　　some of the notes,　　but　　<u>we</u>　　<u>can't predict</u>　　them all.
　主语1　　　谓语1　　　　　　　　　　　　　　　　　主语2　　谓语2

【译文】我们可以预测其中一些音符,但不能预测所有音符。

【解析】两个分句均是主谓结构完整的简单句,且由并列连词连接,故本句为并列句。

4. <u>The ship's next captain</u>　　<u>was</u>　　　an excellent navigator,　　<u>who</u>　　<u>got the best out of</u>
　　　　主语1　　　　　　　系动词(谓语1)　　　　　　　　　　　　主语2　　　　谓语2

both his ship and his crew.

【译文】这条船的下一任船长是一位出色的航海家,他充分发挥了船和船员的能力。

【解析】本句包含who引导的定语从句,为复合句。

5. <u>Music</u>　　<u>triggers</u>　　the production of dopamine.
　主语　　　谓语

【译文】音乐刺激多巴胺的产生。

【解析】本句只有一个主谓结构,为简单句。

第2章　基础句法精讲精练 240 句

第1节　简单句及五种基本句型

Exercise 1

1. <u>Several disasters</u>　　<u>have happened.</u>
　　主语　　　　　　　谓语

【译文】已经发生几起灾难了。

2. <u>The cleanup devices</u>　　closer to shore　　<u>would... reduce</u>　　<u>pollution</u>　　over the long term.
　　　　主语　　　　　　　　　　　　　　　　谓语　　　　　宾语

【译文】长期来看,离海岸更近的清洁设备将更有效地减少污染。

3. <u>Buying cheap and selling dear</u>　　<u>can give</u>　　<u>the collector</u>　　<u>a sense of triumph.</u>
　　　　　主语　　　　　　　　　　　　谓语　　　间接宾语　　　　直接宾语

【译文】低买高卖能给收藏者带来成就感。

4. <u>Those designs</u>　　<u>appear</u>　　<u>counter-intuitive.</u>
　　主语　　　　系动词　　　表语

【译文】那些设计似乎是反直觉的。

5. <u>Being bored</u>   <u>makes</u>   <u>us</u>   <u>more creative</u>.

    主语   谓语   宾语   宾语补语

【译文】无聊的状态让我们更有创造性。

Exercise 2

1. <u>New Zealand</u>   **is**   <u>a small country of four million inhabitants</u>.

    主语   系动词(谓语)   表语

【译文】新西兰是一个拥有400万居民的小国。

2. <u>Over two millennia ago,</u>   <u>the Greek philosopher Plato</u>   **extolled**   <u>its virtues</u>

       状语   主语   谓语   宾语

<u>as a means of developing skills for adult life</u>.

          宾语补语

【译文】两千多年前,希腊哲学家柏拉图称赞它的优点在于它是培养成人生活技能的一种方法。

3. <u>Rochman and her colleagues</u>   **examined**   <u>more than a hundred papers</u>

       主语   谓语   宾语

<u>on the impacts of marine debris</u>.

      papers的后置定语

【译文】罗克曼和她的同事研究了100多篇关于海洋废弃物影响的论文。

4. <u>Our blaming of businesses</u>   <u>also</u>   **ignores**   <u>the ultimate responsibility</u>

      主语   状语   谓语   宾语

<u>of the public for creating the conditions</u>.

      responsibility的后置定语

【译文】我们对企业的指责也忽视了公众负有最大的责任创造条件。

5. <u>They</u> <u>later</u> **passed on** <u>their knowledge of the qanat method</u> <u>to the Romans</u>.

  主语 状语   谓语   宾语   状语

【译文】他们后来将暗渠法的知识传授给罗马人。

Exercise 3

1. <u>In 1999,</u>   <u>Tourism New Zealand</u>   <u>launched</u>   <u>a campaign</u>.

  状语   主语   谓语   宾语

【译文】1999年,新西兰旅游局发起了一项运动。

【解析】本句为"主语+谓语+宾语"的句型。

2. <u>Nutmeg</u>   <u>was</u>   <u>a highly prized and costly ingredient in European cuisine</u>.

  主语   系动词   表语

【译文】肉豆蔻过去是欧洲菜肴中非常珍贵和昂贵的配料。

【解析】本句为"主语+系动词+表语"的句型。

3. <u>Providing support to employees</u>   <u>gives</u>   <u>them</u>   <u>the confidence to perform their jobs better</u>.

        主语   谓语   间接宾语   直接宾语

【译文】为员工提供支持会使他们有信心更好地完成工作。

【解析】本句为"主语+谓语+间接宾语+直接宾语"的句型,其中主语由动名词短语充当。

4. Ideas about play-based learning　　have been developing　　since the 19th century.

  　　　　主语　　　　　　　　　　　谓语　　　　　　　　　　状语

【译文】寓教于乐的理念自19世纪以来一直在发展。

【解析】本句为"主语+谓语"的句型。

5. He　　considers　　the perceived dangers of ocean trash　　as a potential alarm.

  主语　　谓语　　　　　　　　　宾语　　　　　　　　　　　宾语补语

【译文】他认为人们所察觉到的海洋垃圾危害是一个潜在的警告。

【解析】本句为"主语+谓语+宾语+宾语补语"的句型。

第2节　简单句基本成分的变化

Exercise 1

1. Children must enjoy the activity.

  　　　　　谓语

【译文】孩子们一定很享受该活动。

2. More papers on the subject have been published since 2013.

  　　　　　　　　　　　　谓语

【译文】自2013年以来,有更多关于该主题的论文已经被发表。

3. In an oral context, a story won't survive because of one great teller.

  　　　　　　　　　　　　谓语

【译文】在口头传播的背景下,一个故事不会单靠一个伟大的讲述者而流传下来。

4. Knowing more than one language can cause speakers to name pictures more slowly.

  　　　　　　　　　　　　　谓语

【译文】掌握不止一门语言的人需要更长时间才能说出画作的名字。

5. He asked both expert musicians and non-experts to assess six compositions.

  　　谓语

【译文】他要求专业音乐家和非专业人士对六首乐曲进行评估。

Exercise 2

1. are encountered

【译文】许多昆虫种类很少被人类遇到。

【解析】此处考查的是一般现在时的被动语态。句子陈述的是一般事实,故用一般现在时。句末的by human 提示应用被动语态。句首的Many提示主语为复数名词,故填are encountered。

2. have been identified

【译文】从目前研究过的小部分昆虫中,已鉴定出几种有前景的化合物。

【解析】此处考查的是现在完成时的被动语态。由前面的have been investigated可知,主句的谓语动词 identify也应用现在完成时。结合句意, several promising compounds与identify"识别,鉴定"这个动作之间是被动关系,故填have been identified。

3. have been explored

【译文】幸福的意义和价值已经被探讨了许多年。

【解析】此处考查的是现在完成时的被动语态。通过for many years可以判断句子用现在完成时,同时the meaning and value of happiness与explore构成被动关系,另外meaning和value是两个并列的主语,谓语用复数形式,故填have been explored。

4. blaming

【译文】但单靠指责不可能带来变化。

【解析】此句考查的是doing作句子的主语。本句为"主+谓+宾"句型,主语是blaming alone,谓语是is unlikely to produce,宾语是change。

5. was observed

【译文】再次进行实验时,能观察到大脑的所有区域都有活动迹象。

【解析】此处考查的是一般过去时的被动语态。从前面从句的were repeated可知,主句时态也应用一般过去时。根据句意,句子的主语activation"启动,触发"和谓语动词observe"观察"是被动关系,故填was observed。

第3节 简单句的扩展(一)

Exercise 1

1. cultural

【译文】与此同时,文化价值观在全球粮食和农业系统中根深蒂固。

【解析】横线后面的values"价值观"是一个名词,因此选用culture的形容词形式cultural来修饰名词。

2. farmers'

【译文】期货市场过度金融化,可能会导致短期价格波动,使农民的粮食不安全状况恶化。

【解析】横线后面的名词短语food insecurity"粮食不安全状况"与所给单词farmer是所属关系,要用所有格;而且此处farmer是泛指,需要加复数,因此填farmers'。

3. creative

【译文】EMI创造的仿制品仍然完全依赖于原艺术家的创作冲动。

【解析】横线后面的单词impulses"冲动"是名词,横线前的所有格artist's"艺术家的"是impulses的限定词,因此横线也应该填入一个impulses的修饰语,故使用create的形容词形式creative。

4. their

【译文】如果设计师懂得用身体思考,可能会有更好的解决方案。

【解析】横线后面的单词bodies"身体"是名词,所给单词是主格代词they,可知需用对应的形容词性物主代词their修饰bodies。

5. beneficial

【译文】乐趣能产生好的效果,但这种乐趣的设定必须与组织目标和员工特征仔细协调。

【解析】横线后面的单词effect"影响"是名词,横线前有冠词a,因此填benefit的形容词形式beneficial"有益的"修饰effect。

Exercise 2

1. In

【译文】在中世纪,欧洲人用这种香料来给食物调味,尤其是肉类。

【解析】in the Middle Ages是固定搭配,表示"在中世纪这段时期里"。

2. from

【译文】阿拉伯商人和欧洲水手很可能将椰子从南亚和东南亚运到非洲。

【解析】from... to...意为"从……到……",在此处表示地点。

3. Without

【译文】如果没有这些努力，如今存活的物种会更少。

【解析】由 would be 可知，此句使用了虚拟语气，表示假设。根据句意，efforts 和 species 的数量是正相关关系，因此应填 Without 与 fewer 对应。

4. by

【译文】政府可以通过提供基础服务来显著降低农民的风险，如修建道路将农产品更快地运往市场。

【解析】根据句意可知，横线后面的内容是政府用以减少农民风险的手段。"by+doing"表示"通过……（的方式）"，故填 by。

5. of

【译文】事实上，研究表明，60%的补贴受益者不是穷人，而是富有的地主和非农商人。

【解析】"百分比+of"是固定搭配，意为"百分之……的……"。

Exercise 3

1. It might represent **a broader** pattern <u>among **other social** bugs</u>.

【译文】它可能代表了其他社会性昆虫中一种更广泛的模式。

【解析】限定词 a 和形容词 broader 修饰 pattern；限定词 other 和形容词 social 修饰 bugs；介词短语 among other social bugs 修饰 pattern。

2. Animals <u>in **good** zoos</u> get **a varied and high**-quality diet <u>with **all the** supplements **required**</u>.

【译文】在好的动物园里，动物可以获得多样化和高质量的饮食，从中获取需要额外补充的营养。

【解析】形容词 good 修饰 zoos；限定词 a 和形容词短语 varied and high-quality 修饰 diet；限定词 all the 和过去分词 required 修饰 supplements；介词短语 in good zoos 修饰 Animals；介词短语 with all the supplements required 修饰 diet。

3. Mobility will change in **such potentially significant** ways and in association with **so many other technological** developments, <u>such as telepresence and virtual reality</u>.

【译文】有其他如此多的包括远程监控和虚拟现实在内的技术发展助力，移动出行很可能会发生非常深远的变化。

【解析】限定词 such 和形容词短语 potentially significant 修饰 ways；限定词 so many other 和形容词 technological 修饰 developments；介词短语 such as telepresence and virtual reality 修饰 developments。

4. In **many large** cities, **the** wind is not strong enough to clear **the** air <u>**of the massive amounts of** smog</u>.

【译文】在许多大城市，风力不足以清除空气中的大量烟雾。

【解析】限定词 many 和形容词 large 修饰 cities；限定词 the 修饰 wind 和 air；形容词 massive 修饰 amounts；限定词 the massive amounts of 修饰 smog；介词短语 of the massive amounts of smog 修饰 air。

5. **A hybridised** band-tailed pigeon, <u>with **the added nesting** habits of a passenger pigeon</u>, could, in theory, re-establish **that forest** disturbance.

【译文】混合了其他基因的斑尾鸽，额外拥有了旅鸽的筑巢习性，理论上可以帮助重建这种森林干扰。

【解析】限定词 A 和过去分词 hybridised 修饰 band-tailed pigeon；限定词 the、形容词 added 和现在分词 nesting 共同修饰 habits；限定词 that 和名词 forest 修饰 disturbance；介词短语 of a passenger pigeon 修饰 habits；介词短语 with the added... pigeon 修饰 band-tailed pigeon。

Exercise 4

1. By understanding why and how we get sick——方式状语

【译文】通过了解我们为何以及如何生病，我们可以改变我们治疗疾病的方式。

2. In Britain——地点状语；after the repeal of the Excise Act in 1845——时间状语；of the Excise Act、in 1845——repeal 的后置定语

【译文】在英国，现代玻璃工业是在1845年《消费税法》废除后才真正开始发展的。

3. in many different colours——glass containers 的后置定语

【译文】现代玻璃工厂每天可以生产数百万个不同颜色的玻璃容器。

4. between parents and their babies——conversations 的后置定语

【译文】科学家们收集了数千段父母和宝宝之间的30秒对话。

5. Given the current concerns about environmental issues——原因状语；about environmental issues——concerns 的后置定语；of this ancient material——future 的后置定语

【译文】鉴于目前人们对环境问题的关注，这一古老材料再次显得很有前景。

第4节 简单句的扩展(二)

Exercise 1

1. In the past—and nowadays, too, though to a lesser extent—<u>a popular form of collecting</u>,
   主语
   particularly among boys and men, <u>was</u>   <u>trainspotting</u>.
   系动词   表语

   【译文】在过去——现在也是，尽管流行程度变低——流行的一类收集，特别是在男性群体当中，是搜集火车号码。

2. <u>Vehicles</u>   with limited self-driving capabilities <u>have been</u>   <u>around</u> for more than 50 years,
   主语   系动词   表语
   resulting in significant contributions towards driver assistance systems.

   【译文】具有不完全自动驾驶能力的车辆已经问世50多年，为驾驶辅助系统做出了重大贡献。

3. <u>A team</u> made up of more than 30 psychological scientists, anthropologists, and biologists then
   主语
   <u>played</u>   <u>these recordings</u>   to listeners from 24 diverse societies, from indigenous tribes in New
   谓语   宾语
   Guinea to city-dwellers in India and Europe.

   【译文】之后一个由30多名心理科学家、人类学家和生物学家组成的团队向多名听众播放了这些录音，这些听众来自24个截然不同的社会群体，从新几内亚岛的土著部落成员到印度和欧洲的城市居民，都参与其中。

4. At first glance, <u>spending resources</u> to incorporate elements of a seemingly irrelevant trend into
   主语
   one's core offerings <u>sounds</u>   <u>like hardly worthwhile</u>.
   系动词   表语

   【译文】乍一看，花费资源将看似无关的趋势元素整合到一个核心产品中好像几乎完全不值得。

5. <u>A... milestone</u> in the history of glass <u>occurred</u> with the invention of lead crystal glass by the
   主语   谓语
   English glass manufacturer George Ravenscroft.

   【译文】英国玻璃制造商乔治·拉文斯克罗夫特发明了含铅水晶玻璃，这是玻璃历史上的一个重要里程碑。

Exercise 2

1. Travelling

【译文】20世纪90年代,威廉·詹森在泰国各地旅行,对许多家庭屋顶上的基础太阳能加热系统印象深刻。

【解析】此句的主语是William Janssen,系动词是was,因此travel这一动词只能变成非谓语形式。又因为travel与主语William Janssen之间是主动关系,因此使用doing形式作状语,表伴随状态。

2. To make; highlighting

【译文】为了让人们更轻松地计划自驾游,该网站对全国最受欢迎的驾车路线进行了编目,根据季节突出显示不同的路线,并标明距离和用时。

【解析】在本句中, the site catalogued... driving routes已经是完整的"主+谓+宾"结构,因此剩余的两个动词make和highlight都只能充当非谓语。make用不定式to make可以表目的,符合句意。highlight和主语the site之间是主动关系,因此使用doing形式,和and后的indicating形成并列关系。

3. finding

【译文】麻省理工学院在新加坡调查了自动驾驶汽车之后发现,如果实现了全自动汽车共享,需要的车辆数量都不到目前使用的30%。

【解析】本句已有谓语动词investigated,因此动词find只能充当非谓语,且find与主语The Massachusetts Institute of Technology之间是主动关系,因此使用doing形式作状语,表结果。

4. to act

【译文】由于象龟相对而言静止不动并且能够在没有食物或水的情况下存活数月,它们被带到船上,在漫长的海上航行中被当作食物补给。

【解析】本句已有谓语动词was taken,因此act只能充当非谓语。注意,act意为"起作用"时为不及物动词,因此只能选择doing或to do形式。而doing和done作状语时,前面一般有逗号与主句断开(若在句首,则逗号在后面),此题的横线前并没有逗号,因此宜用不定式to act,表目的。

5. damaged

【译文】再野化意味着大规模恢复受损的生态系统。

【解析】此句考查非谓语动词充当定语,修饰名词ecosystems。因为ecosystems与damage之间是被动关系(生态系统被破坏),因此使用done形式damaged。

Exercise 3 （加粗部分为主干）

1. Dr David Beresford-Jones, archaeobotanist at Cambridge University, **has been studying**
　　　　主语　　　　　　　　　　　　同位语　　　　　　　　　　　　谓语

the role of the huarango tree in landscape change.
　　　　宾语

【译文】剑桥大学的考古植物学家大卫·贝雷斯福德–琼斯博士一直在研究牧豆树在环境变化中的作用。

2. In 1866, **he** **gave up** **his business** to open a photographic studio,
　　　　主语　谓语　　宾语　　　　to do短语作目的状语

advertising himself as a portrait and landscape photographer.
　　　　doing短语作伴随状语

【译文】1866年,他放弃了自己的生意,开设了一家摄影工作室,并宣传自己是一名肖像和风景摄影师。

3. **Supported by a rope and harness,**   **you**   **can stand**   on branches no bigger than your wrist.

    done短语作方式状语   主语   谓语

【译文】在绳索和安全带的支撑下，你可以站在不比手腕粗的树枝上。

4. **The BLFC**   **arranged**   **games** between teams representing the north and the south of England.

   主语   谓语   宾语   doing短语作teams的后置定语

【译文】英国女子足球俱乐部安排了分别代表英格兰北部和南部的两支球队进行比赛。

5. **Our... challenge**   **is**   **to address the... causes** of the agricultural system's inability

     主语   系动词   表语

to ensure sufficient food for all.

to do短语作inability的后置定语

【译文】我们最大的挑战是解决导致农业系统无法确保人人获得充足食物的根本原因。

第5节 并列句

Exercise 1

1. By the early 20th century, this region had become the world's largest producer of cork,

                                       分句1

        and   today it accounts for roughly half of all cork production around the world.

并列连词   分句2

【译文】到20世纪初，这一地区已成为世界上最大的软木产地，如今它约占全球软木总产量的一半。

2. He can get you treated by himself,   **or**   he'll send you off somewhere else if necessary.

          分句1   并列连词   分句2

【译文】他可以自己给你看病，或者如果有必要的话，他会把你送到别的地方去。

3. From the 17th century, pirates took a few tortoises on board for food,   **but**   the arrival

                分句1   并列连词   分句2

of whaling ships in the 1790s saw this exploitation grow exponentially.

【译文】从17世纪开始，海盗们就把一些象龟带上船当食物，但18世纪90年代捕鲸船的到来让这种(对象龟的)开发利用呈指数级增长。

4. Corkboard and cork tiles are ideal for thermal and acoustic insulation,   **while**   granules of

                  分句1   并列连词   分句2

cork are used in the manufacture of concrete.

【译文】软木板和软木砖是隔热和隔音的理想材料，而软木颗粒则用于生产混凝土。

5. Her work tracked the ants from the time the pupae became adults,   **so**   she knew their exact ages.

                  分句1   并列连词   分句2

【译文】她的研究从蚁蛹成虫开始就追踪这些蚂蚁，所以她知道它们的确切年龄。

Exercise 2

1. and

【译文】收集一定是最多样化的人类活动之一，而且它也是一种让我们许多心理学家着迷的活动。

2. and

【译文】每个人都带着他或她自己的计划来参加这个项目和课程，并且这些计划甚至不需要涉及获得真正的营销专业知识。

3. but

【译文】健康地理学领域经常被忽视，但它是地理学和医疗保健领域中一块巨大的需求。

4. while

【译文】研究表明，活动是影响游客满意度的关键因素，占比为74%，而交通和住宿占剩下的26%。

5. so

【译文】想象力正在帮助她向创造力迈出第一步，因此将会对她成年后的人生产生重要的影响。

Exercise 3

1. In the 19th century, many collectors amassed fossils, animals and plants from around the globe, **and** their collections provided a vast amount of information about the natural world. 真

   【译文】在19世纪，许多收藏家收集了来自世界各地的化石、动物和植物，并且他们的收藏提供了大量关于自然界的信息。

2. Oxytocin probably does some very basic things, **but** these basic processes could manifest in different ways depending on individual differences and context. 真

   【译文】催产素起的作用可能非常基础，但这些基础作用的过程会根据个体差异和环境以不同的方式表现出来。

3. Intrinsically motivated free play provides the child with true autonomy, **while** guided play can help parents and educators provide more targeted learning experiences. 真

   【译文】内在动机式的自由游戏为儿童提供了真正的自主权，而引导式游戏可以帮助父母和教育者提供更有针对性的学习体验。

4. In some versions of *Little Red Riding Hood*, the wolf swallows up the grandmother, **while** in others it locks her in a cupboard. 真

   【译文】在《小红帽》的一些版本中，狼吞下了祖母，而在另一些版本中，狼把祖母锁在橱柜里。

5. They don't have the money to buy the diesel to run the desalination plants, **so** it is a really bad situation. 真

   【译文】他们没有钱买柴油来运行海水淡化厂，因此这是一个非常糟糕的情况。

第6节 复合句——名词性从句(一)

Exercise 1

1. that

   【译文】他说公司将生产灰色和白色的瓶子。

   【解析】主句的主谓结构为He stated，谓语动词stated后的宾语从句为语义完整的陈述句，因此只需用that连接主句与从句。

2. who

   【译文】催产素如何作用取决于我们与谁互动。

   【解析】主句为Oxytocin's effects vary，其后的depending on...是doing短语作状语，介词on后的宾语从句we are interacting with"我们和……互动"表意不完整，缺少"谁"的含义，故选who。

3. how

【译文】威金斯谴责他故意含糊其词地解释软件的工作原理。

【解析】主句主干为Wiggins condemned him，其后的for...是原因状语，其中介词of后的宾语从句为the software worked"软件工作"。此处worked为不及物动词，从句的结构完整，可推测缺少了状语，故选how表示"如何"。

4. what

【译文】学生需要学习如何做成一件事情，以及事情本身是什么。

【解析】主句的主谓结构为Students need to study，后面有两个并列的宾语，第二个宾语是从句the thing is"事情是……"，结构不完整，缺少表语，故选what表示"什么"。

5. where

【译文】例如，(身体状况)与你生活的地方有关，你不会与生活在不同地理区域的人有同样的健康问题。

【解析】非谓语动词短语depending on后的宾语从句you live"你生活……"结构完整(live为不及物动词)，但表意不完整，缺少地点状语，故选where。

Exercise 2

1. <u>We</u>   <u>know</u>   <u>**how** the land surface of our planet lies.</u>
   主语   谓语   宾语从句

【译文】我们知道地球的陆地表面是如何分布的。

2. <u>This emerging technology</u>   <u>could be used</u>   <u>to fully understand **why** various species went extinct.</u>
   主语   谓语   状语(含why引导的宾语从句，作动词to understand的宾语)

【译文】这项新兴技术可以用来充分了解为什么各类物种会灭绝。

3. <u>In the developing world,</u>   <u>the price</u>   <u>will depend on</u>   <u>**what deal** aid organisations can negotiate.</u>
   状语   主语   谓语   宾语从句

【译文】在发展中国家，价格将取决于援助组织能谈成什么样的协议。

4. <u>Prices</u>   <u>will vary</u>   <u>according to **where** the device is bought.</u>
   主语   谓语   状语(含where引导的宾语从句，作介词to的宾语)

【译文】设备的价格会根据购买地点而有所不同。

5. <u>The UK's Transport Research Laboratory</u>   <u>has demonstrated</u>   <u>**that** more than 90% of</u>
   主语   谓语   宾语从句
   <u>road collisions involve human error as a contributory factor.</u>

【译文】英国交通研究实验室已经证明超过90%的车辆碰撞事故都与人为失误有关。

6. <u>He</u>   <u>wondered</u>   <u>**whether** it could have been the birthplace of the very first Inca, Manco the Great.</u>
   主语   谓语   宾语从句

【译文】他想知道这里是否可能是第一位印加帝国国王——曼科大帝的出生地。

7. <u>Indeed,</u>   <u>environmentalists</u>   <u>estimate</u>   <u>**that** by 2050 there will be more plastic in our oceans than fish.</u>
   状语   主语   谓语   宾语从句

【译文】事实上，环保主义者估计，到2050年海洋中的塑料比鱼还要多。

8. <u>They</u>   <u>wonder</u>   <u>**what** the artist is trying to tell them.</u>
   主语   谓语   宾语从句

【译文】他们想知道艺术家想告诉他们什么。

9. They   carried out   a survey   of **how** the larger area was settled in relation to sources of water.

  主语   谓语   宾语   后置定语(含how引导的宾语从句,作介词of的宾语)

【译文】他们结合水源对当时人们如何在这片更大的地区定居进行了调查。

10. Prospective arson investigators   can learn   all the tricks of the trade

          主语   谓语   宾语

for detecting **whether** a fire was deliberately set.

状语(含whether引导的宾语从句,作动词detecting的宾语)

【译文】未来的纵火调查人员可以学习这一行当所有的诀窍来检测火灾是否人为纵火导致。

第7节 复合句——名词性从句(二)

Exercise 1

1. that

【译文】在今天的英格兰仍然存在古代山丘图案,这个事实证明了当地习俗和信仰具有力量和连续性。

【解析】从句any ancient hill figures survive at all in England today表意和语法结构完整,解释说明了前面抽象名词fact的具体内容,是fact的同位语从句,故选that。

2. What

【译文】令我感兴趣的是这只鸟所指向的概念。

【解析】位于句首的是主语从句,介词in后面缺少宾语,故选What。整个从句意为"我所感兴趣的事"。

3. What

【译文】根据巴雷特的说法,令人惊讶的是这些时期的时间。

【解析】位于句首的是主语从句,从句为"主+系+表"结构,缺少主语,故选What。从句意为"令人惊讶的事情"。

4. It

【译文】人们在不同情况下所表现出来的智慧会有非常显著的差异。

【解析】该句型为"it is+形容词+主语从句",it为形式主语,故选It。该句也可写成How much people can vary in their wisdom from one situation to the next is remarkable,但把主语从句后置,能够平衡句子结构。

5. how

【译文】这就是植物竞相躲避彼此阴影的方法。

【解析】从句plants compete to escape each other's shade跟在系动词is后面,为表语从句。此从句乍看之下似乎语义完整,但若填入没有实际意思的that引导,整个句子意思则为"这是植物竞相躲避彼此阴影",并不通顺。因此,可推断从句缺少了状语,故引导词选how。

Exercise 2

1. The additional information   may be   **what** they did.

        主语   系动词   表语从句

【译文】附加的信息可以是他们做过的事情。

2.   It   's   unlikely   **that** they'll come back.

 形式主语 系动词   表语   主语从句

【译文】他们不太可能回来了。

3. This   is   **why** the tree is so suited to life there.

  主语 系动词   表语从句

【译文】这就是为什么这种树如此适合那里的生活。

4. **It** **is** **clear** **whether** a dominant laugh is produced by a high- or low- status person.
形式主语　系动词　表语　　　　　　　　　　　　　主语从句

【译文】支配性笑声到底是由一个身居高位还是低位的人发出来的,很明显能看出来。

5. **There is** **little doubt** **that** birth order has less influence on academic achievement
There be 句型　　主语　　　　　　　　　同位语从句

than socio-economic status.

【译文】几乎可以确定,出生顺序比社会经济地位对学业成绩的影响小。

6. **How successful they were** **is** **a matter of opinion.**
　　　主语从句　　　　　　系动词　　　表语

【译文】他们有多成功还有待商榷。

7. **What** many millennials prefer to post on social media **are** 'real' (refillable) bottles or even the
　　　　　主语从句　　　　　　　　　　　系动词　　　　　　　表语

once widespread Thermos bottles.

【译文】许多千禧一代更喜欢发布在社交媒体上的是"真实的"(可重复装水的)瓶子,甚至是曾经流行的保温瓶。

8. **They** **never mind** **the fact** **that** these stainless-steel vacuum-insulated water
主语　　谓语　　　宾语　　　　　两个并列的同位语从句

bottles feel oddly out-of-date to anyone over the age of 40 **or that** teenagers in the 1970s would have avoided ever being seen with one.

【译文】他们从不在意这些真空绝缘的不锈钢水瓶对于任何40岁以上的人来说都格外过时了,或者20世纪70年代的青少年会避免被人看到带着它们。

9. **What** seems entirely predictable and controllable on screen **has** **unexpected results**
　　　　　　主语从句　　　　　　　　　　　　　谓语　　　宾语

when translated into reality.
　　　状语

【译文】在屏幕上看起来完全可以预测和控制的东西变成现实后会产生意想不到的结果。

10. **It** **also** **seems** **that** the neurological roots of the bilingual advantage extend to brain
主语　状语　系动词　　　　　　　　　表语从句

areas associated with sensory processing.

【译文】此外,与双语优势相关的神经根似乎也延伸到与知觉处理相关的大脑区域。

第8节　复合句——定语从句

Exercise 1

1. that

【译文】软木是一种可持续的产品,可以轻易回收利用。

【解析】定语从句修饰的先行词是product"产品",指"物",故选that。

2. who

【译文】对那些或多或少容易感到无聊的人的研究提供了更多证据,表明无聊有不好的影响。

【解析】定语从句修饰的先行词是people"人们",指"人",故选who。

3. which

【译文】自由玩耍的机会,在我的童年几乎每天都有,现在却越来越少了。

【解析】定语从句修饰的先行词是 The opportunities for free play "自由玩耍的机会",是"事物",而逗号表明这是非限制性定语从句,在非限制性定语从句中,指代事物只能用 which,不能用 that。

4. whose; who

【译文】在这本关于探索地球表面的书中,我把关注点局限于那些进行真正的旅行,而且不仅仅追求自我发现的人身上。

【解析】两个并列的定语从句都修饰先行词 those "那些人"。第一个从句中,those 与 travels "旅行"是所属关系,故选 whose。第二个从句中,谓语是 aimed at,宾语是 personal discovery,故 those 充当主语,选 who。

5. As

【译文】正如神经科学的研究所表明的,6,000 多年前,我们人类的大脑需要一个新的回路来习得读写能力。

【解析】逗号前的定语从句中,indicates "表明"后缺少宾语,关系词正好充当这个成分,而先行词是后面一整句话,即 the acquisition of literacy necessitated a new circuit in our species' brain more than 6,000 years ago 这件事。由于从句位于句首,关系词只能用 As 不能用 Which。

Exercise 2

1. Psychologically,   this   can give   a purpose   to a life   **that** otherwise feels aimless.
   状语   主语   谓语   宾语   状语   修饰 life 的定语从句

【译文】从心理上看,这能赋予人生一个目标,否则人生就感觉失去了方向。

2. Collecting   gives   a feeling   **that** other hobbies are unlikely to inspire.
   主语   谓语   宾语   修饰 feeling 的定语从句

【译文】收藏带给人的感觉是其他爱好无法激发的。

3. In the Middle Ages,   Europeans   **who** could afford the spice   used   it   to flavour food.
   状语   主语   修饰 Europeans 的定语从句   谓语   宾语   状语

【译文】在中世纪,买得起这种香料的欧洲人用它来给食物调味。

4. People   **who** collect dolls   may develop   an interest   in the way   **that** dolls are made,
  主语   修饰 People 的定语从句   谓语   宾语   后置定语   修饰 way 的定语从句

or the materials   **that** are used.
后置定语的一部分   修饰 materials 的定语从句

【译文】收集娃娃的人有可能会对娃娃的制作工艺和使用的制作材料产生兴趣。

5. This   allowed   them   to determine the genes   **that** have allowed polar bears to survive
  主语   谓语   宾语   宾语补语   修饰 genes 的定语从句

in one of the toughest environments on Earth.

【译文】这使他们能够确定令北极熊得以在地球上最恶劣的一种环境下生存的基因。

6. Mangen's group   asked   subjects   questions about a short story   **whose** plot had
   主语   谓语   间接宾语   直接宾语   修饰 story 的定语从句

universal student appeal.

【译文】曼根的团队向受试者询问有关一篇短篇故事的问题,该故事的情节对学生普遍具有吸引力。

7. There are   still   areas around the world   **where** certain health issues are more prevalent.
There be 句型   状语   主语   修饰 areas 的定语从句

【译文】世界上仍存在一些地区,在那里,某些健康问题更为普遍。

8. Another solution   may be   to reveal more about the algorithms   which AI uses
   主语   系动词   表语   修饰algorithms的定语从句
   and the purposes   they serve.
   表语的一部分   (省略that)修饰purposes的定语从句

   【译文】另一个解决方案也许是揭露更多关于人工智能使用的算法及算法目的的信息。

9. A third approach,   known as 'counteract and reaffirm',   involves   developing
   主语   后置定语   谓语   宾语
   products or services   that stress the values traditionally associated with the category.
                    修饰products or services的定语从句

   【译文】第三种方法被称为"抵制和重申",它要求所开发的产品或服务强调传统上与该类别相关的价值观。

10. A radical solution,   which may work for some very large companies   whose
    主语   修饰solution的定语从句
    businesses are extensive and complex,   is   the professional board   supported by
    修饰companies的定语从句   系动词   表语   后置定语
    their own dedicated staff and advisers.

    【译文】一个激进的解决方案是成立专业董事会,由公司自己的专职人员和顾问提供支持,这个方法对一些业务广泛而复杂的大型公司可能适用。

第9节 复合句——状语从句

Exercise 1

1. when

【译文】当我被邀请去给一个市场营销班学生演讲的时候,我再次意识到这个问题。

【解析】when表示"当……的时候",if表示"如果"。引导时间状语从句用when。

2. because

【译文】被要求从一组物品中"拿起一支马克笔"的俄英双语者会比不懂俄语的人更关注邮票,因为俄语中的"邮票"与英语中的"马克笔"发音相似。

【解析】as if表示"似乎,好像",because表示"因为"。根据句意,连词前后两分句为因果关系,从句说明主句的原因,故选because。

3. although

【译文】那时候有史以来最快的商用帆船是快速帆船,用来在世界各地运输货物,尽管有些也载客。

【解析】for表示"因为";although表示"尽管,虽然",有转折的含义。句子前后意思发生转折,故选although引导让步状语从句。

4. If

【译文】如果我们知道接下来会发生什么,那么我们就不会感到兴奋。

【解析】if表示"如果",although表示"尽管,虽然"。引导条件状语从句用if。

5. so that

【译文】他们的目标是使人工智能技术变得更加可信和透明,以便组织和个人了解人工智能的决策是如何做出的。

【解析】as if表示"似乎,好像",so that表示"以便,为了"。引导目的状语从句用so that。

Exercise 2

1. **If we are asked why happiness matters,**　　we　　can give　　no further external reason.
　　　　　条件状语从句　　　　　　　　　　　　主语　　谓语　　　　　宾语

【译文】假如问我们为什么幸福如此重要,我们给不出任何其他外在原因。

2. The Dutch　took over　　the cinnamon trade　　from the Portuguese　**as soon as** they arrived in Ceylon.
　　主语　　　谓语　　　　　　宾语　　　　　　　　状语　　　　　　　　时间状语从句

【译文】荷兰人一到锡兰就从葡萄牙人手中接管了肉桂贸易。

3. They　　may feel　　empty,　　**now that** the goal that drove them on has gone.
　主语　　系动词　　表语　　　　　原因状语从句(含that引导的定语从句)

【译文】他们可能会感到空虚,因为驱使他们前进的目标已经消失。

4. This chapter　　addresses　　how people conceptualize intelligence,　　**whatever** it may actually be.
　　主语　　　　　谓语　　　　　　宾语从句　　　　　　　　　　　　　让步状语从句

【译文】无论智力实际上会是什么,本章讨论人们是如何理解智力这一概念的。

5. **If the customer's credit card is declined at the till,**　　keep　　your voice　　down　　and
　　　　　　　条件状语从句　　　　　　　　　　　　　　　谓语1　　宾语1　谓语1的一部分　连词

enquire about　　an alternative payment method　　quietly　　**so that** the customer doesn't
　谓语2　　　　　　　宾语2　　　　　　　　　　状语　　　目的状语从句

feel humiliated.

【译文】如果顾客的信用卡被收银机拒收,你要悄悄地小声询问另一种付款方式,这样顾客就不会感到
丢脸。

6. **If we want our soils to survive,**　　we　　need　　to take action　　now.
　　　　条件状语从句　　　　　　　　主语　谓语　　宾语　　　　状语

【译文】如果我们想要土壤继续存在,我们需要立刻开始行动。

7. **Although** the study involves plenty of fancy technology,　　the experiment itself　　was
　　　　　　让步状语从句　　　　　　　　　　　　　　　主语　　　　　系动词

rather straightforward.
　　表语

【译文】尽管这项研究涉及大量复杂技术,但实验本身相当简单。

8. **Since** most of the seats in most cars are unoccupied,　　this　　may boost　　production
　　　　　　原因状语从句　　　　　　　　　　　　　主语　　谓语　　　宾语

of a smaller, more efficient range of vehicles for individual use.
　　production的后置定语

【译文】由于大多数汽车上的大多数座位都是空的,这可能会促使(厂家)生产一系列供个人使用的更小、
使用率更高的汽车。

9. **When** futures markets become excessively financialised,　　they　　can contribute to
　　　　　　时间状语从句　　　　　　　　　　　　　主语　　　谓语

short-term price volatility.
　　宾语

【译文】期货市场过度金融化,可能会导致短期价格波动。

10. When I ask the students to articulate the purpose of their field, they eventually

时间状语从句   主语   状语

generalize to something like, 'The safety and welfare of society'.

谓语   状语

【译文】当我要求学生阐明他们研究领域的目的时，他们最终将其概括为"社会安全和社会福利"之类的东西。

第10节 特殊句式——倒装结构

Exercise 1

1. had we sat

【译文】我们刚在桌子旁坐下，电话铃就响了。

【解析】含有否定意义的副词置于句首时，句子要部分倒装。此处否定词Hardly放在句首，故选had we sat，其正常语序为We had hardly sat down at the table。hardly... when表示"一……就……"。

2. are some recent studies

【译文】以下是一些探索模仿儿语背后科学的最新研究。

【解析】here is/are sth.这一完全倒装结构已变成一种固定句式，用于介绍某物，故选are some recent studies。句子的正常语序为"Some recent studies that... are here."。

3. are obvious risks

【译文】这样做有明显的风险，因而建立明确的指导方针是很重要的。

【解析】此处使用了There be句型这种倒装结构，故选are obvious risks，其正常语序为obvious risks to... are there。

4. has the technology succeeded

【译文】技术从未成功复制那种结构。

【解析】含有否定意义的副词或连词(短语)置于句首时，句子要部分倒装。此处句首有Never，故选has the technology succeeded，其正常语序为The technology has never succeeded in...。

5. will we experience

【译文】只有当我们在这个世界上洒下了我们宏伟的光芒，我们才能体验到真正的意义、真正的满足和真正的快乐。

【解析】句首的时间状语从句前有Only，因此主句要使用部分倒装结构，要把助动词will提前至主语we之前，故选will we experience。句子的正常语序为"We will experience real purpose, real fulfilment, and real joy only when we... on this world."。

Exercise 2

1. EMI created not only compositions in Cope's style, but also that of the most revered classical composers, including Bach, Chopin and Mozart.

【译文】EMI不仅创作出了柯普风格的作品，而且还创作出了包括巴赫、肖邦和莫扎特在内的最受尊敬的古典作曲家的作品。

2. And yet millions of collectors around the world are there.

【译文】然而全世界有数百万的收藏家。

3. Bingham didn't realise the extent or the importance of the site, **and he didn't realise** what use he could make of the discovery, **either**.

【译文】宾厄姆没有意识到这个遗址的大小和重要性，也没有意识到他可以利用这个发现做什么。

4. **The babies were able to** successfully learn the new rule **only** in bilingual situations.

【译文】这些婴儿只有在双语环境下才能成功学会新规则。

5. Low compensation, inadequate benefits, poor working conditions and compromised employee morale and attitudes **are among** the many cited reasons.

【译文】被提及的众多原因包括低薪酬、不充分的福利、糟糕的工作条件以及员工低落的士气和妥协的态度。

Exercise 3

1. None of the donors has a stake in his idea, **nor** does he have any debt. 真

【译文】没有一个捐款人与他的想法产生利害关系，他也没有任何债务。

2. **Never** did *Cutty Sark* live up to the high expectations of her owner. 真

【译文】卡蒂萨克号从未能达到主人的高期望值。

3. **Only** in one place did it grow in the world: a small group of islands in the Banda Sea. 真

【译文】它只在世界上一个地方生长：班达海的一小群岛屿上。

4. **Not only** do direct food distribution systems encourage small-scale agriculture, **but** the systems **also** give consumers more control over the food they consume. 真

【译文】粮食直接分配系统不仅鼓励了小规模农业，而且使消费者能够更好地控制他们所消费的粮食。

5. **Not only** are all people equal as human beings, **but** one person would **also** serve as well as another in almost any position of responsibility in terms of their competencies. 真

【译文】不仅所有人作为人都是平等的，而且就能力而言，几乎在任何负责任的职位上，每个人都能做得同样出色。

第11节 特殊句式——强调句型

Exercise 1

1. that

【译文】正是多亏了拉文斯克罗夫特的发明，光学透镜、天文望远镜和显微镜之类的东西才有可能面世。

【解析】将It is和空格所填的引导词删掉，剩下的部分可组成一个完整的句子："Thanks to Ravenscroft's invention, optical lenses, astronomical telescopes, microscopes and the like became possible.",故该句为强调句，强调部分为thanks to Ravenscroft's invention,故引导词选that。

2. who

【译文】正是富兰克林发现风暴一般是从西往东移动的。

【解析】将It was和空格所填的引导词删掉，剩下的部分可组成一个完整的句子："Franklin discovered that storms generally travel from west to east.",故该句为强调句，强调部分为Franklin,指人。强调句型的引导词只有that或者who,故选who。

3. that

【译文】正是那些物品吸引了考古学家们。

【解析】将It is和空格所填的引导词删掉，剩下的部分可组成一个完整的句子："Those objects are of interest to archaeologists.",故该句为强调句，强调部分为those objects,故选that。

4. that

【译文】我们现在知道，建造过程经历了许多不同的阶段。

【解析】本句中It is和引导词中间是known(know的过去分词形式)，由于强调句型不能强调动词，因此可判断该句不是强调句。根据句意可知，It是形式主语，真正的主语是空格后的部分，即the building process went through many different stages，鉴于这部分意思完整，故该主语从句的引导词选that。

5. that

【译文】这个雕刻图案有可能代表了当地神话中的女神。

【解析】本句中It is和引导词中间是形容词possible "可能的"，故本句不是强调句。根据句意可知，此句通过形式主语It将主语从句后置，从句部分意思完整，故引导词选that。句子还原成正常语序为 "that从句+is possible"，表示 "某事是可能的"。

Exercise 2 （加粗部分为原句的强调内容）

1. **Cutting down native woodland** leads to soil erosion.

【译文】正是砍伐原生林地导致水土流失。

2. The field of health geography comes into its own **in situations like these**.

【译文】正是在这样的情况下，健康地理学领域开始发挥作用。

3. **This uncertainty** triggers the surge of dopamine in the brain.

【译文】正是这种不确定性触发了大脑中多巴胺的激增。

4. **This research** shows we should continually question whether or not our existing assumptions work.

【译文】正是这项研究表明，我们应该不断质疑我们现有的假设是否可行。

5. The number of business schools and graduates has massively increased **over the past 50 years**.

【译文】正是在过去50年里，商学院和毕业生的数量大幅增加。

6. **This simple and ancient molecule** has been used for many different functions.

【译文】正是这种简单而古老的分子被用于许多不同的功能。

7. Scientists first became aware of the influence of oxytocin **through various studies focusing on animals**.

【译文】正是通过对动物的各种研究，科学家们第一次意识到催产素的影响。

8. **This easily understood target** can help shape expectations and encourage action.

【译文】正是这个易于理解的目标有助于培养预期并鼓励行动。

9. Mathematics and physics did **not** become part of meteorology **until the early 20th century**.

【译文】直到20世纪早期，数学和物理学才成为气象学的一部分。

10. **The suspenseful tension of music, arising out of our unfulfilled expectations** is the source of the music's feeling.

【译文】因为音乐(的走向)未满足我们的期望，它产生了一种悬而未决的张力，音乐中的感觉正是来源于这一张力。

第12节 特殊句式——虚拟语气

Exercise 1

1. followed

【译文】如果按时间顺序排列会更好。

【解析】根据主句的谓语动词would be和句意可知，本句是对现在情况的虚拟假设，实际上并没有按时间顺序排列。if非真实条件句中的谓语应用过去式，故选followed。

2. have taken place

【译文】如果没有这些新的能源,工业革命根本不可能发生。

【解析】本句是对过去情况的虚拟假设,事实上工业革命发生了,主句的谓语应用would/could/might/should+have done,故选have taken place。

3. had had

【译文】如果他们的设计师懂得用身体思考,可能会有更好的解决方案。

【解析】根据主句的谓语动词might have been可知本句是对过去情况的虚拟假设,实际上设计师并没有用身体思考。所以if非真实条件句的谓语要用had done形式,故选had had。

4. be linked

【译文】他写信给内政部,建议政府部门通过一套"对话管"连接在一起。

【解析】因主句中有表示"建议"的词suggesting,因此suggesting后接的宾语从句应用虚拟语气,即把谓语动词变成"should+动词原形",其中should可以省略,故选be linked。

5. made

【译文】你早该为这次演讲做准备了。

【解析】本句为It is (high/about) time that句型,that从句用虚拟语气,即谓语动词用过去式或"should+动词原形",故选made。

Exercise 2

1. **If I were you,** I **'d start** looking for another job.
　　条件状语从句　　　主语　谓语　　　　宾语

【译文】如果我是你,就会去另找工作了。

【解析】此句使用了if引导的非真实条件句,假设与现在相反的情况。

2. What **would** life **be** like **if people didn't** have to work?
　疑问词　情态动词　主语　系动词　表语　　条件状语从句

【译文】如果人们不用工作,生活会是什么样子?

【解析】此句使用了if引导的非真实条件句,假设与现在或将来相反的情况。

3. I **wish** I'd taken a diploma in business skills instead of on IT.
　主语　谓语　　　　宾语从句

【译文】我希望我考的是商业技能的文凭而不是IT的。

【解析】wish后的宾语从句表示与过去相反的情况。

4. I **wish** you **wouldn't leave** your clothes all over the floor.
　主语　谓语　　　　宾语从句

【译文】我真希望你以后不把衣服丢得满地都是。

【解析】wish后的宾语从句表示与未来相反的情况。

5. You **would know** what was going on, **if you had listened**.
　主语　　谓语　　　宾语从句　　　条件状语从句

【译文】你若是注意听了就会知道发生什么事了。

【解析】此句中,主句和从句假设的类型并不一致。主句是对现在情况的虚拟,而if引导的非真实条件句则是对过去情况的虚拟。

6. His **proposal**　　**that** the system **should be changed**　　was rejected.
　　主语　　　　　　　　　同位语从句　　　　　　　　　　　谓语

【译文】他提出的修改制度的建议被拒绝了。

【解析】proposal后的同位语从句使用"should型虚拟"。

7. **If** everyone **accessed** books from their own computers at home,　　libraries　　**would be**　　obsolete.
　　　　　　　　条件状语从句　　　　　　　　　　　　　　　　主语　　　系动词　　　表语

【译文】如果每个人都在家里的计算机上阅读书籍,图书馆就会被淘汰。

【解析】此句使用了if引导的非真实条件句,假设与现在或将来相反的情况。

8. What　　**would**　　life　　**have been**　　like　　**if** the Industrial Revolution **hadn't taken place**?
疑问词　　情态动词　　主语　　系动词　　表语　　　　　　　　条件状语从句

【译文】如果工业革命没有发生,生活会是什么样子?

【解析】此句使用了if引导的非真实条件句,假设与过去相反的情况。

9. The US government's Food and Drug Administration　　introduced　　rules
　　　　　　　　主语　　　　　　　　　　　　　　　　　谓语　　　宾语

demanding that the meat industry **abandon** practices associated with the risk of the disease spreading.
rules的后置定语(含that引导的宾语从句, 作动词demanding的宾语)

【译文】美国政府的食品和药物管理局出台规定,要求肉类行业放弃存在疾病传播风险的做法。

【解析】demanding后的宾语从句使用"should型虚拟",此句省略了should。

10.　　It　　**is suggested**　　**that** fathers **use** less familial language to provide their children
形式主语　　谓语　　　　　　　　　　　　主语从句

with a bridge to the kind of speech they'll hear in public.

【译文】有人建议,父亲应该少使用家庭特有的语言,而应该充当桥梁的角色,使孩子知道在公共场合会听到什么样的语言。

【解析】主句出现过去分词suggested,主语从句使用"should型虚拟",此句省略了should。

第13节　特殊句式——分隔结构

Exercise 1

1. In addition,　　the opening of the Suez Canal in 1869,　　the same year that *Cutty Sark* was
　　状语　　　　　　　主语　　　　　　　　　　　　　插入成分(作1869的同位语,含

launched,　　　　　　　　　　　　　　　　had　　a serious impact.
that引导的修饰the same year的定语从句)　　谓语　　宾语

【译文】此外,在卡蒂萨克号下水的同一年,1869年,苏伊士运河开通,影响重大。

2. The lynx　　is　　a specialist predator of roe deer,　　a species　　that has exploded in
主语　　系动词　　表语　　　　　　　　　　roe deer的同位语　　修饰a species 的定语从句
Britain in recent decades,　　　　holding back,　　　　　by intensive browsing,
　　　　　　　　　　　　　　伴随状语,逻辑主语为a species　　插入成分(作方式状语)

attempts to re-establish forests.
伴随状语剩余的部分

【译文】猞猁专门捕食狍,最近几十年在英国,狍的数量急剧增长,它们大量吃草使人们重建森林的努力受阻。

3. She   believes   that... social environment.

主语   谓语   宾语从句

宾语从句: that   oxytocin   acts   as a chemical spotlight   that shines on social clues

引导词   主语   谓语   状语   修饰spotlight的定语从句

—a shift in posture, a flicker of the eyes, a dip in the voice—

插入成分(举例说明social clues)

making people more attuned to their social environment.

伴随状语,逻辑主语为oxytocin

【译文】她认为催产素就像一盏化学聚光灯,照向社交线索——姿势变化、眼神闪烁、声音低沉,使人们更加适应社交环境。

4. The products   stress   the values   traditionally associated with the category   in ways

主语   谓语   宾语   values的后置定语   状语

that allow consumers to oppose   —or at least temporarily escape from—   the aspects of trends

修饰ways的定语从句   插入成分(补充信息)   定语从句剩余的部分

they view as undesirable.

修饰aspects的定语从句

【译文】这些产品强调传统上与该类别相关的价值观,使消费者能够抵抗——或至少暂时逃避——流行趋势中他们认为不可取的方面。

5. Trends   —technological, economic, environmental, social, or political—   that affect how

主语   插入成分(列举Trends的种类)   插入成分(修饰Trends的

people perceive the world around them   present firms with unique opportunities for growth.

定语从句,含how引导的宾语从句)   谓语(present sb. with sth.结构)

【译文】影响人们如何看待周围世界的技术、经济、环境、社会或政治趋势为企业提供了独特的发展机会。

6. The lack of self-imagery in Harappan Civilisation   —at a time when the Egyptians were

主语   插入成分(作定语,含when

carving and painting representations of themselves all over their temples—   is   only part

引导的修饰time的定语从句)   系动词   表语

of the mystery.

【译文】哈拉帕文明缺乏对自我形象的描绘只是谜团的一部分,在同时期的埃及,人们在寺庙的各个地方雕刻和绘画自己的形象。

7. The only question is how to achieve it,   and   here... the way.

分句1("主+系+表"结构)   并列连词   分句2

分句2: here   positive psychology   —a supposed science that not only identifies what

状语   主语   插入成分(作positive psychology的同位语,含

makes people happy but also allows their happiness to be measured—   can show

that引导的修饰science的定语从句,定语从句中又含what引导的宾语从句)   谓语

the way.

宾语

【译文】唯一的问题是如何做到这一点,而现在积极心理学——一门所谓的科学,既能确定什么使人们快乐,又能测量快乐——可以指明方向。

8. In a study published in *Proceedings of the National Academy of Sciences*,   a total of 57 babies
　　　　　　　　　　　　　　　　　　　　状语　　　　　　　　　　　　　　　　　　　　　　　主语

from two slightly different age groups   —seven months and eleven and a half months—
　　　babies 的后置定语　　　　　　　　　　　　插入成分(说明 two age groups)

were played   a number of syllables   from both their native language (English) and a
　谓语　　　　　　　宾语　　　　　　　　　　　　　syllables 的后置定语

non-native tongue (Spanish).

【译文】在《美国国家科学院院刊》发表的一项研究中，研究人员给两个差距较小的年龄组(7个月和11个半月)中的共57名婴儿播放了多个他们母语(英语)和非母语(西班牙语)的音节录音。

9. Alternative explorations   —where experimentation and human instinct lead to progress
　　　主语　　　　　　　　　　　插入成分(修饰 Alternative explorations 的定语从句)

and new ideas—   are effectively discouraged.
　　　　　　　　　　谓语

【译文】事实上，另类的探索被抑制了，而依靠实验和人类直觉，这种探索能带来进步和新想法。

10. They   also   introduced   alien species   —ranging from cattle, pigs, goats, rats and
　主语　　状语　　谓语　　　　　宾语　　　　　　插入成分(alien species 的后置定语)

dogs to plants and ants—   that either prey on the eggs and young tortoises or damage or
　　　　　　　　　　　　　修饰 alien species 的定语从句

destroy their habitat.

【译文】他们还引入了外来物种，从牛、猪、山羊、老鼠和狗到植物和蚂蚁，应有尽有，这些物种要么捕食龟卵和幼龟，要么破坏或毁灭它们的栖息地。

第 14 节　长难句解读——拆分+简化

Exercise 1

1. If the music is too obvious,   it   is   annoyingly boring,   like an alarm clock.
　条件状语从句(“主+系+表”结构) 主语 系动词 　表语　　　　　　　状语

【译文】如果音乐太明显，就会让人感到厌烦，像闹钟一样。

2. It   could be argued   that New Zealand is not a typical destination.
　形式主语　　谓语　　　　主语从句(“主+系+表”结构)

【译文】可以说，新西兰不是一个典型的目的地。

3. Conservationists   accept   that the old preservation-jar model is failing,   even on its own terms.
　　主语　　　　　　谓语　　　宾语从句(“主+谓”结构)　　　　　　　　　　状语

【译文】自然资源保护主义者承认，旧的保存罐模式失败了，即使是根据他们的标准来看。

4. The opportunities for free play,   which I experienced almost every day of my childhood,
　　　主语　　　　　　　　　　　修饰 opportunities 的定语从句(“主+谓+宾”结构)

are becoming   increasingly scarce.
系动词　　　　　表语

【译文】自由玩耍的机会，在我的童年几乎每天都有，现在却越来越少了。

5. The Painting Fool   is   one of a growing number of computer programs   which, so their
　　主语　　　　　系动词　　　　　表语　　　　　　　　　　　　　　　　修饰 computer

makers claim, possess creative talents.

programs 的定语从句(“主+谓+宾”结构，so their makers claim 为插入成分)

【译文】越来越多的计算机程序——据它们的制作者声称——拥有创造性的才能,《傻瓜画画》是其中之一。

6. By contrast, the service sector, and more specifically hotels, has traditionally not extended
状语　　　　　主语　　　　　　插入成分　　　　　　　　谓语

these practices to address basic employee needs, such as good working conditions.
宾语　　　　　　　　目的状语

【译文】相比之下,服务业,更具体地说是酒店业,传统上没有拓展这些做法用于满足员工的基本需求,比如良好的工作条件。

7. In the past, businesses have changed when the public came to expect and require
时间状语　　主语　　谓语　　时间状语从句(谓语为come to do sth.结构,

different behaviour, and to reward businesses for behaviour that the public wanted.
含that引导的修饰behaviour的定语从句)

【译文】在过去,当公众开始期望并要求不同的行为,并为想要的行为奖励企业时,企业就会做出改变。

8. She found that... scientific reasoning.
主语　谓语　　　宾语从句

宾语从句: that children with greater self-control solved problems more quickly
引导词　主语　　后置定语　　　谓语　　宾语　　状语

when exploring an unfamiliar set-up requiring scientific reasoning
时间状语,逻辑主语为children

【译文】她发现,在探索需要做科学推理的陌生装置时,自控能力更强的孩子解决问题的速度更快。

9. Moreover, cork forests are a resource which support local biodiversity, and
状语　　　主语　系动词　表语　　修饰cork forests的定语从句(“主+谓+宾”

prevent desertification in the regions where they are planted.
结构,含where引导的修饰regions的定语从句)

【译文】此外,软木橡树林是一种支撑当地生物多样性的资源,并能防止种植地区荒漠化。

10. When he came to write the *National Geographic* magazine article that broke the story to the
时间状语从句(谓语为come to do sth.结构,含that引导的修饰article的定语从句)

world in April 1913, he knew he had to produce a big idea.
主语　谓语　　宾语从句(“主+谓+宾”结构)

【译文】当他在1913年4月开始撰写《国家地理》杂志的文章,向全世界讲述这个故事时,他知道自己必须创造一个伟大的想法。

11. Until this discovery, the lynx —a large spotted cat with tasselled ears— was presumed
状语　　　　主语　　　　同位语　　　　谓语

to have died out in Britain at least 6,000 years ago, before the inhabitants of these islands
主语补语　　　　状语　　　　　时间状语从句(“主+谓+宾”结构)

took up farming.

【译文】在这项发现之前,猞猁——一种耳朵长有簇毛的大型斑点猫——被认为至少在6,000年前就已经在英国灭绝了,那时英国各个岛屿的居民还未开始从事农业生产。

12. 分句1：

Intent on securing their hold over every nutmeg-producing island,   the Dutch   offered   a trade:
状语   主语   谓语   宾语

分句2：

if the British would give them the island of Run,   they   would in turn give   Britain   a distant
条件状语从句("主+谓+双宾"结构)   主语   谓语   间接宾语   直接宾语

and much less valuable island in North America.

【译文】荷兰人为了保住自己对每一个肉豆蔻出产岛屿的控制权，主动提出交换：如果英国人把伦岛交给他们，他们将相应给回英国一个遥远的、价值较低的北美洲岛屿。

13. Today,   professors   routinely   treat   the progressive interpretation of history and
状语   主语   状语   谓语   宾语

progressive public policy   as the proper subject of study
                                状语

while portraying conservative or classical liberal ideas—such as free markets and self-reliance—
         伴随状语，逻辑主语为professors(含portray sth. as结构)

as falling outside the boundaries of routine, and sometimes legitimate, intellectual investigation.

【译文】如今，教授们通常将对历史的先进解读和先进的公共政策视为恰当的研究课题，同时将保守或经典的自由主义思想，如自由市场和自给自足，描述为超出常规，有时是超出合理学术研究范围的东西。

14. 分句1：

As a sailing ship,   Cutty Sark   depended on   the strong trade winds of the southern hemisphere,
     状语   主语   谓语   宾语

分句2：

and   Woodget   took   her   further south than any previous captain,   bringing her
连词   主语   谓语   宾语   地点状语   伴随状语

dangerously close to icebergs off the southern tip of South America.

【译文】作为一艘大帆船，卡蒂萨克号依靠南半球的强劲信风航行，伍德杰船长将她带到以往任何一位船长都不曾到达的更远的南方，离南美洲南端附近的冰山非常近。

15. 分句1：

However,   this   is   to disregard the role   the human mind has in conveying remote places;
状语   主语   系动词   表语   修饰role的定语从句("主+谓+宾"结构)

分句2：

and   this   is   what interests me:
连词   主语   系动词   表语从句("主+谓+宾"结构)

分句3(作分句2中this的同位语从句)：

how   a fresh interpretation,   even of a well-travelled route,   can give   its readers
引导词   主语   插入成分   谓语   间接宾语

new insights.
直接宾语

【译文】然而，这无视了人类思维在传达偏远地区信息方面的作用；而这正是让我感兴趣的地方：哪怕是热门路线，对它的全新解读也能给读者带来新的见解。